Howard Kleyn has been keenly interested in Shakespearean drama ever since, as a boy, he took the part of Hermia in an all-male production of *A Midsummer Night's Dream*. In subsequent roles he often found that the text of a play was imperfectly understood by the audience and even on occasion by the cast. This book was written to help all those who would welcome a clear narration of these world-famous plays.

Nichola Bartlett, whose drawings complement the text, was born in London on 23rd April, 1968. She studied costume and illustration at Southend School of Art and illustration at Norwich School of Art where she gained a BA (Hons). She now lives in Essex.

The Play's The Thing

by HOWARD KLEYN

Illustrations by Nichola Bartlett

Howard's Corner

Published in 1996
by Howard's Corner
The Cottons
Outwell
Wisbech
PE14 8TP

The author asserts the moral right to be identified
as the author of this work.

Copyright Howard Kleyn 1996

ISBN 0-952-7387-1-6

Printed and set in the UK by Clanpress Ltd,

King's Lynn 01553 772737

Set in Palatino

For Mark, John and Tony,
whose enthusiasm and forbearance made it all possible

Introduction

"The play, I remember, pleased not the million; 'twas caviare to the general."

(Hamlet, Act II, Scene 2)

William Shakespeare is generally regarded as the foremost English poet and playwright. Many people consider him the world's greatest dramatist of all time. In the modern era his work has translated well onto cinema and television screens, where *Richard III, Hamlet* and *Henry V* have been particularly successful. However with the exception of Stratford-upon-Avon, the National Theatre and now The Globe comparatively few professional productions of Shakespeare in the live theatre are seen these days and even amateur productions are declining in number.

There is little doubt that a major factor in this decline is the difficulty encountered by contemporary audiences with the language of the plays. The unfamiliar phraseology, outmoded usage, archaic words and obscure allusions prevent today's playgoer from following the dialogue with ease.

It is true that scholarly treatises are available to elucidate Shakespeare's text (such as the synopses in Campbell's *A Shakespeare Encyclopaedia*) but these tomes cannot be consulted during a performance. The outcome is that the playgoer is liable to miss a vital twist in the plot or fail to understand the relationships between the various characters, especially when some of them are masquerading as others.

One answer to the problem is to present the plays in up-to-date English — and even contemporary dress. As Colin Burrow has remarked, "Modern critics and theatre directors often feel the need to drag Shakespeare forcibly into the 20th century, perhaps in order to compensate for the way his language seems a furlong or so more distant now that it did to our grandparents." Unfortunately this treatment largely robs them of Shakespeare's imagery and poetry — the reason for their pre-eminent quality. Another answer is to study the text with the aid of a glossary before seeing the play, a rather daunting task for someone who is merely in search of theatrical entertainment.

The present guide seeks to offer an easier solution. It presents the stories of Shakespeare's plays in colloquial English, derived directly from the text without augmentation. Anyone thinking of going to the theatre to attend a Shakespearean production, at The Globe or elsewhere, is invited to consult the relevant story before setting out. Having done so, he or she will then be able to concentrate on the poetry, aided by the costumes and setting, and thus enjoy Shakespeare in the same way as medieval audiences and latter-day scholars.

Other authors such as Marchette Chute have related the stories of these plays in narrative form, the most notable being Charles and Mary Lamb. This book is therefore in no sense innovative. However it exhibits a number of major differences from most previous publications.

First, the Lambs' Tales from Shakespeare cover little more than half of the canon of thirty seven plays of which Shakespeare was the sole author (or possibly joint author in the cases of *Henry VIII* and *Pericles*). Even study guides such as the excellent York Notes published by Longman go no further. The present volume encompasses every play and is based on the authentic texts, as far as these are known to us.

Second, the Tales are narrated in the past tense and contain comments and other material by the authors. This is acceptable since they were intended to be read for entertainment as a collection of stories. They are also enhanced by dramatic prose and a little extra guidance for the reader. This book, on the other hand, uses the present tense, mirroring Shakespeare's speeches, and strives to avoid introducing opinions on the characters and their motivation. The aim is to tell the story of each play without omission or embellishment of any kind.

Third, the Tales concentrate on the central characters and plot. Subsidiary characters, however significant, are omitted. For instance in *Twelfth Night* no mention is made of Malvolio with his yellow cross-gartered stockings, nor of Sir Andrew Aguecheek and Sir Toby Belch, all of whom are characters of considerable importance in Shakespeare's version. Similarly in *A Midsummer-Night's Dream* the mechanicals and their 'very tragical mirth' of Pyramus and Thisbe are not to be found, other than Bottom with his ass's head. Thus several important scenes have disappeared.

The distinctive feature of this volume is that it follows the plays in close detail, scene by scene, thus ensuring that the structure of each play is preserved. It includes all the named characters and refers to the attendants, musicians, soldiers and others as appropriate. Moreover all the most famous Shakespeare quotations appear in their places, reminding us of who originally spoke them and in what context.

In commending this book to the playgoer, the author wishes to emphasise that it is primarily a work of reference. It is of course possible to read through the stories in the normal way and the reader is encouraged to do so. However the reader may find himself or herself battling through thickets of characters rather than strolling along the path of the plot. These are, after all, stage plays and full enjoyment of them should be sought in the theatre for which they were intended. Nevertheless it is hoped that such enjoyment will be both anticipated and heightened by these explanatory narratives.

Some notes on the presentation of the plays in Shakespeare's time will be found in the Preface.

Index

A Midsummer-Night's Dream

Preface

When contemplating all thirty seven of Shakespeare's plays it is tempting to seek to group them in some way, for convenience of study. The most natural grouping would appear to be by category (as was done in the first Folio). However as James Brodie has noted it is unwise to classify the plays neatly as comedies, tragedies, romances etc. since some of the comedies have tragic episodes, some of the tragedies moments of humour and the historical plays elements of both. For example, while Romeo and Juliet is of course a love story it is also undeniably a tragedy. We should therefore be wary of attaching definitive labels of this kind to the plays.

Another possibility is to group the plays in chronological sets although here again the assignment of a play to a particular set must be somewhat arbitrary, taking into account that many of the dates of composition are conjectural. We can perhaps recognise five Shakespearean periods, the labels being no more than indicative:

1. Development (1590 - 1593). This period comprises *Love's Labour's Lost, The Comedy of Errors, The Two Gentlemen of Verona, King Henry VI Part 1, Part 2* and *Part 3, Romeo & Juliet, King Richard III* and *Titus Andronicus.* (Total 9)

2. Poetry (1593 and 1594). In this period the narrative poems *Venus and Adonis* and *The Rape of Lucrece* were written while the theatres were closed during the Plague.

3. History, Drama, and Comedy (1594 - 1601). This major period comprises *King Richard II, A Midsummer Night's Dream, King John, The Merchant of Venice, The Taming of the Shrew, King Henry IV Part 1* and *Part 2, King Henry V, The Merry Wives of Windsor, Hamlet, Much Ado About Nothing, Julius Caesar, As You Like It, Twelfth Night* and *All's Well That Ends Well.* (Total 15)

4. Tragedy (1602 - 1609). The period comprises *Troilus & Cressida, Measure for Measure, Othello, King Lear, Macbeth, Antony & Cleopatra, Coriolanus, Timon of Athens* and *Pericles.* (Total 9)

5. Romance (1610 - 1613). The last period includes *Cymbeline, The Winter's Tale, The Tempest* and *King Henry VIII.* (Total 4)

In addition Shakespeare turned out more than 150 sonnets and other poetry such as *The Lover's Complaint* and *The Passionate Pilgrim* during part of the foregoing periods.

But whereas the chronology of the plays is of interest, in illustrating the dramatist's increasing mastery of his craft, it does not assist the student to recognise a particular play by its type.

However, a further differentiation may be helpful, as follows: Nearly half of Shakespeare's plays, sixteen in all, are based (sometimes very loosely) on historical events. These include four from Roman times, *Julius Caesar, Coriolanus, Titus Andronicus* and *Antony & Cleopatra* and one in ancient Grecian times, *Troilus & Cressida.*

Of the 'native' eleven, Cymbeline is set in early Britain. The other ten have come to be known as Shakespeare's 'history plays', meaning those dealing specifically with English history. One of these is *King John* and another is *Henry VIII*, a possible collaboration with John Fletcher. The remaining eight form a more or less continuous English history-cycle of the fifteenth century from the reign of Richard II (which ended in 1399) to the coronation of Henry VII, the first of the Tudor kings, in 1485.

In historical (but not compositional) order the history-cycle depicts the deposition and murder of Richard II, the troubled reign of Henry IV (parts 1 and 2), the conquests of Henry V, the defeats and civil war in the time of Henry VI (parts 1, 2 and 3) and finally the villainous schemes of Richard III.

The twenty one non-historical plays may be classed broadly as (a) dramatic, comprising *Timon of Athens, Macbeth, Othello, Measure for Measure, Hamlet, The Merchant of Venice, Pericles, The Winter's Tale,* and *King Lear,* (b) romantic, comprising *Romeo & Juliet, Twelfth Night, Much Ado About Nothing,* and *All's Well That Ends Well,* (c) comic, comprising *The Two Gentlemen of Verona, The Merry Wives of Windsor, The Comedy of Errors* and *The Taming of the Shrew* and (d) lyric, comprising *As You Like It, A Midsummer Night's Dream, Love's Labour's Lost* and *The Tempest.*

Thus the 37 plays may perhaps be regarded as:

Classical	5
Historical	11
Dramatic	9
Romantic	4
Comical	4
Lyrical	4

Alternatively the plays can be ordered roughly by chronological periods. A possible sequence may be found in the table at the end of the book although many of the dates are no more than guesses. Finally, they can merely be listed alphabetically, as is done in the Index, which also includes a few of the major characters under each title for quick reference.

Some observations on the construction of the plays may be useful when reading the narratives. It will be noticed that the scenes are curiously uneven in length (a matter of no great consequence when the stage set remained unchanged, as in Elizabethan times). Shakespeare divided some of his plays into five acts but in most cases the division into acts and scenes was undertaken by others.

A number of scenes consist of little more than a single speech. Thus Act V, Scene 4 of *The Merry Wives of Windsor* is only four lines in length. (Other examples of brief scenes include *As You Like It*, Act II, Scene 6, *Pericles*, Act IV, Scene 5, *Coriolanus*, Act I, Scene 7, *Timon of Athens*, Act V, Scene 3 and three scenes in *Cymbeline*). On the other hand some scenes run to 500 lines or more (e.g. *The Tempest*, Act I, Scene 2, *Richard III*, Act IV, Scene 4, *Timon of Athens*, Act IV, Scene 3, Part 1 of *Henry IV*, Act II, Scene 4 and especially *Love's Labour's Lost*, Act V, Scene 2). In *Antony & Cleopatra* no complete agreement on scene division exists.

A common pattern is the alternation of scenes of high drama and low comedy. This type of contrast may be seen in *Much Ado About Nothing* and *Twelfth Night* and especially in Part 2 of *Henry IV* where the two story lines make little contact until the middle of Act IV. Plays or masques within plays afford an opportunity for similar contrasts, such as those in *Hamlet*, *A Midsummer Night's Dream*, *Cymbeline*, *The Merry Wives of Windsor* and *Love's Labour's Lost*. In the first Folio the whole of *The Taming of the Shrew* is an example.

The plays were also much influenced by both the limitations and capabilities of the Elizabethan theatre. At the end of the sixteenth century one limitation was the absence of a curtain round the stage, which projected or 'thrust' into the audience. Therefore a Shakespearean character who is to die often makes an exit or is carried out, since if he expired on stage the corpse could not very well get up and walk off before the next scene, especially when some 'swells' might actually be seated on the rear corners of the stage.

Typical instances occur in the first Act of *Henry VI, part 1* and also include the dragging off of Polonius (*Hamlet*, Act III, Scene 4) and Clarence (*Richard III*, Act I, Scene 4), the collapse of Regan (*King Lear*, Act V, Scene 3) and the bearing out of John of Gaunt (*Richard II*, Act II, Scene 1) and King Henry (Part 2 of *Henry IV*, Act IV, Scene 5).

As to capabilities, a number of scenes make use of a parapet or upper window, utilising features behind a 'thrust' stage as used in wrap-around theatres like *The Globe*, *The Fortune* and *The Swan*. These include the famous balcony scene in *Romeo and Juliet* (Act II, Scene 2), *Henry V* at the gates of Harfleur (Act III, Scene 3), the confrontation with the schoolmaster in *The Taming of the Shrew* (Act V, Scene 1), Jessica's elopement with Lorenzo (*The Merchant of Venice*, Act II, Scene 6), the elevated senate-house in *Julius Caesar* (Act III, Scene 1) and others.

Certain dramatic devices recur in the plots. Much use is made of impersonation, particularly where the impersonator is of the opposite sex. At a time when the female parts were played by boys this added to audience enjoyment. Examples include the impersonation of Fidele by Imogen (*Cymbeline*), Diana by Helena (*All's Well That Ends Well*), Brook by Ford (*The Merry Wives of Windsor*), Ganymede and Aliena by Rosalind and Celia (*As You Like It*), Isabella by Mariana and Friar Lodowick by the Duke of Vienna (*Measure for Measure*), Dr. Balthazar by Portia (*The Merchant of Venice*), Cesario by Viola (*Twelfth Night*) and many more.

In an age when there were no such things as identity cards or passports, rings were a frequent method of authentication (and hence a fruitful cause of misunderstandings). Shakespearean use of rings includes those of Thaisa (*Pericles*), Bertram and Helena (*All's Well That Ends Well*), Bassanio and Gratiano (*The Merchant of Venice*), Proteus and Julia (*The Two Gentlemen of Verona*) and Posthumus' ring and Imogen's bracelet (*Cymbeline*).

Narcotics which counterfeit death are another favourite device. They are mentioned in *Antony & Cleopatra*, Act I, Scene 5 and employed in *Cymbeline* (Imogen), *Pericles* (Queen Thaisa) and *Romeo and Juliet* (Juliet). In other cases deaths are feigned by swooning, through cowardice or even by posing as a statue (*Pericles*).

The narratives of the plays themselves now follow. In the stories, square brackets [like these] contain information not derived directly from the text.

"...the play's the thing,
Wherein I'll catch the conscience of the king."

(Hamlet, Act II, Scene 2)

All's Well That Ends Well

Like *Cymbeline*, the story is one of those in Boccaccio's *Decameron*, included in William Paynter's *Palace of Pleasure* published in 1566. The play may be regarded as the last of the major group of histories, comedies and drama (1594-1601), after which Shakespeare turned to the tragedies. It is set in France and Italy.

Act I

Scene 1

The Countess of Rousillon, her son Bertram and Helena, a gentlewoman, are in mourning after the recent death of the Count. Bertram is taking leave of his mother in her palace, having been summoned to attend the King of France by Lafeu, an elderly lord. Lafeu informs them that the King is suffering from an ulcer and has given up hope of being cured by his physicians.

The Countess recalls that Helena's father, Gerard de Narbon, had been a famous physician and Lafeu confirms that the King had spoken highly of him. The Countess explains that on his death she became the protector of his only child and gently reproves Helena for weeping excessively. She counsels Bertram to be like his father ("Love all, trust a few, Do wrong to none") and leaves. Bertram and Lafeu depart, leaving Helena to express her forlorn love for Bertram and her sorrow at his going, for which her tears are really being shed.

She is joined by an effeminate follower of Bertram, Parolles, whom she regards as a notorious liar, a fool and a coward. Parolles tries, with no success, to convince her that virginity is against the rule of nature and should be abandoned; he is called away to Bertram by a page.

Scene 2

To a fanfare of cornets the King of France enters a room in his palace in Paris, reading letters with news of factional fighting in Tuscany. Although he will not aid Florence he is willing to allow some French cavaliers to prove themselves in battle. The arrival of Bertram, Lafeu and Parolles is announced. The King welcomes Bertram, now Count of Rousillon, and praises his father and Gerard de Narbon, both deceased.

Scene 3

Back at Rousillon the Countess' jester Lavache asks her for leave to marry his Isabel. The Countess tells him she will decide later and, on the prompting of Rinaldo, her steward, bids him go and fetch Helena. While waiting, Rinaldo tells the Countess that he has overheard Helena confessing her love for Bertram and lamenting the difference between his high rank and hers. The Countess thanks him and dismisses him as Helena comes in.

The Countess, remembering her own youthful passions, remarks to Helena that she is a mother to her. When Helena reacts to the remark she realises that Helena is indeed in love with Bertram and hence would not have him for a brother. Helena admits as much while acknowledging the hopelessness of her position. She goes on to say that her father left her some powerful prescriptions, among which the most potent is one suitable for the King's malady. The Countess supports her proposal to go to Paris and offer treatment to the King, despite his physicians.

Act II

Scene 1

At the palace the King bids farewell to the young bloods on their way to the Florentine war and leaves. Before departing, the lords try to persuade Bertram to join them, supported by Parolles who tells Bertram to show more enthusiasm for their enterprise.

The King re-enters and receives Lafeu who informs him that a young doctor has brought him a marvellous remedy. He ushers Helena in and leaves her with the King. Helena tells the King of her father, whom he knew, and the wonderful properties of the medication which he left her. She overcomes the King's initial reluctance by staking her life on its efficacy. However in return for his certain recovery she asks for the hand of any man she wishes, apart from one of royal blood. The King assents.

Scene 2

In Rousillon Lavache tells the Countess facetiously that he can answer any question with phrases like "O Lord, sir!" and "Spare not me." The Countess waves his drollery aside and gives him letters to take to Bertram and Helena in Paris.

Scene 3

Back at the palace Lafeu and Bertram discuss the King's miraculous recovery while Parolles sycophantically repeats their words. As Helena enters with the King and some lords Parolles is astonished to see her. The King tells Helena to select a noble husband, in accordance with his undertaking. When she chooses Bertram he protests that she is nothing but a poor physician's daughter brought up by his parents. The affronted Helena is ready to let him go but the King, whose honour is at stake, tells him that if her rank is the only consideration he will confer a title on her. He commands Bertram to marry Helena that day or fall from favour. The court moves off.

Lafeu, left with Parolles, pours contempt on his fancy clothes and mincing ways before leaving. The newly married Bertram re-enters swearing that he will go off to the Tuscan wars and send Helena back to Rousillon rather than bed her. Parolles urges him on his way.

Scene 4

Elsewhere in the palace Lavache conveys the Countess' greetings to Helena. Parolles comes to tell her of Bertram's departure on a "very serious business".

Scene 5

In another room Bertram speaks of Parolles' valour, to Lafeu's surprise. Parolles reports to Bertram while Lafeu again expresses his doubts before leaving. When Helena enters Bertram excuses himself, telling her he was unprepared for such a sudden and unwanted marriage; he hands her a letter for his mother and makes haste to depart without even the kiss for which Helena hoped.

Act III

Scene 1

Two French lords advise the Duke of Florence in his palace that the French king will not lend him assistance although some of the young nobility will support his cause.

Scene 2

At Rousillon the Countess reads the letter brought by the jester Lavache. In it Bertram writes that he has sent her a daughter-in-law whom he has wedded but not bedded and that he has "run away". Lavache, who has gone out, returns briefly to announce the arrival of two soldiers who have brought Helena a letter. They confirm that Bertram has gone with Parolles to serve the Duke of Florence.

Helena shows the Countess the letter from Bertram which says that she may call him husband only when she can get a ring from his finger "which never shall come off" and show him a child of which he is the father. Helena mournfully quotes a further line: "Till I have no wife, I have nothing in France." The Countess attempts to console her and takes the soldiers off to give them a letter for Bertram.

Helena is overcome with remorse at having driven Bertram from the court and perhaps to his death; she resolves to fly from Rousillon.

Scene 3

Near the palace in Florence the Duke appoints Bertram to the post of general commanding his cavalry.

Scene 4

Back at Rousillon Rinaldo reads the Countess a letter left by Helena. She hears that Helena has undertaken a barefoot pilgrimage to the shrine of St. Jacques le Grand. The Countess reproves Rinaldo for letting her go and instructs him to write to Bertram conveying her grief and calling on him to return.

Scene 5

Outside the walls of Florence the widow Capilet is waiting to see the Count of Rousillon with her daughter Diana and two neighbours, Violenta and Mariana. They talk of Bertram's exploits and Parolles' licentiousness. Helena comes along in a pilgrim's habit seeking lodgings; the widow offers her own house, the *St. Francis*, where other pilgrims are staying, and asks her to wait for the Florentine army. She relates Bertram's story to Helena, including Parolles' denigration of his wife, and mentions that Diana is resisting the Count's advances.

A party of soldiers passes by with drum and colours, headed by Bertram (in a plume) with Antonio, the Duke's eldest son, Escalus, a courtier, and Parolles who is adorned in scarves and mentions a lost drum.

Scene 6

In a camp near Florence two lords impress on Bertram that Parolles is not only a liar but a coward. The first suggests that he be sent to recapture the lost drum; they will then ambush him in the guise of adversaries and convey him to a tent where they are confident that under examination Bertram will hear Parolles betray him.

When Parolles joins them they provoke him to undertake to recover the drum, in a fit of bravado. After he sets out the lords assure Bertram that he will return not with the drum but with a tissue of falsehoods. Bertram invites the second lord to take a look at a virtuous girl, Diana, who has coldly returned presents that he sent her via Parolles.

Scene 7

Helena decides to tell the widow Capilet in her house who she really is; she offers the widow a purse of gold and solicits her aid in a scheme to win Bertram, who comes every evening to serenade Diana. Diana is to beg Bertram to give her his ring, which has come down to him through several generations, in return for an assignation. Helena will then take Diana's place and, if all goes well, will add three thousand crowns to Diana's dowry. The widow readily agrees.

Act IV

Scene 1

Near the Florentine camp the first French lord organises the ambush, warning his men to use garbled words. Parolles comes by, wondering what plausible story he can tell to account for failing to secure the drum. The Florentines seize Parolles and blindfold him, speaking in strange tongues. He is led away while one of the soldiers is sent to inform the Count.

Scene 2

In the widow's house Diana initially repulses Bertram as a married man. When she demands his ring, being equivalent to the jewel of her chastity, he reluctantly hands it over. She tells him to knock at her bedroom window at midnight; if he promises not to speak she will entertain him for one hour, during which time she will place another ring on his finger.

Scene 3

The two lords gossip in the Florentine camp. Bertram has received his mother's letter and is planning to seduce Diana that night. Furthermore it seems that Helena has died of grief at the pilgrimage shrine. A servant reports that Bertram has taken leave of the Duke and will be going back to France in the morning.

Bertram himself enters complacently, having said his farewells, written to the Countess and enjoyed success in a certain affair which is not yet ended. The lords send for Parolles, who has been languishing in the stocks and confessing his sins to a man he thought was a friar.

Under questioning Parolles states that the Duke has five or six thousand horses and fifteen thousand men but the commanders are weak and the troops scattered. He goes on to describe one of the lords, Captain Dumain, as a drunken thief of an officer whom the Duke, in a letter, wanted dismissed from his service. The soldiers search Parolles and duly find a letter but it is from him to Diana, warning her that the Count is a dangerous and lascivious fool. Dumain and Bertram are both enraged at this calumny.

The soldier who has been taking notes pretends to confer with 'the general', returning to tell Parolles that he is to be beheaded for traitorously betraying the secrets of the army and vilifying its officers. Parolles beseeches him to let him live or at least see his death. The soldier removes the blindfold and Parolles is greeted scornfully by Bertram and the lords. After they have left he is thankful that he is still alive.

Scene 4

Back in Florence Helena tells the widow that while she is rumoured to be dead she must go to the King in Marseilles. She needs one more favour from Diana and her mother before "all's well that ends well."

Scene 5

The Countess in her palace at Rousillon mourns the death of Helena while Lafeu endures Lavache's banter. While Lavache is out of the room Lafeu tells the Countess that the king has agreed that Bertram shall be affianced to Maudlin (Lafeu's daughter, to whom he had been promised before he was precipitately married to Helena). Lavache returns to announce the arrival of Bertram, who has a scar on his cheek.

Act V

Scene 1

Helena, accompanied by the widow Capilet, Diana and two attendants in a Marseilles street, meets a goshawk-keeper whom she has seen at court. She asks him to present a petition to the King and learns that the King has already left for Rousillon.

Scene 2

In the inner court of the Countess' palace at Rousillon Parolles, in soiled clothes, asks Lavache to deliver a paper to Lafeu. Lavache refers him to Lafeu, who enters at that moment, and leaves. Lafeu gives him some money and promises him food.

Scene 3

Trumpets sound as the King enters another room in the palace with the Countess, Lafeu, members of the court and guards. They discuss Bertram. Lafeu comments that he has offended the King and his mother but most of all himself in losing a beautiful and admirable wife.

A courtier fetches Bertram who asks the King's pardon for his wrongs. The King forgives him and notes his engagement to Maudlin. Lafeu asks Bertram for a token for his daughter. Bertram gives him a ring which he immediately remembers having seen on Helena's finger. Bertram denies its identity but the King takes the ring, recognising it as one that he himself had given to Helena. Lafeu and the Countess attest to it. Bertram maintains that the ring was thrown to him by a girl from a casement in Florence. The King accuses him of lying and orders the guards to take him away.

The goshawk-keeper enters with a petition from Diana Capilet and leaves. The petition states that Bertram seduced her, promising to marry her when his wife was dead; now that he is a widower she has come to Rousillon and calls upon the King to compel Bertram to honour his vow.

Bertram is recalled, followed by the goshawk-keeper with the widow and Diana, who introduce themselves to the King. Bertram admits his involvement with Diana but claims that she was nothing but a camp follower. However as proof Diana produces the Rousillon family ring which he gave her. Moreover she identifies 'her' ring, now on the King's finger, as one that she gave Bertram in bed. Bertram admits it.

Parolles is brought in by an attendant. After some equivocation he confirms that Bertram took Diana to bed and promised to marry her. Bertram castigates him as an inveterate liar but the King turns from him to Diana, demanding to know where she obtained Helena's ring. Diana tries to change her story, increasing the King's suspicious wrath. He orders her to tell what she knows or she will be taken to prison and put to death within the hour. In desperation Diana sends her mother to fetch the

Act V, Scene 3

The widow Capilet brings Helena de Narbon before the King of France in the palace at Rousillon. Helena hands Bertram his ring and the letter in which he promised to be her husband if she could get the ring from his finger and become the mother of his child.

'jeweller' who supplied the ring; she describes the stratagem in Florence and reveals that Helena is not only alive but is pregnant by Bertram.

To the astonishment of the King the widow returns with Helena, who hands Bertram his ring and the letter in which he promised to be her husband if she could get the ring from his finger and become the mother of his child. Bertram declares his love for her while Lafeu weeps; the King offers to provide a dowry for Diana when she chooses a husband.

Epilogue

The King tells the audience that "The king's a beggar, now the play is done: All is well ended if this suit be won That you express content."

Antony and Cleopatra

The source of the play is North's *Plutarch,* on which Shakespeare also based *Julius Caesar* and *Coriolanus.* Cleopatra was the daughter of Ptolemy XI, Auletes. Mark Antony, Octavius Caesar and Marcus Aemilius Lepidus were Roman triumvirs, i.e. men sharing imperial power. The action, covering the end of the Ptolemaic dynasty of Egypt, is represented by twelve separate days and runs roughly from 40 to 30 BC.

Act I

Scene 1

Demetrius and Philo, two friends of Mark Antony, comment on his infatuation with Cleopatra, queen of Egypt, in her palace in Alexandria. Antony enters in a stately procession with Cleopatra, who is fanned by eunuchs.

A messenger arrives from Rome but Cleopatra scoffs that he is bringing either a command from Caesar or a scolding from his Antony's wife Fulvia. She cajoles Antony into discussing some leisure diversion and ignoring the messenger.

Scene 2

Three of Cleopatra's attendants chat in another room. Alexas gets Charmian to show the palm of her hand to a soothsayer to be read, while her friend Iras looks on. Domitius Enobarbus of Antony's party enters and calls for a banquet to be brought in. The soothsayer tells Charmian that she will become fairer and will outlive Cleopatra; he predicts similar good fortune for Iras.

Cleopatra appears, looking for Antony; however when he enters with the messenger and others she waywardly sweeps out with Enobarbus and all her attendants. The messenger reports that Labienus and his Parthians have conquered the Middle East while Fulvia, after battling Antony's brother Lucius, allied herself with him against Caesar and suffered defeat.

Another messenger arrives with a letter conveying the news that Fulvia has died of an illness. A saddened Antony calls Enobarbus and informs him of Fulvia's death. He means to leave the unpredictable Cleopatra and, at the behest of his "contriving friends", return to Rome where Sextus Pompeius, son of Pompey the Great [Pompeius Gnaeus], is gaining popularity and opposing Caesar.

Scene 3

Elsewhere in the palace Cleopatra despatches Alexas to find Antony, as if by chance, and hint that if he is sad she is merry and vice versa. Charmian feels that to hold Antony it would be better not to taunt and cross him in this way but Cleopatra disagrees.

When Antony enters she sullenly says she is sick. She dismisses Charmian and berates Antony for leaving her to go to Rome. Antony professes his love but maintains that he must go to deal with his wife's death and the young Pompey's challenge. Cleopatra relents and wishes him well.

Scene 4

The two other triumvirs discuss Antony in Octavius Caesar's house in Rome. Caesar thinks he is going soft in Alexandria but Lepidus defends him.

A messenger comes to report that Pompey is approaching by sea and many malcontents are flocking to the ports to meet him, while the pirates Menecrates and Menas have a free hand. Caesar calls for the council to assemble and looks forward to Antony's return.

Scene 5

Back in Alexandria a despondent Cleopatra sighs for Antony and in his absence asks Charmian for mandrake [a strong narcotic] to drink. She contrasts her feelings with those of the eunuch Mardian while Iras listens. Alexas brings her a pearl which was given a farewell kiss by Antony before he rode off. Cleopatra makes ready to write to him, repudiating any comparison with her earlier love for Julius Caesar in her "salad days" when she was "green in judgment".

Act II

Scene 1

At his house in Messina, Sicily, Pompey reviews his position with Menecrates and Menas. He refuses to believe that Caesar and Lepidus are in the field in strength, as Menas has heard from Silvius (an officer serving Antony's colleague Ventidius). Varrius, another friend, arrives to report that Mark Antony is expected hourly in Rome; Pompey knows that Antony is the best soldier of the triumvirs but hopes that since his wife and brother fought against Caesar he will fall out with him.

Scene 2

Lepidus, at home, enjoins Enobarbus to have Antony speak softly to Caesar. Antony comes in by one door with Ventidius as Caesar enters by another with his companions Agrippa and Mecaenus [perhaps Maecenas]. When Lepidus calls them together Caesar reproaches Antony for the actions of his wife and brother and accuses him of failing to lend him arms and aid. Mecaenas attempts to placate him and Agrippa suggests that Antony, now a widower, marry Caesar's sister Octavia, the widow of Caius Marcellus. Caesar consents; the two shake hands and depart with Lepidus to visit Octavia.

Mecaenas and Agrippa ply Enobarbus with questions about his sumptuous life style in Egypt.

He describes Cleopatra's initial meeting with Antony on a river at Tarsus in Turkey. Her barge boasted perfumed sails and a gold poop, in which she lay dressed in cloth-of-gold surrounded by mermaids and prettydimpled boys. The besotted Antony will never leave this wanton Venus, he goes on; "Age cannot wither her, nor custom stale Her infinite variety."

Scene 3

In Caesar's house he and Octavia bid Antony good night and retire. A soothsayer enters and urges Antony to return to Egypt since Caesar's fortunes will be better than his. Antony acknowledges that the prediction is probably accurate; he sends Ventidius to Parthia and decides to return to Egypt after his remarriage.

Scene 4

Lepidus, in the street, hurries Mecaenas and Agrippa off to war, on Antony's heels.

Scene 5

In the palace in Alexandria with her attendants Cleopatra calls for music, "moody food Of us that trade in love" [see the opening lines of *Twelfth Night*]. She idly changes her mind, suggesting a game of billiards with Charmian or Mardian. Then she proposes to go fishing and pretend that each fish is Antony, a catch, mischievously recalling how she arranged for a diver to attach a fish to his hook when they were angling on a previous occasion.

When a messenger arrives Cleopatra plays fast and loose with him, promising him gold for good news and death for bad. The messenger timidly reports that Antony is well and is reconciled with Caesar — but is married to Octavia! Cleopatra strikes him in a tantrum; he flees when she draws a knife. Charmian restrains her and is sent to recall the terrified messenger, who confirms his report and leaves. Cleopatra sends Alexas after him for details of Octavia's appearance. Finally Iras, Charmian and Mardian lead her away to her chamber.

Scene 6

Pompey and Menas, with drum and trumpet, meet Caesar, Antony, Lepidus, Enobarbus and Mecaenas near Misenum [a port in Pozzuoli Bay near Naples] for a parley, each side having hostages from the other. The triumvirs offer Sicily and Sardinia to Pompey in return for ridding the sea of pirates and paying a tribute of wheat to Rome. He is surprised to see Antony but accepts the offer and invites them to a feast on his galley.

Menas and Enobarbus, who are acquainted, are left to compare notes. They discuss Antony's political marriage to the austere Octavia and predict trouble when he returns to "his Egyptian dish".

Scene 7

Some servants provide a banquet aboard Pompey's galley lying off Misenum and comment on the uneasy friendliness of the Romans. Trumpets sound the entry of Caesar, Antony, Lepidus, Pompey, Agrippa, Mecaenus, Enobarbus and Menas with other officers. Antony discourses on the flood-control of the Nile while they ply Lepidus with drink and tease him.

Menas draws Pompey aside and suggests that they put to sea and cut the triumvirs' throats; Pompey will then rule the world. Pompey observes that Menas should have gone ahead without telling him; his own honour precludes his taking such action. The disappointed Menas mutters to himself that he will no longer follow a man who cannot grasp a golden opportunity.

The befuddled Lepidus is carried ashore. Enobarbus places the others in a linked circle while a boy sings a drinking song. Eventually Caesar and Antony take their party ashore while Enobarbus arranges to stay in Menas' cabin.

Act III

Scene 1

A Roman triumphal procession winds over a Syrian plain, the corpse of Pacorus (son of the Parthian King Orodes) being borne before Ventidius and his officers. Ventidius is urged by Silius to pursue the routed Parthians into Mesopotamia but he fears provoking the triumvirs if he is too successful and proposes to meet Antony in Athens.

Scene 2

Agrippa and Enobarbus meet in Caesar's house in Rome. They outdo each other in praise of Lepidus' attachment to the other triumvirs. They watch as the triumvirs and Octavia enter. Antony promises Caesar to look after Octavia. As farewells are said Octavia whispers in her brother's ear, bringing a solemn look to his face.

Scene 3

Back in Alexandria the apprehensive messenger is again called before Cleopatra and her attendants. Being questioned, he tells the jealous queen that Octavia is about thirty, is not so tall as she, has a round face and a low voice and moves without grace. A mollified Cleopatra gives him gold and dismisses him. Charmian agrees with her that Antony surely cannot find such a woman attractive.

Scene 4

Antony grumbles to Octavia in his house in Athens that Caesar has disparaged him and has waged new wars with Pompey. Octavia laments the friction between her husband and her brother. Antony accedes to her request to return to Rome in due course to put matters right.

Scene 5

In another room Eros, another of Antony's friends, calls Enobarbus to attend Antony, who is walking abstractedly in the garden. He reports that Caesar has arrested Lepidus after the war against Pompey

Act IV, Scene 4

In her palace in Alexandria Cleopatra, Queen of Egypt, helps Mark Antony to don his armour before he is called away by his officers and men to lead them in battle against Octavius Caesar.

and that Antony deplores Lepidus' fate and is railing against the officer who assassinated Pompey.

Scene 6

Caesar, in his house in Rome, describes to Agrippa and Mecaenus how Antony and Cleopatra have been enthroned in Alexandria with Caesarion [Cleopatra's son by Octavius' father Julius Caesar] and their own children at their feet. Antony has made Cleopatra queen of Lower Syria, Cyprus and Lydia as well as Egypt and proclaimed his sons kings of various other countries. Furthermore Antony has complained that he was not allotted one third of Sicily after Pompey's defeat and disagrees with the treatment of Lepidus.

Caesar tells them that he has written to Antony justifying Lepidus' detention and offering him one third of Sicily if Antony will similarly concede part of all the territories he has conquered.

Octavia enters with her train and explains that she has come without ceremony on her own initiative to smooth relations between him and her husband. Caesar is not impressed; he informs her that Antony has sailed from Athens to Alexandria to be with Cleopatra and has assembled many kings (including Herod) for warlike purposes. Agrippa and Mecaenus confirm this account and welcome Octavia to Rome.

Scene 7

In Antony's camp near the Actium peninsula Enobarbus remonstrates with Cleopatra for being there and distracting Antony. Antony enters with his lieutenant-general, Canidius, wondering how Caesar has moved so swiftly across the peninsula to Brindisi from Taranto and over the Ionian sea to occupy Toryne [Tirana in modern Albania]. He resolves to fight him at sea rather than on land, against the advice of Enobarbus and Canidius.

When Antony, Cleopatra and Enobarbus have left, Canidius confides to a soldier that he will keep Antony's nineteen legions and twelve thousand horse on land.

Scene 8

On a plain near Actium Caesar commands his lieutenant-general, Taurus, not to fight on land until after the sea battle. Separately, Antony and Enobarbus dispose their squadrons within sight of the sea. The two armies, under Taurus and Canidius respectively, march off and the sound of a sea-fight is heard.

Enobarbus returns with Scarus, another friend of Antony, bemoaning the flight of the Egyptian ships to the Peloponnese and Antony after them. He is followed by Canidius who prepares to surrender his legions and horse to Caesar.

Scene 9

In the palace in Alexandria Antony bids his attendants take his ship and its treasure and make peace with Caesar. Charmian, Iras and Eros enter, followed by Cleopatra. They urge her to console Antony. She asks his pardon for turning tail in the naval battle, not thinking that he would follow.

Scene 10

Antony has sent his children's tutor, Euphronius, to Caesar's camp in Egypt. Three of Caesar's friends, Agrippa, Dolabella and Thyreus [or Thidias], listen as Euphronius conveys Antony's plea to be allowed to live in Egypt or Athens as a private citizen, while Cleopatra asks to retain the monarchy. Caesar replies that if Cleopatra will drive Antony out of Egypt he will heed her request. He sends Thyreus to win Cleopatra with promises.

Scene 11

Cleopatra, who is with Charmian and Iras at the palace in Alexandria, is assured by Enobarbus that Antony is at fault for fleeing from the naval action and not she. Antony comes by, hearing Caesar's response from Euphronius and determining to write challenging him to a duel. An attendant announces the arrival of Thyreus who persuades Cleopatra to agree that she did not so much love Antony as submit to him. Enobarbus quickly goes to apprise Antony of this while Cleopatra instructs Thyreus to tell Caesar that she kneels to him and lays her crown at his feet.

A furious Antony returns with Enobarbus and calls attendants to take Thyreus out and have him whipped. Then he turns on Cleopatra and castigates her for her faithlessness. Thyreus is brought back, having been flogged, and despatched to tell Caesar that if he likes he can have Antony's bondman, Hipparchus, scourged in return. After he has gone Antony recovers his poise and proposes a last night of music and revelry to celebrate Cleopatra's birthday. Enobarbus privately decides to leave his service.

Act IV

Scene 1

At his camp near Alexandria Caesar scornfully reads out Antony's letter to Agrippa and Mecaenus. He bids them prepare for a last battle on the morrow.

Scene 2

In Alexandria Antony informs Enobarbus that Caesar will not fight him hand to hand. In the presence of Cleopatra, Iras, Alexas and others he commends a group of servants and excites their pity by asking them to serve him well one last time at supper that night.

Scene 3

Some soldiers on guard at the palace find it strange to hear music on the eve of the battle.

Scene 4

Inside the palace Antony, with Cleopatra and Charmian, orders Eros to bring his armour. Cleopatra helps him to put it on before he is called away by his officers and men. Charmian leads Cleopatra off to bed.

Scene 5

In his camp Antony learns from a soldier that Enobarbus has defected to Caesar. He instructs Eros to send his belongings after him with a courteous note.

Scene 6

In the other camp Caesar tells Agrippa that he wants Antony taken alive. He orders the deserters from Antony's army to be placed in the front line. Enobarbus muses that Caesar has hanged Alexas for persuading Herod to switch his allegiance. Canidius has also abandoned Antony. When Enobarbus learns from a soldier that his possessions have been sent on by Antony on muleback he is overcome with remorse.

Scene 7

Agrippa falls back on the field of battle. One of Antony's men, Scarus, has been wounded. Eros assures him and Antony that the enemy is in retreat.

Scene 8

Antony and Scarus arrive under the walls of Alexandria with their men. Antony thanks them for their valour. Cleopatra comes to meet them; a march is planned through the city.

Scene 9

Enobarbus wanders past some sentries on duty at Caesar's camp; stricken with guilt at his desertion he commits suicide. The sentries carry his body to the guard room.

Scene 10

Antony and Scarus on the one hand and Caesar on the other march forward with their troops. Antony goes to observe progress from a lone pine and returns with the news that all is lost. Caesar has captured his fleet and the sailors of both sides are carousing together. He orders Scarus to go and tell his men to fly. Cleopatra appears and is sent away with a flea in her ear, after which Antony leaves, calling for Eros.

Scene 11

In the palace Charmian, Iras and Mardian urge Cleopatra to lock herself in her tomb for safety. She assents, ordering Mardian to inform Antony that her last word was 'Antony' before she slew herself.

Scene 12

In another room Antony tells Eros that Cleopatra has betrayed him. When Mardian comes to report Cleopatra's suicide a grieving Antony tells Eros to disarm for "the long day's task is done And we must sleep". He sends Mardian and Eros out but calls Eros back to put an end to his life. Eros refuses, shocked. When pressed, he draws his sword and tells Antony to turn his face away; however he then kills himself.

Antony is shamed by the heroism of Cleopatra and Eros. He falls on his sword but does not die. A friend, Dercetas, enters with guards. Antony begs them to finish him off but the guards refuse and leave, followed by Dercetas carrying his blood-stained sword.

One of Cleopatra's attendants, Diomedes, finds Antony and tells him that Cleopatra had sent word of her death, fearing Antony's wrath, but is actually alive and locked in her tomb. He calls the guards to carry Antony to the tomb.

Scene 13

Antony, preceded by Diomedes, is borne to the tomb at the top of which Cleopatra is waiting with Charmian and Iras. After some passionate exchanges Antony is hauled up to her. He declares his love, warns her to trust no-one around Caesar except Proculeius and dies in her arms. Cleopatra swoons but recovers to speak of a ceremonial funeral for Antony.

Act V

Scene 1

Dercetas brings Antony's sword to Caesar, who is in his camp with Agrippa, Dolabella, Mecaenus, Gallus and Proculeius. Caesar mourns the noble Antony's suicide. An Egyptian informs him that Cleopatra is confined in her tomb. Caesar sends Proculeius and Gallus to calm her fears.

Scene 2

Proculeius and Gallus arrive at the tomb and convey Caesar's greetings to Cleopatra, Charmian and Iras. Cleopatra asks to be allowed to retain Egypt for her son. Gallus orders Proculeius to guard her and leaves.

Proculeius and two guards climb a ladder to apprehend her while other guards open the lower part of the tomb. Cleopatra draws a dagger but is disarmed by Proculeius. She tells him that she will fast to death rather than be scorned by Octavia and mocked in Rome.

Dolabella appears; he orders Proculeius to turn Cleopatra over to him and report to Caesar. Cleopatra reveres Antony's memory and is assured by Dolabella that Caesar will do her honour.

Caesar himself enters with Gallus, Proculeius, Mecaenas and some of Cleopatra's attendants including her treasurer Seleucus. Cleopatra kneels to Caesar, as promised, and hands him an inventory scroll of her possessions. She is enraged when Seleucus mentions that some items have been kept back and insists that they are only a few toys and some gifts for Livia (Caesar's wife) and the widowed Octavia. Caesar magnanimously waves the matter aside and departs.

Cleopatra despatches Charmian on a whispered errand. Dolabella looks in to tell her that within three days she and her children are to be sent ahead of Caesar on his journey through Syria. At this, Cleopatra confirms to Iras her suspicions that they are to be exhibited as prisoners in Rome. When Charmian returns she sends for her royal robes.

A guard ushers in a jester with a basket of figs. The jester warns Cleopatra about its contents but is assured that she knows what she is doing. She dons the robes and crown brought by Iras and kisses her and Charmian. Iras falls dead. Cleopatra takes two asps [probably horned vipers] from the basket, applies them to her breast and arm and dies. Two guards rush in but they are just too late to prevent Charmian from taking another asp and dying from its bite.

Dolabella re-enters, followed by Caesar and his train. At first Caesar believes that the women died of poisoned figs but Dolabella and a guard find traces of the asps. Sadly he gives orders for Cleopatra to be buried next to Antony; the Roman army will attend the funeral before returning to Rome.

Act I, Scene 2

On the lawn of Duke Frederick's palace Rosalind rewards Orlando de Boys with a locket after he has defeated Charles, the Duke's wrestler. Charles is carried away, watched by the angry duke.

As You Like It

The story of the play, probably written in 1599, is based on the romance of *Rosalynde* (1590) by Thomas Lodge which in turn was partly based on the pseudo-Chaucerian *Tale of Gamelyn*. The title illustrates Shakespeare's disregard for the naming of his works [see *Twelfth Night* and *Much Ado About Nothing*]. Most of the action takes place in Duke Frederick's palace and in the Forest of Arden (between Coventry and Birmingham).

Act I

Scene 1

Orlando, the youngest son of Sir Rowland de Boys, deceased, is talking to his father's old servant Adam in the family orchard. He grumbles that his older brother Oliver will not give him the thousand crowns left him by his father or a decent education, although his other brother Jaques is kept properly at school. When Oliver comes up they quarrel, while Adam tries to keep the peace.

Oliver dismisses the other two in a fury and calls his servant Dennis, who brings Charles, Duke Frederick's wrestler. Charles reports that the old duke has been banished by his younger brother (his own master, Duke Frederick) and has taken to living in the forest like Robin Hood. Meanwhile the usurping Frederick holds court at the palace, with his daughter Celia and her cousin Rosalind, the old duke's daughter.

Charles is scheduled to wrestle the next day before Duke Frederick and has learned that Orlando means to contend with him in disguise. He asks Oliver how he should handle Orlando and is told not to hold back but to break his neck.

Scene 2

While chatting on the palace lawn Celia warns Rosalind not to love any man too earnestly. The court jester, Touchstone, comes to summon Celia to her father. Le Beau, a courtier, brings news of the wrestling while the others chaff him ("Well said: that was laid on with a trowel."). Le Beau tells them that Charles has wrestled with three sons of an old man and injured all of them.

Duke Frederick arrives with Orlando, Charles and the court. Rosalind falls in love with Orlando at first sight, despite Celia's advice, and begs him not to challenge Charles. Orlando, however, is indifferent to danger; he wrestles and succeeds in throwing Charles, who is carried away. Rosalind rewards Orlando with a locket but Duke Frederick, initially warm, is disappointed to learn that he is the son of an enemy, namely Sir Rowland.

When the court and the girls have gone Le Beau returns to warn Orlando of Duke Frederick's displeasure.

Scene 3

Inside the palace Rosalind confesses her love for Orlando to Celia. Duke Frederick enters and angrily orders Rosalind to leave the court, accusing her of being a traitor, apparently because she is seen to outshine Celia. Celia is distraught; she declares that she will accompany Rosalind into exile. Rosalind will be disguised as a young man called Ganymede and Celia will be 'his' sister Aliena. They plan to take Touchstone with them.

Act II

Scene 1

In the Forest of Arden the old duke muses with Amiens and other lords on their carefree existence ("our life...finds...books in the running brooks, sermons in stones,").

Scene 2

Back in the palace the disappearance of Touchstone and the girls is reported to Duke Frederick. Suspecting that Orlando is with them he sends for Oliver to go in search of his brother.

Scene 3

Orlando meets Adam near Oliver's house and learns from him that Oliver is planning to burn down his lodgings while he sleeps and thus cause his death. Adam offers him his savings of five hundred crowns and begs to go away with him as his servant. Together they set out to seek their fortune.

Scene 4

Touchstone is found in the forest, with a weary Rosalind (Ganymede) in boy's clothes and Celia (Aliena) dressed as a shepherdess. They overhear a young shepherd, Silvius, telling an older colleague, Corin, about his love for a shepherdess called Phebe. They ask Corin for food and shelter; he takes them to a cottage with a flock of sheep in a pasture and they agree to purchase it.

Scene 5

Elsewhere in the forest Lord Amiens sings to his colleague Jaques and the others ("Under the greenwood tree Who loves to lie with me") before going to summon the old duke to a banquet.

Scene 6

Adam is too weak from hunger to go further through the forest so Orlando leaves him to search for food.

Scene 7

Still in the forest a table has been set out in the banished duke's encampment. Jaques enters in melancholy mood and describes an encounter with a motley fool (Touchstone). He is interrupted by Orlando who demands food, brandishing his drawn sword. The old duke greets him civilly. Orlando apologises for his hostility and goes off to fetch Adam to the feast.

Jaques speaks of life and humanity ("All the world's a stage, And all the men and women merely players:"). "One man in his time plays many parts" Jaques says, going on to describe the seven ages of man as roles in a play. Orlando returns with Adam, to be welcomed by the old duke, while Amiens sings again ("Blow, blow, thou winter wind,").

Act III

Scene 1

At the palace Duke Frederick commands Oliver to bring in his brother Orlando dead or alive within twelve months or all his property will be seized from him.

Scene 2

Back in the forest Orlando hangs poems in praise of Rosalind on various trees. Corin asks Touchstone how he likes being a shepherd; Touchstone equivocates with witticisms. Rosalind (Ganymede) comes by, reading one of Orlando's verses. Celia (Aliena) appears with another. After the men have gone ("though not with bag and baggage,") Celia informs Rosalind that the poet is none other than Orlando, to whom she gave her locket when he defeated the wrestler.

Rosalind is eagerly questioning Celia about Orlando when he arrives with the melancholy Jaques, who wanders off after hearing about Orlando's infatuation. Rosalind, as Ganymede, banters with Orlando and queries the strength of his love. She offers to cure him by getting him to woo her at her cottage as if she were his Rosalind and responding inconstantly.

Scene 3

In another part of the forest, while Jaques looks on, Touchstone professes his love for Audrey, a country wench who herds goats. He reveals that he has arranged for Sir Oliver Martext, the vicar of the next village, to marry them in the forest. The vicar arrives and asks who is to give the bride away. Jaques comes forward to rebuke Touchstone and urge the two to get married in church in the proper manner.

Scene 4

Also in the forest Rosalind sadly tells Celia that Orlando has not come to see her, as he promised. Corin drops by to tell them that if they want to see love spurned they should eavesdrop on Silvius and Phebe.

Scene 5

They find Silvius being scorned by Phebe. Rosalind (Ganymede) comes forward to chide Phebe and urge her to accept Silvius. She leaves with Celia and Corin while Phebe, somewhat taken with Ganymede, consents to be at least a friend to Silvius.

Act IV

Scene 1

Still in the forest, gloomy Jaques seeks to be friends with Ganymede (Rosalind) and Aliena (Celia). Orlando arrives, an hour late, to woo "Rosalind", as arranged. Rosalind scoffs at Orlando's being ready to die for love, but later she mischievously gets Celia to 'marry' them. While Orlando departs for a couple of hours Rosalind tells Celia of her deep love for Orlando.

Scene 2

Jaques enquires of some lords and foresters who killed a deer. One lord acknowledges the kill and a second is required to sing a song to accompany the gift of the deer to the banished duke.

Scene 3

Rosalind, with Celia, is awaiting Orlando's return. Silvius appears with a letter for her from Phebe. Unaware of its contents, he is chagrined when Rosalind reads it out, showing it to be a love letter from Phebe to 'Ganymede'. In pity she bids Silvius tell Phebe that Ganymede commands her to love Silvius since Ganymede will not have her unless Silvius pleads her cause.

Oliver comes along, looking for a sheepcote set about with olive trees where he hopes to find Orlando with the girls. Celia directs him to it but remarks that it is empty at present. Oliver recognises Celia as the new owner of the cottage; he produces a blood-stained handkerchief and the message that Orlando cannot keep his appointment with Rosalind.

He explains that Orlando, pacing through the forest, frightened a snake away from attacking Oliver himself while he was asleep. Orlando then battled with a lioness, who also made to attack the sleeper. Subsequently Orlando took the awakened Oliver, now reunited with his brother in gratitude, to the old duke. Orlando, stripping off his clothes in a cave, passed out when a wound made by the lioness in his arm was revealed. Oliver bound up the wound and has come to tell the story.

Ganymede (Rosalind) faints at the news. She pretends that the swoon was counterfeit but Oliver sees through the pretence; he returns to Orlando while Rosalind is helped back to the cottage by Celia.

Act V

Scene 1

In yet another part of the forest Touchstone counsels patience when Audrey grumbles that they could have been married by the priest despite the intervention of Jaques. William, a young suitor for Audrey, comes across them but is intercepted and sent on his way by Touchstone with a flea in his ear.

Scene 2

Oliver confesses to Orlando that he and Aliena (Celia) are engaged to be married the next day; he intends to become a shepherd and bequeaths his inheritance to Orlando on the spot. As he leaves, Rosalind, as Ganymede, arrives to confirm that it was love at first sight. Orlando wishes that he could marry his Rosalind at the same time. Ganymede tells him that through 'his' magic powers 'he' can bring it about.

Silvius arrives with Phebe, who scolds Ganymede for reading out her love letter. Orlando sighs for Rosalind, Silvius sighs for Phebe, she for Ganymede and Ganymede for no woman. However 'he' promises that all their wishes will come true the following day.

Scene 3

Touchstone and Audrey look forward to their wedding. Two of the old duke's pages sing to them ("It was a lover and his lass, With a hey, and a ho, and a hey nonnino,").

Scene 4

The next day Amiens, Jaques, Orlando, Oliver and Celia assemble with the old duke in the forest. They are joined by Rosalind (still as Ganymede), Silvius and Phebe. The duke agrees that if Rosalind appears she will be bestowed on Orlando. Phebe wants to wed Ganymede but if that is not possible she undertakes to marry Silvius. Rosalind then leaves with Celia to prepare for the nuptial celebrations.

Audrey arrives with Touchstone, who is recognised by Jaques as the motley fool that he has seen in the forest. Touchstone asks the old duke if he may marry Audrey ("an ill-favoured thing, sir, but mine own") and addresses the company on the subject of courtiers, with their responses ranging from "the retort courteous" to "the lie direct".

Hymen, the god of married love, enters leading Rosalind in woman's clothes and Celia in court dress. Orlando now realises that the young man he 'wooed' is indeed Rosalind while Phebe agrees to marry Silvius since Ganymede turns out to be a girl. Hymen pronounces blessings on the couples and sings a hymn.

Jaques de Boys (not the other Jaques but the youngest brother of Oliver and Orlando), arrives with the news that Duke Frederick, having set out to slay the old duke in the forest, has encountered a hermit; as a result he has been converted to a religious life and in remorse has turned over his crown and lands to his older brother, the banished duke. The lugubrious Jaques decides to join Duke Frederick while the others make ready to celebrate the young people's marriages.

The epilogue, usually delivered by a man, is spoken by Rosalind. She tells the audience, "If it be true that good wine needs no bush, 'tis true that a good play needs no epilogue." She asks the women and men in turn to approve of the play and to bid her farewell when she curtsies.

Act I, Scene 1

In the shipwreck off Epidamnum Aemilia lashes the younger of each set of twins to a jury mast. Aegeon ties the older twins to another mast and attaches his wife and himself to the other ends of the masts.

The Comedy of Errors

The plot of this experimental comedy is taken from the *Menaechmi* of Plautus (translated by William Warner) and to a lesser extent from the same author's *Amphitruo*. The action takes place in Ephesus, a lost city situated somewhere on the west-facing coast of Asia Minor (see note to Act III, Scene 2 of *Pericles*).

Act I

Scene 1

Aegeon, an old merchant from Syracuse in Sicily, appears before Solinus, the Duke of Ephesus, in the hall of his palace, attended by a gaoler and other officials. The Duke reminds him that by law any Syracusan found in Ephesus (or Ephesian found in Syracuse, for that matter) is to be executed and his goods confiscated unless he pays a fine of one thousand marks. Since Aegeon cannot afford even one hundred marks he is condemned to die.

Asked by the Duke why he has dared to come to Ephesus Aegeon tells his story. He was born at Syracuse, was happily married there and became wealthy. Being detained by business for six months in Epidamnum [probably a port in the Peloponnese] on the death of his factor there he sent for his wife Aemilia to join him. Not long afterwards she gave birth to identical twin sons. By coincidence a poor woman lodging at the same inn was also delivered of identical twin sons at that time.

He adopted the second set of twins and brought them up to attend his own sons. They all set out to return home but one league [three miles] from Epidamnum a violent storm arose and the sailors abandoned the sinking ship. Aemilia lashed her last-born child to one end of a jury mast together with the younger of the servant twins. Aegeon tied the other children to the end of another mast. Then he attached his wife to the opposite end of that mast and himself to the first.

As the ship drifted on towards Corinth they saw two vessels approaching, one from there and the other from Epidaurus. However when they were yet thirty miles apart the ship split upon a rock and foundered. Aemilia and the two older children with her were rescued by Corinthian fishermen while he and the younger two were picked up by the second ship which was unable to overtake the first. Thus the family was separated.

Years passed and at the age of eighteen his son, the younger twin, asked to be allowed to search for his brother, together with his attendant who was in the same situation. He reluctantly let them go and has now spent five years roaming Greece and other countries, finally arriving in Ephesus.

The sympathetic Duke is unable to change the law but gives Aegeon a day of grace to beg or borrow the money for the fine. Aegeon leaves with the gaoler on his hopeless quest.

Scene 2

A merchant in the marketplace tells recent arrivals Antipholus and his servant Dromio of Syracuse about Aegeon's predicament. As he pays them for goods he advises them to make out that they come from Epidamnum, to avoid a similar fate. Antipholus (of Syracuse) tells Dromio (S) to take the money to the *Centaur* where they are lodging; he will be along later.

Antipholus (S) invites the merchant to look round the town and then dine with him. The merchant is engaged until five o'clock but agrees to meet him then and spend the evening with him.

Antipholus (S) thinks he sees Dromio approaching but in fact this is the older twin, Dromio of Ephesus, who has been living in the city with his own older twin, Antipholus of Ephesus, for twenty years. The first of many misunderstandings occurs as Antipholus (S) wonders why he is returning so soon while Dromio (of Ephesus) reproaches him for not coming home to lunch. Antipholus (S) wants to know what he has done with the thousand marks he gave him; Dromio (E) denies knowledge of it and bids him join his wife at the *Phoenix*. The puzzled and indignant Antipholus (S) beats him till he scampers off and follows him, as he thinks, to the *Centaur*, fearing that his money is lost.

Act II

Scene 1

Adriana, the wife of Antipholus (E), grumbles to her unmarried sister Luciana that neither her husband nor his servant have come home to lunch. Luciana counsels patience and suggests that they have their meal as it is two o'clock [an anachronism].

Dromio (E) comes in, complaining that his master has denied having a wife, demanded money of him and boxed his ears. The jealous Adriana sends him back "like a football" and rants to Luciana that her husband must have another woman.

Scene 2

Antipholus (S) encounters Dromio (S) in a public place and beats him for his imagined previous insolence. Dromio (S) tries to divert him with jests since "in the why and the wherefore is neither rime nor reason".

Adriana, accompanied by Luciana, finds Antipholus (S) and accuses him of philandering. He is amazed, since he has been in Ephesus only two hours. When Dromio (S) denies having called on him to come home she blames Antipholus (S) for involving his servant in his deception. Antipholus (S) wonders if he is dreaming when Adriana directs him to lunch privately with her while Dromio (S) stands guard at the gate.

Act III

Scene 1

Arriving at his house with two guests — a merchant, Balthazar, and a goldsmith, Angelo — Antipholus (of Ephesus) asks the latter to explain his lateness to his wife. He is to say that Antipholus (E) had lingered to watch him making her carkanet [jewelled collar], which he will deliver tomorrow. Seeing Dromio (E) he calls him an ass and enquires why, at the market, Dromio had said falsely that he (Antipholus) had given him money and denied having a wife.

When he finds the door locked he orders Dromio (E) to get the servants to let them in. From inside Dromio (S) tells them to go away, startling Dromio (E) by identifying himself as Dromio the gatekeeper. Dromio (E) hears the voices of Adriana and Luce, her servant, and a shouting match ensues.

Antipholus (E) calls for a crowbar to break down the door but is restrained by Balthazar who proposes that they repair to the *Tiger* for lunch and that Antipholus (E) return quietly in the evening. Antipholus (E) suggests lunch at the *Porpentine*; to spite his wife he sends Angelo to fetch a chain as a gift for the hostess, the courtesan with whom he is accused of having an affair. He and Balthazar leave.

Scene 2

At the same place Luciana admonishes Antipholus (S), telling him to be more attentive to her sister. He wonders how she knows his name. Protesting that he has no wife he makes advances to her, which she parries before leaving. Dromio (S) appears and tells him a frantic story of a grossly fat kitchenmaid called Nell or Dowsabell who claimed that he was her fiancé. Antipholus (S) sends him to find out if an offshore wind is blowing, in which case they will both depart from this place that "witches do inhabit".

Angelo brings Antipholus (S) the chain, saying that he will call at suppertime to collect the money for it. A bemused Antipholus accepts the chain and confirms his resolution to take the first ship out with his servant.

Act IV

Scene 1

Another merchant who is leaving for Persia threatens to have Angelo arrested in the street by an officer for a debt owed him since Pentecost. Angelo tells him that at five o'clock Antipholus (E) will be paying him that sum and three ducats more for the chain and invites him to accompany him to Antipholus' house.

Antipholus (E) and Dromio (E) come by on their way back from the courtesan's house. Dromio (E) is sent to buy a rope with which to chastise Adriana. When Antipholus (E) is accosted he tells Angelo to take the chain to his house, where his wife will pay him for it. Angelo insists that he already gave him the chain half an hour earlier and an argument develops. Eventually the officer arrests both Angelo and Antipholus (E) in the name of the Duke.

Dromio (S) returns to inform Antipholus (E) that a bark [small sailing ship] called Expedition that is about to sail for Epidamnum is waiting for him to board. Antipholus (E), having sent Dromio for a rope, is baffled. He gives Dromio (S) a key and sends him to his wife with instructions to unlock a desk and send him back with a purse of five hundred ducats. Dromio (S) is reluctant to return to the house where Dowsabell claimed him but complies.

Scene 2

In Antipholus (E)'s house Luciana has told Adriana about his advances to her. Adriana is riven with jealousy. Dromio (S) enters and asks for the purse from the desk; Luciana fetches it for him and he leaves.

Scene 3

In a public place Antipholus (S) cannot understand why people keep greeting him and inviting him to accept various commodities. Dromio (S) brings him the purse and is glad to see him out of prison. He informs Antipholus that because of his arrest he has missed the bark and will now have to sail on the *Delay*, a hoy [one-decked sloop].

The courtesan comes up, invites Antipholus (S) to dinner and asks if the chain he is holding is the one he promised her. Dromio (S) suggests a long spoon, for "he must have a long spoon that must eat with the devil". When the courtesan insists on either the chain or a ring worth forty ducats that she gave him at lunch Antipholus (S) and Dromio (S) dash off.

Scene 4

In the street Antipholus (E) assures the officer that he will not seek to escape. Dromio (E) meets them with the rope but no money. Antipholus (E), under the impression that he has given all the five hundred ducats for the rope, beats him.

Adriana, Luciana and the courtesan come along with Pinch, a schoolmaster and spiritualist. As Antipholus (E) continues to beat his servant the courtesan asks if he is not mad. When Pinch tries to take Antipholus' pulse and exorcise his 'Satan' he beats him as well. A further quarrel develops as Adriana denies that he was locked out of his house and Dromio (E) denies receiving any gold. Adriana calls some men to bind Antipholus (E) and take him home; the officer points out that Antipholus is his prisoner. The men then bind Dromio (E), at Pinch's behest, and take him away with Antipholus (E).

Adriana learns from the officer that Angelo is owed two hundred ducats for a chain which the courtesan saw in his hands. When Antipholus (S) and Dromio (S) approach with drawn rapiers, on their way to the boat, Adriana, Luciana and the officer flee, thinking that they have escaped their captors.

Act V

Scene 1

Near an abbey Angelo apologises to the merchant for the fact that the well-respected Antipholus has made off with his chain. They spot Antipholus (S) with the chain round his neck walking with Dromio (S) and challenge him with drawn swords. Adriana appears with Luciana, the courtesan and others and attempts to disarm Antipholus (S). He and Dromio (S) take refuge in the abbey.

The abbess emerges and calms the throng. She tells Adriana that Antipholus has probably been driven out of his mind by her upbraiding and forbids anyone to enter the abbey until she has restored him to health and sanity. When she departs Luciana urges her sister to complain to the Duke. The second merchant recalls that the Duke is due at five o'clock to attend Aegeon's execution.

Duke Solinus comes past in procession with Aegeon, the executioner and other officers. Adriana importunes him to have Antipholus and Dromio released from the abbey so that she can take Antipholus home. Since Antipholus (E) has served the Duke loyally in time of war he agrees to speak to the abbess. A servant comes to report that Antipholus and Dromio, far from being in the abbey, have broken loose, burned Pinch's beard and doused him with mire. The Duke and the others are guarded by halberds [long-shafted axes] as Antipholus (E) and Dromio (E) arrive.

Antipholus (E) cries for justice against Adriana who locked him out of his house. She tells the Duke that on the contrary she lunched with her husband. Antipholus relates the whole story of the goldsmith, the chain and his own detention. Angelo and the second merchant contradict him and give their versions of events. Aegeon is happy to find a couple of people at last who know him well but is distraught when Antipholus (E) swears he has never set eyes on him and has never even visited Syracuse.

The abbess brings in Antipholus (S) and Dromio (S). Adriana and the others are flabbergasted to see the doubles before them. Aegeon is further amazed when the abbess reveals that she is Aemilia, the wife whom he lost in the shipwreck years before. Antipholus (E) confirms that he was brought to Ephesus by Duke Menaphon, the Duke's uncle, who had acquired him and his servant from the Corinthian fishermen. Antipholus (S) takes the opportunity to renew his courtship of Luciana and the matter of the chain and the purse of ducats is sorted out, while the diamond ring is returned to the courtesan.

The abbess invites the Duke, Aegeon, the courtesan, the merchant, Angelo and the attendants into the abbey to go over the affair in detail. Antipholus (E) leaves with Adriana and Antipholus (S) goes off with Luciana. Dromio (S) thanks his stars that the fat kitchen wench will be his sister rather than his wife and departs with his twin brother.

Coriolanus

Little is known about the provenance of this play. It appears to have been written in 1608, immediately after *Antony & Cleopatra*, and is similarly based on North's *Plutarch*. The story is based on the suspect legend that the patrician Gaius (or Caius) Marcius was accorded the surname Coriolanus through his bravery at the siege of Corioli in 493 BC.

Act I

Scene 1

It is a time of famine in Rome. Some mutinous citizens carrying weapons resolve to kill Gaius Marcius over the high price of corn while others urge restraint. The shouts of another crowd are heard as they encounter the elderly Menenius Agrippa, a friend who is like a father to Marcius, in the street.

Menenius relates a parable in which the belly is accused by the head and limbs of being a useless food cupboard which does not see, feel, walk or share the labour of the body. The belly replies that, unseen, it distributes nourishment like flour to all parts of the body, retaining only the bran. The senators of Rome are the belly; the dearth of food is due to the gods, not the patricians [i.e. the aristocracy].

Marcius comes along and rebukes the rioters for their greed and volatility. He tells them to go home, saying that the other mob has dispersed, having been promised five tribunes [magistrates who defend the rights of the plebeians, or commoners]. A messenger rushes up to report that the Volsces [a marsh people of southern Latium] are up in arms.

The group is joined by two generals, Titus Lartius and Cominius (who is also a consul), two tribunes, Junius Brutus and Sicinius Velutus, and some senators. Marcius and the generals agree to oppose the Volscian general, Tullus Aufidius, and call upon the mutineers to follow them. The two tribunes are left alone; they commend Marcius' nobility and wonder how he will fare as second-in-command to Cominius.

Scene 2

In the senate-house at Corioli Aufidius reads a letter to the senators warning them that the Romans have mobilised and appear to know the Volsces' intentions. The senators order Aufidius to take the field while they guard Corioli.

Scene 3

Marcius' mother Volumnia and his wife Virgilia are seated on stools, sewing, in his house in Rome. Volumnia speaks of her pride in Marcius' valour but Virgilia fears for his safety. A gentlewoman announces the visit of Virgilia's friend Valeria, Publicola's sister, who enters with an usher. After talking about Virgilia's young son (also Marcius) the other two press her to visit a sick friend. Virgilia declines, wishing to wait for the return of her husband from the siege of Corioli which he is conducting with Lartius.

Scene 4

Near Corioli a messenger comes to tell Marcius and Lartius that the Roman and Volscian armies have met a mile and a half away but Cominius has not yet spoken to Aufidius. Lartius consequently wins a horse in a wager but he lends it back to Marcius for fifty years (!).

While distant drums are heard a parley is sounded. Two senators appear on the town walls to tell the Romans that Aufidius is attacking their forces. A Volscian force emerges from the city and pushes the Romans back to their trenches. Marcius curses the Romans' cowardice.

The fight is renewed and now the Volsces are driven back into Corioli. Marcius follows them and is trapped as the gates swing shut. Lartius is shaken but sees Marcius, wounded, being assaulted by the enemy. He and some Roman troops join the fray and they all pour into the city.

Scene 5

Roman soldiers are carrying away spoils in the streets of Corioli. Marcius orders Lartius to secure the city while he, although injured, goes to the aid of Cominius.

Scene 6

A messenger has been driven out of his way by a Volscian patrol. He reports to Cominius, who is in retreat, that the besieging forces have been forced back to their trenches. However Marcius arrives and tells Cominius that Corioli has fallen and that Lartius is directing its affairs. He excuses the messenger's delayed report, hinting that his bravery saved the day and offering to take up the fight against Aufidius. When Cominius acquiesces he rallies the soldiers and, to their cheers, departs with a selected group.

Scene 7

Lartius emerges from the gates of Corioli to seek out Cominius and Marcius, instructing a lieutenant to guard the city and to despatch some centuries [troops of one hundred men] if he sends for them.

Scene 8

Marcius and Aufidius meet on the field of battle and fight. Some Volsces come to Aufidius' aid but Marcius forces them to give ground.

Act I, Scene 9

*After the battle Cominius presents Marcius with an oak garland
outside the gates of Corioli and declares that he is to be known
henceforth as Gaius Marcius Coriolanus. His men acclaim the distinction.*

Scene 9

Cominius extols Marcius, whose arm is in a sling, at the Roman camp. In Lartius' hearing he offers Marcius a tenth of all the booty; Marcius modestly refuses it. Cominius then presents him with an oak garland and declares that he is to be known as Gaius Marcius Coriolanus. He prepares to write despatches for Rome as the men acclaim the distinction.

The newly styled Coriolanus asks Cominius to release a poor Volscian prisoner who had accommodated him in Corioli and shown him kindness. Lartius, on his way back to the city to assemble the hostages, enquires the man's name but the weary Coriolanus has forgotten it.

Scene 10

In the Volscian camp Aufidius, having been beaten five times by the hated Marcius, swears revenge. He sends a soldier to spy on the Roman city garrison and report to him at a cypress grove south of Corioli.

Act II

Scene 1

Back in Rome Sicinius and Brutus consider Marcius proud and boastful as well as unpopular. Menenius pours scorn on their judgement, recalling that they take two days to decide a dispute over threepence between a fruiterer and a hardware merchant. Volumnia comes by with Virgilia and Valeria. She informs Menenius that Marcius has written to everyone and is on the way home. He has won a third garland but has suffered wounds in the shoulder and left arm to add to twenty five previous ones.

To a flourish of trumpets and a heraldic proclamation of his new title Coriolanus enters between Cominius and Lartius, followed by the ranks of the Roman army. He kneels to his mother and queries his wife's tears of happiness. The procession resumes its march to the Capitol, leaving the two tribunes maliciously considering Marcius' downfall if he is appointed consul [one of two chief magistrates].

Scene 2

Two officers gossip about Coriolanus, one of three candidates for the consulship, while laying out cushions in the Capitol. They find him worthy but careless of the opinions of the common people, to the point where he seems to court their disapprobation.

Trumpets sound the entry of a procession led by lictors [officers bearing fasces, i.e. bundles of rods symbolic of magisterial power]. They are followed by Cominius (as a consul), Menenius, Coriolanus, other senators and tribunes including Sicinius and Brutus. Menenius calls on Cominius to speak about Coriolanus but Brutus mutters some doubts. Coriolanus withdraws despite being entreated to stay.

Cominius makes a speech reviewing Coriolanus' outstanding career and his heroic exploits at Corioli. Coriolanus is recalled and informed that the senate appoints him a consul. He accepts but tries to avoid the customary colloquy with the people, fearing to be thought a braggart. After the ceremony Sicinius and Brutus continue to voice their disquiet.

Scene 3

A group of citizens in the forum have not forgotten Coriolanus' treatment of them over the price of corn. He enters with Menenius, wearing a gown of humility and still at a loss as to how to converse with the multitude.

Coriolanus tells the first two citizens who come past that it is not his desire to be there; he has to be prompted to ask kindly for their support. Another couple come by, commending his military prowess but observing that he has not loved the common people. He grudgingly promises a better attitude and takes the opportunity to canvass three more people.

Menenius, Brutus and Sicinius return to conduct Coriolanus to the senate-house; he goes off with Menenius to change his clothes. The citizens then return. All but one of them remark to Brutus and Sicinius that they felt that Coriolanus was mocking them. They say that he did not show them his wounds and implied that he was seeking their approval only because custom required him to do so.

The tribunes tell them that they should have challenged his record of oppression and contempt for the lower classes; he would then either have made them promises which would have to be honoured or flown into a rage and disqualified himself. They resolve not to confirm him as consul and scatter to drum up more opposition, urged on by Brutus and Sicinius who hurry to the Capitol to see the outcome.

Act III

Scene 1

In a street in Rome Cominius addresses Coriolanus as "lord consul" in the company of Menenius, Lartius and other senators and patricians, thinking that his appointment has been approved by both the nobility and the commoners. He and Lartius tell him that the armed force newly raised by Aufidius is exhausted and that Aufidius has retired to Antium to nurse his hatred of Coriolanus.

Sicinius and Brutus appear and warn Coriolanus not to go on to the marketplace as the crowd may lynch him for having tried to prevent the distribution of free corn. Coriolanus accuses them of stirring up the rabble and remarks petulantly that he may as well be an ordinary tribune like them. He scorns any placation of the people, saying that it will lead to mob rule, and is affronted by Sicinius' uncompromising words.

Brutus and Sicinius are disgusted at his arrogance and summon an aedile [a magistrate in charge of police and public events]. The aedile fetches his colleagues and returns with a crowd of people, while Coriolanus rants in fury. The mob surround Coriolanus. Menenius asks Sicinius to calm them but he tells them that Coriolanus will deprive them of their liberty. He and Brutus call upon the commoners to put Coriolanus to death by hurling him from the Tarpeian rock [a place of execution on the Capitoline Hill].

Despite Menenius' efforts Coriolanus draws his sword and challenges the rabble. They lay hands on him but are beaten off by him and the patricians, aided by Menenius. The tribunes, the aediles and the people retreat; Coriolanus and Cominius depart, leaving Menenius to reason with them later.

Brutus and Sicinius bring the crowd back again, intent on killing Coriolanus. Menenius calls for temperance, painting Coriolanus as a rough soldier who has served Rome valiantly. They eventually agree to let Menenius and the senators counsel him and bring him to the marketplace to answer the charges against him.

Scene 2

Among the patricians in his house Coriolanus is obdurate. Volumnia enters, followed by Menenius and the senators, and pleads with him eloquently to go and speak softly and humbly to the people.

Cominius comes to report that an angry mob is waiting in the marketplace and the tribunes are preparing even more serious accusations. A resentful Coriolanus reluctantly agrees to go and speak "mildly" to the people.

Scene 3

In the forum Brutus and Sicinius plan to provoke Coriolanus by accusing him of tyranny and failing to share out the spoils of war. They tell an aedile to get the crowd to support them when they call for a fine or banishment or death. As Coriolanus enters with Menenius, Cominius, other patricians and senators the aedile returns with the citizens.

Menenius asks for consideration of Coriolanus' distinguished military record but Sicinius refers to him as a traitor. As foreseen, this enrages him and he defies his accusers. The crowd roars approval as Sicinius calls for him to be banished from Rome. Coriolanus curses them bitterly as they prepare to hustle him out of the city.

Act IV

Scene 1

At one of the city gates Coriolanus bids farewell to Volumnia, Virgilia, Menenius, Cominius and a group of young patricians. Cominius offers to accompany him for the first month of his banishment but Coriolanus bids them dry their tears and nobly sets off alone.

Scene 2

In a nearby street Brutus and Sicinius tell an aedile to send the people home. They cannot avoid meeting Volumnia, Virgilia and Menenius returning from the gate. The women give vent to their grief and despisal, while Menenius again attempts to act as peacemaker.

Scene 3

Nicanor, a Roman, meets Adrian, a Volsce, on the highway between Rome and Antium. Nicanor tells him of friction between the Roman plebeians and the patricians, who resent the banishment of Coriolanus. Adrian reports that the Volsces are once more making ready for war.

Scene 4

Coriolanus, in ragged clothes and muffled, has reached Antium and asks a passer-by for directions to Aufidius' house.

Scene 5

Some of Aufidius' servants ask Coriolanus how he got past the porter and into the hall of their house. He pushes them about and bandies words with them until Aufidius is fetched. When Coriolanus is not recognised he reveals himself as Gaius Marcius surnamed Coriolanus; he describes his banishment and offers his services, or his life, to Aufidius.

Aufidius' hatred melts. He embraces "noble Marcius" and offers him command of half the forces he is about to lead into the field. The two go to talk to the Volscian senators while the servants tell each other that they knew all the time that the visitor was more than a beggar. One servant comes in to report that Coriolanus is now seated at the top of the senators' table, inspiring them to go to war.

Scene 6

Back in Rome Brutus and Sicinius greet Menenius and observe that Coriolanus, of whom there is no news, is not being missed. Menenius admits that all seems well but feels that things would have been even better had Coriolanus temporised.

At that moment an aedile enters to tell the disbelieving tribunes that two Volscian armies have entered Roman territory. A messenger comes to confirm the news, reporting that the Volscian commanders are Aufidius and Marcius (Coriolanus). He is followed by another messenger who calls them to attend the senate.

Cominius arrives and, supported by Menenius, castigates the tribunes for bringing this fate upon Rome. A number of fearful citizens rush in, maintaining that they consented to the banishment of Coriolanus against their will. Sicinius manages to disperse them.

Scene 7

In his camp near Rome a lieutenant reports to Aufidius that the Volscian soldiers are all turning to the prestigious Coriolanus and regrets that command of the army has been divided. Aufidius reassures him that although Coriolanus will capture Rome he will yet trip over something left undone.

Act V

Scene 1

Within the city Cominius describes to Menenius, Sicinius, Brutus and others how he was repulsed by Coriolanus when he sought mercy for Rome. Menenius enquires what else he expected. Being pressed, he agrees to mediate and leaves to ask pardon of Coriolanus while Cominius doubts that he will be given a hearing, after his own experience.

Scene 2

Menenius arrives at the Volscian camp near Rome, to be told by the guards that Coriolanus will not see him. While he is insisting on an audience Coriolanus enters with Aufidius. Menenius begs him to spare Rome, saying that he has been prevailed upon to come, as the only man to whom Coriolanus will listen. Coriolanus waves him away but before departing hands him a paper. Menenius leaves, to the discomfiture of the guards.

Scene 3

Coriolanus confers with Aufidius in his tent. Virgilia and Volumnia enter in mourning, leading young Marcius, Valeria and their attendants. He kneels to them but Volumnia raises him and kneels to him in turn. She introduces Valeria and on behalf of Rome pleads at length for forgiveness. Coriolanus finally softens and agrees to make peace with the Romans. Aufidius signifies his acquiescence but privately resolves to profit from Coriolanus' weakness.

Scene 4

Back in Rome Menenius tells Sicinius that Volumnia has no chance of persuading Coriolanus to relent.

A messenger comes to report that the plebeians have seized Brutus and will put him to death if the Roman ladies do not succeed in their mission.

A second messenger brings the good news that the ladies have prevailed; Coriolanus and the Volsces have withdrawn. Shouting is heard, with sounds of trumpets, oboes and drums. To cries of 'Welcome!' a procession passes through, including Volumnia, Virgilia, Valeria, senators, patricians and plebeians.

Scene 5

In a public place in Corioli Aufidius hands his attendants a paper for the lords of the city. Three or four conspirators enter; they agree that the people of Corioli are dismayed by the fact that a Roman, elevated to command, has prevented their army from sacking Rome and winning booty. The city lords arrive and welcome Aufidius. They endorse the view in his paper, that Coriolanus should not have concluded a treaty that deprives the Volsces of their potential spoils.

Coriolanus appears with an escort, followed by a crowd. He tells the lords that the negotiated spoils will cover a third of the cost of the campaign and that peace has been achieved with both the Antiates and the Romans.

The lords decline to scan the treaties. They address him as 'Marcius' and brand him a traitor for giving up the prize of Rome at the behest of his mother. He rounds on Aufidius, calling him a liar, but he and the conspirators draw their swords and kill Coriolanus.

Standing on Coriolanus' body Aufidius justifies the deed. He joins the others in bearing the noble corpse away, to the sound of a funeral march.

Cymbeline

The play is based on one of the stories in Boccaccio's *Decameron* (Day 2, No. 9) and possibly also on one of the tales in an English book called *Westward for Smelts*. Posthumus' dream in Act V, Scene 4, is thought to be an interpolation by another author. The action appears to take place a few years after the birth of Christ, when Augustus Caesar was the Roman emperor.

Act I

Scene 1

Two gentlemen are chatting in the palace garden of Cymbeline, King of Britain. Their conversation reveals that Imogen, the king's daughter by his first wife, has married a worthy commoner and childhood sweetheart, Posthumus Leonatus, without her parents' prior knowledge. Cymbeline, who had intended Imogen to marry Prince Cloten, the queen's only son by her first husband, has ordered Posthumus to be banished from the country.

(Posthumus is the orphan son of Sicilius who was killed in battle against the Romans while in the king's service. Cymbeline brought him up because his own two sons from his first marriage twenty years ago were stolen from their nursery, never to be seen again, one being newborn and the other three years old).

The queen enters with her stepdaughter and Posthumus as the gentlemen leave. She slyly undertakes to go and intercede with her husband on behalf of Posthumus. Meanwhile Imogen swears her love for Posthumus, who tells her that he will suffer his banishment at the house of his father's friend, Philario, in Italy. The queen returns briefly to warn them that Cymbeline is coming; Imogen gives her husband a diamond ring of her mother's and he clasps a bracelet on her arm.

Posthumus hurries off as Cymbeline enters with his retinue and rails at Imogen, who responds in kind. The queen comes back again and endeavours to calm them. Cymbeline stalks off and Posthumus' servant Pisanio appears with a report that Cloten and Posthumus have drawn their swords on each other but have been parted.

Scene 2

Prince Cloten blusters to two lords that he would have defeated Posthumus had he not been prevented; at least one of the lords is not impressed.

Scene 3

Pisanio, who has been left behind in the palace in Imogen's service, tells her how Posthumus set sail, waving a sorrowful goodbye. She sighs with love before being called away to the queen.

Scene 4

In his house in Rome Philario, an old comrade of Sicilius, tells a friend, Iachimo, about Posthumus in the company of a Frenchman, a Dutchman and a Spaniard. When Posthumus enters the Frenchman refers to a previous wrangle in which each man upheld the unassailable virtue of his own countrywomen. Iachimo taunts Posthumus, against Philario's wishes. He wagers ten thousand ducats against Imogen's diamond ring that he can go to England and seduce her. Posthumus accepts, challenging him to a duel if he loses.

Scene 5

In Cymbeline's palace the queen despatches her ladies to collect flowers and commands Cornelius, a physician, to produce the poison she had ordered. The mistrustful Cornelius hands her a small box, observing to himself that it contains only a stupefying drug. As he leaves, Pisanio enters and picks up the box which the queen has dropped. She lets him keep it, commenting that it contains a restorative that has already revived the king five times; she bids him summon her ladies again. Pisanio is not deceived by her overtures.

Scene 6

Elsewhere in the palace Imogen laments her situation, having a cruel father, a false stepmother, a foolish suitor and a banished husband. Pisanio introduces Iachimo from Italy, who presents her with a letter from Posthumus and sends Pisanio to look after his own servant. Iachimo then plies Imogen with ambiguous compliments and insinuates that her husband is living the life of a libertine in Rome, on her money. When Imogen angrily rebuts the story he retracts it, maintaining that he was merely testing her constancy. She forgives him and grants his request that she store a chest containing a costly present for the Emperor in her chamber overnight for safekeeping.

Act II

Scene 1

Near the palace Cloten grumbles to his companions about losing a game of bowls on the last delivery. He learns from them that an Italian stranger has turned up at court.

Scene 2

At midnight Imogen dismisses her attendant, Helen, and settles down to sleep. Iachimo emerges from a large trunk in her bedchamber and takes note of his surroundings. He removes the bracelet from her arm, noticing a five-spotted mole on her left breast, and hides in the trunk again.

Act II, Scene 2

At midnight Iachimo emerges from a trunk in Imogen's bedchamber in the palace of Cymbeline, King of Britain. He removes a bracelet from her arm, noticing a five-spotted mole on her breast.

Scene 3

At dawn Prince Cloten, with his suite and musicians, enters the adjoining anteroom and sings an aubade ("Hark! hark! the lark at heaven's gate sings,") to no effect. As the musicians leave, the king and queen arrive and reassure Cloten that in due time Imogen will accept him. A messenger comes to call Cymbeline to meet an ambassador from Rome, General Caius Lucius.

Left alone, Cloten knocks vainly at Imogen's door; when a lady approaches he tries to bribe her to open it. At that moment Imogen appears and makes it clear that she will have nothing to do with him. When Pisanio enters she asks him to help her maid Dorothy look for the bracelet missing from her arm. Cloten sweeps out in a huff.

Scene 4

In Rome Posthumus and Philario discuss Caius Lucius' visit to Britain and a possible Roman invasion. Iachimo arrives and boasts that he has won the bet. To prove it he describes Imogen's bedchamber in detail but Posthumus points out that he could have heard a description of it. Iachimo then produces the bracelet and Posthumus, convinced, prepares to hand over the diamond ring.

Iachimo cunningly acknowledges that the bracelet could have been filched by a maid or even sent to Posthumus by his wife. However he clinches the matter by claiming that he kissed the mole on her breast. Posthumus cries out that he has been cuckolded and vows to go to Britain and tear Imogen limb from limb.

Scene 5

Posthumus rants on in the next room, cursing all women for their volatility and deception. He even suspects that his true father was a lover of his mother's.

Act III

Scene 1

Cymbeline with the queen, Cloten and their courtiers receive Caius Lucius and his aides in the palace hall. Lucius demands an annual tribute of three thousand pounds, as agreed by Cymbeline's uncle Cassibelan. When the royal family refuse to pay it Lucius threatens war on Britain in the name of Augustus Caesar.

Scene 2

Pisanio reads a letter from Posthumus accusing Imogen of adultery and entreating him to kill her. He is appalled. When Imogen enters he gives her another letter which asks her to meet Posthumus in Milford Haven, Cambria. She at once prepares to ride to Wales with Pisanio.

Scene 3

Belarius, a banished nobleman living under the name of Morgan, emerges from his cave in the Welsh mountains with Guiderius and Arviragus. He celebrates the open-air existence which he has lived for twenty years and sends off the young men, whom he calls Polydore and Cadwal, to hunt for venison. In a soliloquy he reveals that they are really Cymbeline's sons whom he stole in infancy out of revenge for his unjust banishment, together with their nurse Euriphile, now dead, whom they took to be their mother.

Scene 4

Near Milford Haven Imogen cross-questions Pisanio who shows her the letter in which he is instructed to kill her. In despair she invites him to do so but the loyal Pisanio advises her to don some clothes he has brought and pass herself off as a man; she can then enlist with Lucius, who is due in Milford Haven the next day. In that way, he suggests, she may reach her husband in Rome. He gives her the box of 'restorative' to combat seasickness on the way.

Scene 5

Back at the palace Cymbeline bids farewell to Lucius and provides him with an escort to Milford Haven. Hearing from an attendant that Imogen does not answer her door he goes to look for her. The queen orders her son to join the search, realising that if Imogen has fled to Rome Prince Cloten will succeed to the throne. Cloten returns to report that Imogen has indeed disappeared and sends the queen to soothe Cymbeline's wrath.

When Pisanio appears Cloten interrogates him so fiercely that Pisanio has to show him the letter from Posthumus. He gives Pisanio money, induces him to agree to serve him and gets him to bring some of Posthumus' garments from his lodgings. His evil plan is to kill Posthumus at Milford Haven and ravish Imogen in her husband's clothes; however Pisanio's loyalty to Posthumus does not waver.

Scene 6

Imogen, in boy's dress, stumbles wearily upon Belarius' cavern and enters. Morgan (Belarius) arrives with his 'sons' and is startled to see a figure in his cave, eating. Imogen emerges and offers them money for the food. She gives her name as Fidele and they welcome 'him'.

Scene 7

In a Roman square two senators and some tribunes discuss the raising of a civilian force to supplement the legions in Gallia (France) for an invasion of Britain, the other forces being occupied with the Dannonian uprising.

Act IV

Scene 1

Cloten, in Posthumus' clothing, nears Belarius' cave with his sword unsheathed.

Scene 2

At the cave entrance Imogen, still weak from hunger and exhaustion, swallows some of the drug in the small box and retires. Belarius, catching sight of Cloten, takes Arviragus away, leaving Guiderius to deal with him. Cloten identifies himself and calls on Guiderius, as a mountain outlaw, to yield to him; Guiderius resists and their fight carries them away. Belarius and Arviragus come back, to be joined by Guiderius carrying Cloten's severed head. Belarius fears retribution.

As Guiderius goes to dispose of the head Arviragus tiptoes into the cave to see how Fidele is faring. The two return, Arviragus carrying Imogen's inert body. They lament the death of the 'boy' and decide to bury 'him', along with Cloten, next to Euriphile. The brothers sing a threnody ("Golden lads and girls all must, As chimney-sweepers, come to dust"). Belarius brings Cloten's body and they lay the two corpses down, covered in herbs and flowers, before departing.

Later, Imogen wakes and finds the headless body in Posthumus' clothes next to her. In her grief she raves against Cloten and Pisanio for the apparent murder and falls weeping across the corpse.

She is found by Lucius and some of his officers. They inform him that the legions garrisoned in France have landed and are to be followed by a civil force under Iachimo. A soothsayer prophesies success for the Romans. They rouse Fidele (Imogen) who offers to join them now that, as she says, her master is slain. Lucius accepts the 'boy' while his men prepare a deeper grave for Cloten's cadaver.

Scene 3

At the palace, with his wife ill and his daughter and stepson missing, the downcast Cymbeline is informed that the Roman legions and civil force have landed in Wales. He tries in vain to extort information from Pisanio who is in genuine ignorance of Imogen's fate and Posthumus' whereabouts.

Scene 4

Amid the sounds of conflict in Wales Arviragus and Guiderius persuade Belarius to join the resistance against the Roman invaders.

Act V

Scene 1

In the Roman camp Posthumus, filled with remorse for having procured Imogen's death, decides to side with the British.

Scene 2

The battle is joined. Posthumus, in the garb of a poor Roman soldier, detaches Iachimo from Lucius' train, disarms him and vanishes. Cymbeline is taken prisoner but is rescued by Belarius, Arviragus and Guiderius with the aid of Posthumus. Lucius and Iachimo advise Fidele (Imogen) to fly from the scene.

Scene 3

Elsewhere on the field Posthumus relates to a doubting British lord how he with Morgan (Belarius) and his two sons held off the Roman army valiantly in a narrow lane. The lord departs and two British captains appear with their men, talking about the capture of Lucius. They arrest Posthumus and deliver him to Cymbeline when he arrives with his Roman captives. Cymbeline hands him over to a gaoler.

Scene 4

Two warders leave Posthumus locked in a prison cell. Resigned to his fate, he falls asleep. In a dream the apparitions of his father, Sicilius, his mother and two brothers dressed as wounded warriors materialise. The phantoms circle him and summon Jupiter to his aid. Jupiter descends in thunder and lightning seated on an eagle. He tells the spirits to lay a tablet on Posthumus' breast and promises that Posthumus shall be 'lord of Lady Imogen'. He ascends and the ghosts vanish.

Posthumus wakes up, remembers his dream and reads the encouraging metaphors on the tablet. The gaolers come to conduct Posthumus to the gallows but a messenger arrives in the nick of time, ordering them to strike off his manacles and bring him to the king.

Scene 5

In his tent Cymbeline recognises the bravery of Belarius, Guiderius and Arviragus by knighting them in the presence of Pisanio and his lords and officers. Cornelius enters with the ladies to report that the queen has died in a frenzy. However she first confessed that she had never loved Cymbeline, only his royal status. She also hated Imogen and was planning to kill them both with slow poison in order to set her son Cloten on the throne.

Lucius enters with Iachimo and other Roman prisoners including the soothsayer, followed by Posthumus and Fidele. Lucius acknowledges his fate and requests that Fidele, a Briton, be ransomed and not put to the sword. Cymbeline assents and grants Fidele a boon. Lucius is taken aback when Fidele does not pray for Lucius to be spared; instead 'he' asks to speak to Cymbeline confidentially. As the two confer privately Belarius realises with a shock that Fidele is the boy whom he and the others had laid out, dead, near their cave.

Cymbeline steps forward and commands Iachimo to answer Fidele's question. Fidele calls on Iachimo to explain how he came by his diamond ring. Iachimo tells the whole story of the wager and how he deceived Posthumus by claiming to have seduced Imogen. Posthumus comes forward in wild grief to admit that he arranged her death subsequently. When Fidele seeks to play the story down he strikes the boy, who falls. Pisanio quickly reveals that the 'boy' is in fact Imogen. She spurns Posthumus for having tried to poison her but Cornelius explains that the box contained only an anaesthetic drug. Imogen embraces Posthumus joyfully and kneels to the king.

Pisanio relates how Cloten came to be dressed in Posthumus' garments and Guiderius admits having decapitated him. For that Cymbeline condemns him to death but Belarius steps in to reveal his identity and recount the story of the kidnap of the baby princes twenty years before. He introduces Polydore as Guiderius and Cadwal as the younger Arviragus to their father and sister. Finally Posthumus is identified as the lone soldier who assisted Belarius and the others to defeat the Romans; Iachimo confirms his account and returns the ring and bracelet to him. Cymbeline pardons all concerned.

Posthumus describes his dream of Jupiter and his family and produces the tablet which he found on his chest afterwards. The soothsayer interprets the riddles on the tablet to mean that Posthumus and Imogen will be happily wed and Cymbeline will enjoy a period of peace and harmony in the Roman empire, to which he agrees to pay tribute. Cymbeline proposes sacrifices to the gods and a triumphant feast.

Hamlet
PRINCE of DENMARK

The outline of the plot of Shakespeare's longest play lies in Scandinavian legends recorded in the *Historica Danica* of Saxo Grammaticus (early thirteenth century). The saga reached Shakespeare via François de Belleforest's *Histoires Tragiques*. In the mythology Hamlet, or Amleth, was born to Gerutha, the daughter of Rorik, King of Denmark. The scene is set in Elsinore [Helsingör] on the Danish coast.

Act I

Scene 1

At midnight Francisco, a soldier, is shivering on sentry duty at Elsinore Castle [north of Copenhagen]. He is glad when an officer, Bernardo, comes to take over ("For this relief, much thanks;"). Marcellus, another officer, comes along with Horatio, a friend of Hamlet's. Bernardo and Marcellus start to tell Horatio about a wraith in armour that they have seen twice when suddenly it re-appears. They recognise it as the ghost of the Danish king who died two months before.

Horatio speaks to the ghost but it stalks away. He sees it as an omen relating to an impending war with Norway, brought about by Hamlet's slaying of the father of Fortinbras, the young Norwegian prince, and the acquisition of his lands. The ghost returns and seems about to speak when a cock crows and it vanishes.

Scene 2

Inside the castle Hamlet's uncle Claudius, the new King of Denmark, is addressing Queen Gertrude, the Lord Chamberlain Polonius, his son Laertes and Hamlet in the company of Voltimand, Cornelius and other courtiers. He sends Voltimand and Cornelius to make peace with Fortinbras' uncle, the King of Norway. Laertes asks him for leave to return to France, now that the coronation is over; Polonius having agreed, Claudius allows Laertes to go. The king and queen then call on Hamlet to cease his mourning and remain in Denmark instead of returning to school in Wittenberg.

Left alone, Hamlet reflects miserably on his father's death ("O! that this too too solid flesh would melt,") and his mother Gertrude's precipitate remarriage to his uncle ("Frailty, thy name is woman!"). He is joined by Horatio, Marcellus and Bernardo. Horatio tells him about the appearances of his father's ghost, with its "countenance more in sorrow than in anger", and Hamlet arranges to watch for it that night.

Scene 3

In Polonius' house Laertes takes leave of his sister Ophelia, advising her not to pay too much attention to Hamlet's advances, since his marriage will have to be a politically arranged one. His father Polonius enters to bid Laertes farewell with sage advice ("Neither a borrower, nor a lender be....This above all: to thine own self be true....Thou canst not then be false to any man.") After Laertes has left for France Polonius endorses his warnings about Hamlet to Ophelia in even stronger terms.

Scene 4

Hamlet is with Horatio and Marcellus upon the castle battlements when they hear the sound of trumpets and cannon accompanying the king's revels. He observes to them that though he is "native here And to the manner born, — it is a custom more honour'd in the breach than the observance."

The ghost appears, beckons Hamlet away from the others and identifies itself as the spirit of his father, about to descend to Hades. The spirit tells Hamlet that the story that his father was fatally stung by a serpent while sleeping in his orchard is false. The truth is that his brother Claudius murdered him in the orchard by pouring henbane into his ear. Hamlet swears revenge on his uncle the king.

When Marcellus and Horatio rejoin him Hamlet gets them to swear solemnly on his sword that they will not reveal what they have seen ("There are more things in heaven and earth, Horatio, Than are dreamt of in your philosophy.") and to take no notice if he behaves irrationally.

Act II

Scene 1

Polonius, at home, instructs his servant Reynaldo to take some money and letters to Laertes in Paris. While there he is to drop hints that Laertes is somewhat wild in order to tempt his cronies to reveal whether Laertes is in fact gambling and visiting brothels.

Ophelia comes to tell her father that while she was sewing in her closet Hamlet visited her with distraught looks and disordered clothing, clutched her arm for a while but said nothing. Polonius, thinking that Hamlet is lovesick, takes her along to inform the king.

Scene 2

In the castle the king is disturbed by Hamlet's behaviour. He and the queen send two old school friends of Hamlet, Rosencrantz and Guildenstern, to find out what is wrong with him.

Polonius brings in Voltimand and Cornelius who inform Claudius that the King of Norway has given Fortinbras three thousand crowns and commissioned him to switch his attack to Poland, if his

Act III, Scene 2

When the player 'king' is murdered in the performance in Elsinore Castle hall by having henbane poured into his ear Claudius, King of Denmark, rises in agitation, halts the drama and dismisses the court.

troops may have permission to pass through Denmark.

When they have left Polonius tells the king and queen bluntly ("since brevity is the soul of wit") that Hamlet is unhinged, showing Claudius a passionate letter from him to Ophelia, to prove it. He arranges to hide with Claudius behind an arras [tapestry curtain] when Hamlet next meets Ophelia.

The court retires and Hamlet wanders in, reading a book. Polonius suspects his ravings ("Though this be madness, yet there is method in't.") As he leaves, Rosencrantz and Guildenstern find a melancholy Hamlet, who soon discovers their mission. He learns that they have passed some young itinerant players who are to provide some Lenten entertainment.

Polonius returns to announce the arrival of the actors. When they enter Hamlet quotes from a play that "'twas caviare to the general" and the leading actor continues a long speech on the death of Priam. While Polonius sees to their lodging Hamlet asks their leader to present The Murder of Gonzago to the court, with an extra speech inserted by himself. Left alone, he reveals his plan, which is to see if Claudius reacts guiltily when the play simulates the murder of Hamlet's father.

Act III

Scene 1

Rosencrantz and Guildenstern report to the king and queen that they cannot discover the cause of Hamlet's strange behaviour. Claudius sends Gertrude away and withdraws with Polonius to eavesdrop on Hamlet's meeting with Ophelia. In a famous soliloquy ("To be or not be: that is the question:") Hamlet ponders on suicide and possible terrors to follow. He shocks Ophelia by telling her that he does not love her ("Get thee to a nunnery"). Claudius realises that Hamlet's trouble is not infatuation; he decides to send him away to England to collect tribute.

Scene 2

In the castle hall Hamlet instructs the players in stagecraft ("Speak the speech, I pray you....trippingly on the tongue.") He asks Horatio also to watch Claudius for signs of guilt when he sees the play.

The court assembles and some actors mime the action of the play, in which a king is killed by poison poured in his ear and the poisoner subsequently woos and wins his queen. The cast then perform the play, in which the queen declares vehemently that she will not remarry if she is widowed. Gertrude comments that "The lady doth protest too much, methinks." When the player king is murdered Claudius rises in agitation, halts the drama and dismisses the court.

Hamlet and Horatio are joined by Rosencrantz and Guildenstern who describe the anger and amazement of the king and queen. Hamlet agrees to speak to Gertrude.

Scene 3

Claudius orders Rosencrantz and Guildenstern to accompany Hamlet to England; Polonius comes in to tell him that he will hide behind the arras to overhear what Hamlet says to the queen. A remorseful Claudius prays for forgiveness; Hamlet sees him on his knees and shrinks from killing him thus.

Scene 4

The queen tells Hamlet in her apartment that he has offended his father; he retorts that she has offended his father (i.e. his real father) and threatens her. Polonius calls for help from his concealment and Hamlet, thinking he may be the king, kills him with a thrust of his sword through the arras. Discovering his mistake he continues to revile his mother for marrying a murderer.

The ghost re-appears, being invisible to the queen, and Hamlet speaks to it, thus convincing Gertrude that her son is indeed deranged.

Act IV

Scene 1

Gertrude reports Hamlet's accidental killing of Polonius to Claudius. The king orders Rosencrantz and Guildenstern to take Polonius' body from Hamlet and place it in the chapel.

Scene 2

The two attempt to do so but Hamlet says that he has disposed of the body already.

Scene 3

Hamlet accompanies Guildenstern to the king and Rosencrantz to state that Polonius has been interred, possibly under the lobby stairs. The king hastily despatches Hamlet to England where he plans to have him killed.

Scene 4

Out in the country Fortinbras sends one of his captains to Claudius to let him know that he and his soldiers will be marching through Denmark. Hamlet, with Rosencrantz and Guildenstern, intercepts the captain and learns the Norwegian plan, which seems to be futile.

Scene 5

Back at Elsinore a gentleman informs the queen and Horatio that Ophelia has gone out of her mind. He fetches her in and she babbles on as the king enters. He grieves over her and sends Horatio to look after her when she goes.

Laertes bursts in, armed and ready to avenge the death of his father; Claudius manages to persuade him that he is innocent of the murder. Laertes is shocked when Ophelia returns, strewing flowers with crazy murmurings.

Scene 6

Some sailors bring a letter from Hamlet to Horatio, informing him that on the way to England Hamlet was captured by pirates while Rosencrantz and Guildenstern went on.

Scene 7

Claudius explains to Laertes that he has not taken action against Hamlet because he is much loved by both the queen and the people. A messenger arrives with letters from Hamlet, advising his return. The king, having heard from a gentleman of Normandy about Laertes' skill with the rapier, suggests that he challenge Hamlet to a fencing match. The rapier will be tipped with poison and, to ensure the outcome, Hamlet's wine chalice will also be poisoned.

The queen enters with the news that Ophelia has fallen into a brook from an overhanging willow. She apparently made no attempt to save herself while she was still buoyant; eventually her sodden clothing pulled her down and she has drowned. Laertes is further inflamed.

Act V

Scene 1

Two labourers debate the morality of suicide as they prepare a grave in the churchyard. Hamlet comes along with Horatio; when the first gravedigger throws up two skulls he recognises one of them as that of the king's jester ("Alas! poor Yorick. I knew him, Horatio;")

The funeral procession approaches and Hamlet learns that the grave is Ophelia's. Laertes, frantic with grief, leaps into the grave. Hamlet follows, professing his own love for Ophelia, and grapples with him until they are parted by the mourners. The king and queen are now fully convinced of Hamlet's insanity.

Scene 2

In the hall of the castle Hamlet tells Horatio that on the ship to England he read the despatches from Claudius to the English king entreating his own murder and that of his companions. He resolves to kill the king before a reply is received from England.

A courtier, Osric, comes to tell Hamlet that the king has wagered six Barbary horses against six French rapiers with poniards and three carriages that Hamlet will score three more hits than Laertes in a dozen rounds of fencing. Hamlet agrees to fence, against Horatio's advice.

The court enters and Hamlet asks Laertes' pardon before they fence. The king sets out the wine as the bout begins and Hamlet scores two hits. The queen unknowingly drinks from the poisoned cup. Laertes succeeds in wounding Hamlet but in a scuffle the rapiers are exchanged and Hamlet wounds Laertes.

The queen falls dead and the stricken Laertes reveals the king's use of poison on the swordpoint and in the wine. Hamlet stabs the king to death with the poisoned rapier. Horatio offers to drink the rest of the poisoned wine but Hamlet, before expiring, insists that Horatio live to tell the tale and clear his name. Horatio mourns Hamlet ("Good night, sweet prince, And flights of angels sing thee to thy rest!").

Fortinbras marches in with his troops from Poland together with ambassadors from England. They report that Rosencrantz and Guildenstern have been done to death, as requested by Claudius. Fortinbras pays a tribute to Hamlet as the bodies are carried off to the sound of a funeral march.

Julius Caesar

This is the first of Shakespeare's 'Roman' plays, which are based on Plutarch's *Lives* as published by Sir Thomas North in 1580. Since the eponymous Caesar dies at the beginning of Act III a more appropriate title might have been The Fall of Julius Caesar. Most of the action takes place in Rome in the year 44 BC but there are additional scenes in the field near Sardis and Philippi respectively.

Act I

Scene 1

The commoners of Rome are out and about on the streets. Two tribunes [people's magistrates], Flavius and Marullus, rebuke them for being in leisure clothes on a working day. The crowd, with considerable badinage, tell them that they have taken a holiday to see Caesar and rejoice in his triumph.

The tribunes recall how Romans used to welcome Pompey and scold the fickle people for now celebrating the return of Pompey's conqueror [at Pharsalus]. Flavius, deploring any further homage to Caesar, disperses the crowd and instructs Marullus to take down the decorations from the statues, although it is the festival of Lupercal [on February 15th, a celebration of the founding of Rome].

Scene 2

Caesar's procession is passing through a public square. He calls on his wife, Calphurnia, to stand close to the route to be taken by Marcus Antonius (Mark Antony) on his run through the city as a religious rite. He reminds Antony to touch Calphurnia so that, according to belief, her sterility will be cured [Lupercus being the Roman god of fertility]. A soothsayer in the crowd warns Caesar to "Beware the ides of March!" [i.e. March 15th, a month ahead]; Caesar dismisses him as a dreamer and passes on.

Cassius Longinus, left behind in conversation with Marcus Brutus, wonders why his friend has grown cool towards him. Brutus professes his continuing friendship and ascribes any coolness to preoccupation with private worries. Cassius offers to be a 'mirror' to allow Brutus to see into himself.

On hearing a distant uproar Brutus fears that the people are acclaiming Caesar as a king. Cassius, encouraged, plays on his fear, pointing out that ambitious Caesar is a mere mortal and telling stories of his past weaknesses and cowardice. Why should Caesar be allowed to become a god or even a king? ("The fault, dear Brutus, is not in our stars but in ourselves..."). Brutus confesses uneasiness but adjures Cassius to say no more for the time being.

The procession returns from the Lupercalian games. As it passes by, a disturbed-looking Caesar draws Antony's attention to sinister Cassius, with his "lean and hungry look" and self-deprecating smile. Casca, another friend, detained by Brutus, recounts what happened at the games. He says that Mark Antony offered Caesar a crown three times; each time Caesar put it aside, with increasing reluctance, eventually suffering an epileptic fit (to Cassius' contempt). Afterwards, Casca goes on, Cicero made a speech in Greek ("for mine own part, it was Greek to me.") and Marullus and Flavius were apprehended for pulling scarves off Caesar's images.

Cassius, Casca and Brutus agree to meet again. After Brutus takes his leave Cassius muses, planning to toss notes purporting to come from various citizens through Brutus' windows extolling Brutus and hinting at Caesar's ambitions.

Scene 3

A thunderstorm is raging. Casca, with drawn sword, meets Cicero and tells him of direful sights including a lion loose near the Capitol and a slave whose left hand was coldly aflame. Cicero departs for home and Cassius appears. He revels in the storm and the strange portents, comparing them with puny Caesar. When Casca notes that the senators may establish Caesar as a king Cassius sounds him out and mentions an enterprise involving some noble-minded Romans.

Cinna, another acquaintance, comes along and Cassius introduces Casca as one of the conspirators. He tells Cinna to leave a note in the chair of the praetor [senior magistrate ranking below a consul] and throw another in at Brutus' window before joining the conspirators in Pompey's porch. Casca observes that the inclusion of Brutus would confer legitimacy on the enterprise; he and Cassius go off to persuade him.

Act II

Scene 1

Brutus, strolling in his orchard, calls his servant Lucius to light a taper in his study. He soliloquises that Caesar, once crowned, will become a tyrant. Lucius brings him a paper, found near the closet window, which urges Brutus to awake, to strike and to redress. Lucius reminds him that the next day is the ides of March; he answers a knock at the door and ushers in the conspirators: Cassius, Casca, Decius Brutus, Cinna, Metellus Cimber and Trebonius with veiled faces.

Cassius whispers with Brutus and invites him to swear an oath with the others. Brutus refuses, deeming their cause noble enough not to require oaths. Cassius suggests recruiting Cicero but Brutus disagrees. Decius and Cassius think Mark Antony

Act III, Scene 1

At the foot of Pompey's statue in front of the Capitol in Rome Mark Antony apostrophises Caesar's body and the place where it has fallen, promising that the foul assassination shall be avenged.

should be eliminated along with Caesar but Brutus again demurs, feeling that Antony will be powerless without Caesar. However when Metellus Cimber proposes that one Caius Ligarius should join them Brutus agrees to recruit him. Decius undertakes to persuade Caesar to go to the Capitol on the morrow.

After the conspirators leave, Brutus' wife Portia comes to him to ask why he is so distrait. Brutus first claims a slight indisposition but eventually agrees to divulge everything to Portia. He dismisses her upon the arrival of Ligarius who, although he is not well, readily agrees to support Brutus in any action.

Scene 2

The storm is still raging after midnight as Caesar, at home in his nightgown, bids a servant ascertain the auguries from the priests. Calphurnia comes to dissuade him from venturing out that day, in view of the ominous "horrid sights" seen by the watchmen, but Caesar is not deterred until the servant returns to tell him that the sacrifices confirm that he should not go out. He then agrees to stay at home.

However Decius then arrives to take him to the senate-house. When he explains to Decius that Calphurnia has had a nightmare in which his statue spurted blood Decius interprets it as a happy vision of Rome sucking reviving blood from mighty Caesar. He also hints that if Caesar does not attend, the senate may revise its view of a coronation.

Caesar changes his mind again and decides to go; the conspirators with Mark Antony arrive to accompany him.

Scene 3

In a street near the Capitol Artemidorus, a sophist [teacher of philosophy] of Cnidos, is reading over a paper warning Caesar to beware of the conspirators. He plans to hand the paper to Caesar as he approaches the Capitol.

Scene 4

Further along the street near Brutus' house Portia orders Lucius to run to the Capitol and report what is happening between Brutus and Caesar. The soothsayer comes by and deepens her fears.

Act III

Scene 1

In front of the Capitol the senate is sitting in the senate-house. Artemidorus presses his schedule [warning paper] on Caesar while Decius urges acceptance of a petition from Trebonius. Popilius Lena quietly wishes Cassius success with his enterprise, causing him and Brutus to suspect that their plot has been discovered. At the foot of Pompey's statue Trebonius draws Mark Antony out of the way while Metellus Cimber, supported by Brutus and Cassius, pleads with Caesar to end the banishment of his brother, Publius Cimber. Caesar is unyielding.

On Casca's signal the conspirators surround Caesar and stab him to death; his last words are, "Et tu, Brute? [You also, Brutus?] Then fall, Caesar!"

Amid the ensuing uproar Cinna and the others proclaim liberty and freedom while Cassius exults and Brutus tries to reassure the senators and people. A servant enters to ask if Mark Antony may safely approach. When Brutus acquiesces, Mark Antony arrives, mourns Caesar's death and, on being assured that there was good reason for the assassination, shakes hands with the conspirators. He asks to speak at the funeral, to Cassius' alarm. Brutus placates Cassius, pointing out that he will speak first from the pulpit and explain why Caesar had to die.

The conspirators depart, leaving Mark Antony with Caesar's body. He apostrophises it, promising that the foul deed shall be avenged and that Caesar's spirit shall "cry 'Havoc!' and let slip the dogs of war." A servant of Octavius Caesar's comes to tell Antony that his master is within seven leagues [21 miles] of Rome. Antony gives him a message telling Octavius Caesar to come no nearer but first he and the servant carry Caesar's body away.

Scene 2

Brutus and Cassius arrange to address separate meetings in the Forum. Brutus harangues the crowd, explaining that although he loved Caesar, the dictator had to be slain for his ambition. ("Who is here so vile that will not love his country? If any, speak; for him have I offended.") The crowd roars approval and praise for the noble Brutus, who, as he leaves, enjoins them to listen to Antony. With some suspicion they do so.

In a famous speech over the corpse ("Friends, Romans, countrymen, lend me your ears...") Antony works on the emotions of the throng, increasingly querying Caesar's supposed ambition. He weeps as he recalls how Caesar thrice refused a kingly crown offered by himself. Was this ambitious? He then produces Caesar's will, and grieves over Caesar's blood-stained mantle ("If you have tears, prepare to shed them now").

By this time the crowd are ready to riot and kill the traitorous murderers but Antony holds them by reading the will, in which Caesar has left every Roman citizen seventy five drachmas together with the use of all his walks, arbours and orchards. The crowd, now further inflamed, disperses to burn the traitors' houses.

The servant returns to inform Antony that Octavius, Caesar's nephew, has reached Rome and is with Lepidus, a gallant general, at Caesar's house, while Brutus and Cassius have fled from the city. Antony is satisfied.

Scene 3

The mutinous crowd come upon Cinna, a poet, in the street. He gives them his name and tells them that he is on his way to Caesar's funeral. Despite his desperate protests the crazed rabble take him for Cinna, one of the conspirators, and lynch him.

Act IV

Scene 1

Octavius and Lepidus are sitting at a table with Antony in his house. As newly-appointed triumvirs [i.e. three sharing political power] they are 'pricking' names on a list of those who are to die. Lepidus is sent to fetch Caesar's will; in his absence Antony suggests to Octavius that Lepidus is 'a slight unmeritable man' unfit to share in the spoils as a triumvir. Octavius defends him as a valiant soldier and the matter is dropped while the two strike up an alliance to oppose Brutus and Cassius, who are gathering their forces.

Scene 2

In a camp near Sardis Brutus receives Pindarus, Cassius' servant, in front of his tent, with Titinius and Lucilius, mutual friends. Lucilius remarks that lately Cassius has been less open and friendly. Cassius himself arrives and immediately accuses Brutus of having wronged him. Brutus hastily arranges a withdrawal into his tent, so that that their armies shall not overhear a quarrel.

Scene 3

Inside the tent Cassius airs his grievance. Lucius Pella had been condemned by Brutus for taking bribes from the Sardians while Cassius' letters, pleading his cause, were ignored. Brutus tells Cassius that not only was he wrong to take up the case but that Cassius himself has "an itching palm", unworthy of a man who had slain for justice on the ides of March. Cassius is livid with fury but Brutus is undaunted and belittles him, recalling that Cassius had refused him gold to pay his legions.

Cassius descends from rage to self-pity and eventually the two are reconciled. Too late, a poet forces his way in to quell the argument and is dismissed. The two commanders share a bowl of wine and Brutus tells Cassius that his wife, Portia, has committed suicide. Cassius consoles him.

Together with Titinius and Messala Valerius Corvinus they pore over despatches which state that Octavius, Antony and Lepidus have put to death many senators, including Cicero, and are leading an expedition to Philippi. In discussion Cassius is in favour of letting the enemy seek them but Brutus is determined to march to Philippi and confront them. ("There is a tide in the affairs of men which, taken at the flood, leads on to fortune;").

Cassius and the others depart for bed. Brutus calls Varro and Claudius to sleep on cushions in his tent. A tired Lucius sings him a lullaby but falls asleep over his lyre. Left alone to read a book Brutus is startled by the apparition of Caesar. The ghost tells Brutus that it is his evil spirit, which he will see again at Philippi; it then vanishes. In a panic Brutus wakes the others but they all deny seeing anything or crying out in their sleep.

Act V

Scene 1

Octavius and Antony note the enemy's descent to the plains of Philippi and squabble over their order of battle. The two sets of commanders meet and exchange insults, Antony referring to the conspirators as flatterers. When they part, to return to their armies, Cassius, whose birthday it is, confesses his misgivings to Messala and takes a last farewell of Brutus, in case they never meet again.

Scene 2

Brutus gives Messala despatches directing the legions on the other side of the battle line to attack Octavius' wing, which seems weak.

Scene 3

On another part of the battlefield Titinius tells Cassius that Brutus has given his orders too early; his soldiers are off pillaging while Cassius' men are surrounded by those of Antony. Cassius sends Titinius to reconnoitre; he rides off. Being short-sighted, Cassius asks his bondman, Pindarus, to watch from a hillock. Pindarus reports that Titinius has been captured and killed. Cassius, overcome with remorse, instructs Pindarus to run him through while his face is covered. Pindarus does so and flees.

Titinius, who in reality is uncaptured, and Messala appear with a victory wreath, only to discover Cassius' corpse. Messala goes to look for Pindarus while Titinius, overcome in his turn by Cassius' tragic error, commits suicide. Messala returns with Brutus and others. They mourn the deaths of Cassius and Titinius; Brutus summons Lucilius, Cato, Labeo and Flavius to continue the fight with him.

Scene 4

Brutus and his companions charge the enemy. Cato falls; in the confusion Lucilius pretends to be Brutus and attempts to bribe the enemy soldiers to kill him; they refuse. Antony arrives, recognises him and orders him taken captive.

Scene 5

Elsewhere on the battlefield Brutus tries to get Clitus or Dardanius to despatch him but neither will do so. Volumnius will not assist him either but finally his servant Strato agrees to hold his sword while he impales himself on it.

Octavius and Antony come upon Brutus' body and learn from Strato what happened. They pardon Brutus' followers. Antony, recognising that Brutus was the only conspirator with purity of motive, delivers the epitaph ("This was the noblest Roman of them all;") and he and Octavius depart from the field.

King Henry IV, Part 1

In historical chronology the two parts of *Henry IV* are the second and third plays in the so-called history-cycle, falling between *Richard II* and *Henry V*. This first part covers a period of about ten months leading up to the battle of Shrewsbury on 21st July, 1403. It introduces the famous character of Sir John Falstaff who was originally a caricature of the 15th-century Lollard martyr Sir John Oldcastle; the substituted name is adapted from Sir John Fastolfe [see part 1 of *Henry VI*, Act I, Scene 1].

Act I

Scene 1

In the royal palace in London King Henry IV (Henry Bolingbroke) finds the country weary of "civil butchery" and announces that he will lead a crusade to the Holy Land, as he has been meaning to do for a year. He asks the Earl of Westmoreland how the Council intends to support the expedition. The Earl informs him that their discussion was interrupted by the news that Edmund Mortimer, the Earl of March, had been captured by Welshmen led by Owen Glendower; a thousand men of Herefordshire were killed and mutilated.

Westmoreland goes on to say that a battle has been fought at Holmedon [Homildon] between the English under Hotspur (Henry Percy, son of the Earl of Northumberland) and the Scots under Archibald, the Earl of Douglas. Through a report from Sir Walter Blunt the king is able to tell him that Hotspur has been victorious, his forces having slain ten thousand Scots and taken many prisoners.

Henry rues the difference between the gallant Hotspur and his own riotous son, Prince Hal. Hotspur, however, has displeased him by keeping all but one of his prisoners instead of turning them over to him. Westmoreland suggests that Hotspur's uncle, Thomas Percy, the Earl of Worcester, has influenced him malevolently.

Scene 2

A conversation between Prince Hal and Sir John Falstaff in the prince's apartment reveals Falstaff to be a jovial but disreputable braggart and spendthrift. Hal is captivated by him but not mesmerised ("Sir John....will give the devil his due.") Hal's attendant, Edward Poins, enters and proposes a robbery at Gad's Hill at four o'clock the following morning. He says they will obtain purses full of crowns from rich traders and Canterbury pilgrims, aided by a ruffian called Gadshill (!).

Hal demurs but after Falstaff leaves Poins elaborates on the planned escapade. Falstaff and Gadshill, he says, will be left to waylay the victims, together with two accomplices, Bardolph and Peto; then Hal and he, in disguise, will rob them of the loot in turn. He looks forward gleefully to the lying claims that Falstaff will make afterwards about the encounter. Poins goes off to make preparations, leaving Hal to soliloquise on his tolerance of the rogues and his eventual intended reform.

Scene 3

At the palace Henry feels that he has been too lenient with the Percys; when Worcester reminds him that they helped him to depose Richard II and ascend the throne Henry irritably dismisses him. Then, while his father listens, Hotspur describes how, in his exhaustion after the battle of Holmedon, a perfumed popinjay appeared and demanded his prisoners on behalf of the king. His careless refusal, in the circumstances, is defended by Blunt.

Henry, unconvinced, points out that Hotspur is still retaining the prisoners and is demanding, in return for them, that he (Henry) ransom his wife's brother Mortimer (who has married Glendower's daughter). Henry considers Mortimer a traitor but Hotspur declaims Mortimer's long and valiant combat with Glendower on the banks of the Severn. Henry doesn't believe him; he orders him peremptorily to deliver up the prisoners and departs with Blunt.

Hotspur rants on as Worcester returns, especially when he learns that Mortimer had been proclaimed heir to the throne by Richard II and might now have been king. He blames Worcester and his father for elevating Henry Bolingbroke but Worcester has a scheme to placate him. Hotspur must use the bargaining value of his prisoners as a means of forming an alliance with Archibald, Earl of Douglas. Meanwhile his father Northumberland will enlist Richard Scroop, the Archbishop of York, who has been alienated by the execution of his brother Stephen at Bristol. After that they will all foregather with Mortimer and Glendower in Wales.

Act II

Scene 1

In the middle of the night two carriers are grumbling about the poor forage and flea-ridden chambers in the yard of an inn at Rochester [on the Medway in Kent]. Gadshill enters and attempts to borrow a lantern from them. When they depart he learns from the chamberlain that an auditor and a yeoman carrying gold will soon be setting out.

Scene 2

In the dawn half-light in a narrow lane near Gad's Hill [between Rochester and Canterbury] Falstaff is looking for Poins, who has hidden his horse. Hal pretends to go in search of him. Gadshill, Bardolph and Peto arrive; Hal and Poins leave the four to make

Act II, Scene 4

In the Boar's Head tavern in Eastcheap, London, Sir John Falstaff adopts the role of King Henry IV while Prince Hal, as a suppliant, rehearses his defence of his involvement in the Gad's Hill robbery.

the initial confrontation.

The travellers come by on foot, to spare the horses on the hill, and Falstaff yells threats as the thieves set upon them. The robbery is carried out. Falstaff complains of the cowardice of Hal and Poins but when they re-appear in disguise with a challenge he and the others flee in terror, leaving the booty behind.

Scene 3

Hotspur is reading a letter at Warkworth Castle [north of Newcastle-upon-Tyne] in Northumberland. The letter warns him not to proceed with his plot but he scornfully disregards the advice. His wife, Lady Katharine Percy, enters and wants to know why he has been distant and has experienced troubled dreams for the past fortnight. In between giving orders to servants he evades her questions but assures her that she will be with him when success is achieved.

Scene 4

Hal and Poins play a mocking game with Francis, one of the serving boys in the *Boar's Head* tavern in Eastcheap (London), until he is called away by the vintner. A bombastic Falstaff enters with Gadshill, Bardolph and Peto ("A plague of all cowards!") Drinking Spanish wine, Falstaff boasts of the way in which he and his three companions tackled at least sixteen travellers and tied them up. Then, he goes on, another band of men freed them although Falstaff himself fought heroically against an ever-increasing number of assailants.

Eventually he trips over a detail and Hal reminds him of what really happened, including his own cowardly flight. Falstaff recovers quickly, brazenly insisting that he knew Hal's identity all the time but would not run the risk of killing the heir apparent.

The hostess, Mistress Nell Quickly, comes to tell Hal that an old courtier, Sir John Bracy, is at the door; Falstaff goes to deal with him while Bardolph and Peto reveal what Falstaff did to his weapon and clothes to make it appear that he had been in a sword fight. Falstaff returns with the news that Worcester has stolen away and the rebels are gathering. Hal is to go to his father, who will undoubtedly rebuke him severely.

Falstaff suggests that Hal rehearse his defence. Accordingly he plays the part of Henry, with a cushion for a crown, and Hal bows to him. From the 'throne' Falstaff reproves Hal for the low company he keeps and lauds the virtues of the goodly noble Falstaff. Hal, affronted, decides to take the role of the king while Falstaff becomes Prince Hal. Speaking as Henry he denounces 'Hal' for consorting with a fat old man who is but a white-bearded Satan. Falstaff, as Hal, pleads sentimentally that to be old and merry is no sin.

Together with Francis, Mistress Quickly and Bardolph answer a knock at the tavern door; they report that it is the sheriff and the watch [night guard]. Hal quickly hides Falstaff behind the arras and sends the others upstairs, leaving him with Peto. The sheriff enters with one of the carriers who were robbed, seeking Falstaff. Hal swears that Falstaff is not there but promises to despatch him to the sheriff by dinnertime the next day. After the sheriff has gone Falstaff is found to be fast asleep behind the arras, with a bill for more than two gallons of sack [Spanish wine] in his pocket. The others leave him there while Hal undertakes to repay the stolen money and prepares to go to the wars.

Act III

Scene 1

Mortimer, Glendower and Hotspur gather in the archdeacon's house in Bangor [north Wales] along with Worcester. After Glendower exchanges compliments with Hotspur he talks impressively of the earthquake and heavenly fires that signalled his birth; he even claims to command the spirits. Hotspur ridicules this mumbo-jumbo ("tell truth and shame the devil.")

They turn to the archdeacon's map, which assigns Wales and all the land west of the Severn to Glendower, southern and eastern England to Mortimer and all the land to the north of the Trent to Hotspur. The bickering continues as Hotspur grumps that his share is smaller, due to the encroaching curves of the river Trent. After a further squabble about the value of poetry Glendower gives in over the land and goes to fetch the ladies. In his absence Mortimer remarks that his father-in-law wouldn't take such insolence from anyone but Hotspur; he and Worcester warn Hotspur to be less rash and provocative.

Glendower returns with his daughter and Lady Percy. Lady Mortimer speaks only Welsh and her husband only English but they exchange tender looks and caresses; Hotspur's relationship with his wife is equally loving but more playful. They listen to a Welsh song from Lady Mortimer before Hotspur drags Mortimer off to the campaign.

Scene 2

In his palace in London Henry arranges a private conversation with Hal. As anticipated, he reproves Hal for his vulgar pursuits and the low company he keeps. He refers to his own dignity and discretion compared with Richard II's craving for common popularity and reminds him that he (Hal) has lost the Court's approbation and also his place on the Council. Hal promises to reform himself; when Henry holds up the example of the valorous Hotspur, casting doubts on Hal's loyalty, Hal pledges to redeem himself in battle.

Sir Walter Blunt enters to report that the Scottish and English rebels have gathered at Shrewsbury. Henry responds that Westmoreland has set forth with Prince John of Lancaster and that he and Hal will join forces at Bridgnorth (Shropshire) the following week.

Scene 3

Falstaff, in the *Boar's Head*, fears he is losing weight and pokes fun at Bardolph's shining red face. When Mistress Quickly comes in to discuss the twenty four pounds he owes her he complains that his pocket has been picked in her tavern and thereby he has lost a signet ring of his grandfather's worth forty marks. (Previously he had claimed that Prince Hal owed him a thousand pounds).

Just as Nell Quickly mentions that the prince has said repeatedly that the eightpenny ring was only copper, Hal himself enters with Poins. Falstaff hastily changes his story, audaciously suggesting that Hal picked his pocket and 'forgiving' the hostess, who leaves. Hal tells Falstaff that the money from the robbery has been repaid. He sends Bardolph off with letters to Prince John and Westmoreland, orders Poins to saddle up and arranges to meet Falstaff the next day at Temple Hall.

Act IV

Scene 1

Hotspur and Douglas greet each other in the rebel camp near Shrewsbury. A messenger brings letters from Hotspur's father Northumberland, who is sick. Northumberland explains in the letters that he has not appointed a deputy, having found no-one sufficiently trustworthy. Worcester comments that the absence of his forces may lead others to think that the rebels are disunited but Hotspur is not daunted.

Sir Richard Vernon enters to announce the approach of Westmoreland and Prince John with seven thousand men. Henry and Hal have also started for Shrewsbury in fine fettle; furthermore Glendower cannot assemble his army for another two weeks. Douglas and Worcester agree that these are ominous tidings since the king's force will amount to some thirty thousand men.

Scene 2

Falstaff, marching along a road towards Sutton Coldfield, sends Bardolph into Coventry to buy more sack but neglects to give him any money. He muses on the methods he has used to pressgang a hundred and fifty 'scarecrows', including allowing better men to buy themselves out. Encountering Hal and Westmoreland he cynically maintains that his "pitiful rascals" will do for cannon-fodder.

Scene 3

Back at the rebel camp Hotspur and Douglas want to be in action immediately but Vernon and Worcester restrain them since the mounted men have not all arrived. Trumpets sound a temporary truce and Blunt arrives with an offer of peace and pardon from the king if the rebels have legitimate grievances. Hal replies at length that when Henry returned from exile to inherit the Dukedom of Lancaster the Percys gave him their support. However he then enacted popular measures and beheaded the deputies of Richard II who was absent at war in Ireland. Finally he deposed the king and left Mortimer unransomed

in Wales. Having finished, Hotspur tells Blunt that his uncle will bring Henry a definitive reply in the morning.

Scene 4

In his palace at York the Archbishop fears that Hotspur's rebels, without Mortimer and Glendower, will not be strong enough to defeat the king's army at Shrewsbury. Anticipating that a victorious Henry will turn upon him next he gives a friend, Sir Michael, some letters aimed at raising another army.

Act V

Scene 1

Henry, Hal, Lancaster, Blunt and Falstaff are joined by Worcester and Vernon at the king's camp near Shrewsbury. It is a blustery morning. Worcester has come to give the rebels' answer to the peace terms. Henry deprecates his presence since he has disloyally fomented the rebellion. Worcester reminds him again of how he (Henry) took advantage of Richard II's absence in Ireland to seize the throne, only to cast out the Percys, who had helped him, as a cuckoo ejects sparrows' eggs.

To avert the slaughter if the two armies are engaged Hal offers to fight Hotspur single-handed to decide the issue. Henry reluctantly agrees whereupon Worcester and Vernon leave to impart the offer to Hotspur and Douglas. Hal and Henry, not believing that they will agree, go off to prepare for battle. Falstaff asks Hal, vainly, to protect him if he falls; he concludes by deeming the concept of honour to be of little or no worth.

Scene 2

At the rebel camp Worcester presses Vernon not to mention Henry's peace offer to Douglas, fearing subsequent treachery. When Hotspur and Douglas enter he suppresses the proposal and Douglas goes to free Westmoreland, who has been held hostage against Worcester's safe return. Douglas re-enters to say that Westmoreland is taking a defiant answer back to Henry.

Worcester tells his nephew about Hal's offer to fight him singly, made with modesty and respect. Hotspur cannot credit this change of attitude on Hal's part; as messengers warn of Henry's advance he urges his men on with the Percys' battle cry.

Scene 3

Several noblemen are disguised as Henry on the battlefield. Douglas, having slain one of them, Lord Stafford, encounters Blunt similarly dressed and kills him after a fight. Hotspur comes along and identifies Blunt, thus reviving Douglas' grim resolve to slay the real Henry; they go off together.

Falstaff, with only three of his men left, happens upon Blunt's corpse. Hal enters and tries to borrow Falstaff's sword. When Falstaff offers a pistol instead the holster is found to be holding nothing but a bottle of wine. Hal hurls it at him and leaves.

Scene 4

Henry urges the wounded Hal to withdraw with Westmoreland's assistance but he courageously refuses. On the departure of Westmoreland and Lancaster Hal praises the valour of his brother who, it appears, has even held off Hotspur. As he leaves Douglas enters to find "another king!" Discovering that it is indeed Henry this time he fights with him until Hal comes to the rescue; he continues to fight with Hal and is driven off. Henry lauds his son's bravery before departing to support one of his commanders, Sir Nicholas Gawsey.

Hotspur appears; Hal identifies himself as the Prince of Wales and they fight. In the background Falstaff is engaged by Douglas and is seen to fall dead. Hotspur is wounded and expires, speaking of death before dishonour. Hal delivers a speech over the body, honouring Hotspur; seeing Falstaff's body he takes his leave of him also and departs.

Falstaff now rises from his feigned death, which he justifies as "The better part of valour is discretion." He coldbloodedly stabs Hotspur's corpse and hoists it onto his back. Meeting the princes Hal and Lancaster he throws the body down, claiming to have killed the mighty Hotspur and brazening it out when Hal states that he himself was responsible. Nevertheless Hal is indulgent as the trumpets sound retreat.

Scene 5

Elsewhere on the field Henry, Hal, Lancaster and Westmoreland have taken Worcester and Vernon prisoner. Henry blames the carnage on Worcester's failure to convey his peace terms to Douglas and condemns him and Vernon to execution. Hal has Douglas captive; given leave to dispose of him he authorises Lancaster to release him as a reward for his valour.

Finally Henry despatches Lancaster and Westmoreland to York to deal with Northumberland and the Archbishop while he and Hal march on to Wales to oppose Glendower and Mortimer.

King Henry IV, Part 2

This play covers a historical period of nearly ten years, running on from the battle of Shrewsbury at the end of part 1 to the coronation of Henry V on 9th April, 1413. The events are taken from Holinshed's *Chronicles of England, Scotland and Ireland* and are, as usual, adapted and compressed for dramatic purposes. (Act V, Scene 4 is often omitted from the stage presentation).

Act I

Induction

The character Rumour explains that although Henry IV was in fact victorious at Shrewsbury he (Rumour) has reached Warkworth in Northumberland to the effect that Prince Hal was slain by Hotspur and the king himself by the Earl of Douglas.

Scene 1

At the gate of his castle at Warkworth [on the coast about 25 miles due north of Newcastle-upon-Tyne] the Earl of Northumberland emerges from the orchard to greet Lord Bardolph. As Rumour has indicated, Lord Bardolph informs Northumberland that he has heard from "a gentleman well bred" that Henry IV has been fatally wounded, Hal has been killed, Falstaff taken prisoner and other supporters of the king have fled. However Travers, one of Northumberland's retainers, arrives with a contradictory story from another traveller that "Harry Percy's spur was cold", i.e. that Northumberland's son Hotspur had been defeated.

Finally a second retainer, Morton, brings news direct from Shrewsbury that in reality Douglas is alive but captured, Hotspur has been killed by Hal and Worcester has been executed. Thus the battle has been lost by the rebels. Northumberland, in his grief, is determined to rally his forces and take revenge for the loss of his son. Morton supports him, remarking that his ally the Archbishop of York, Richard Scroop, will lend the sanctity of religion to the rebellion.

Scene 2

Sir John Falstaff is accompanied by his page Robin, who is carrying his sword and buckler, on a London street. He complains that he is the butt of others' jokes and that a tailor, Master Dombledon, will not give him credit. He encounters the Lord Chief Justice of the King's Bench and his servant. The judge tells him that his valiant service at the battle of Shrewsbury has offset his participation in the Gad's Hill robbery [in part 1] but warns him to keep out of trouble.

He goes on to note that the king has separated Hal and Falstaff, who is to join the forces of Prince John of Lancaster against the Archbishop and Northumberland. Falstaff treats the situation with levity, impudently attempting to borrow money from the judge.

Scene 3

In his palace at York the Archbishop confers with Lord Hastings, Lord Bardolph and Mowbray, the Earl Marshal. Having mustered 25,000 men they consider that they can successfully oppose Henry, whose armies have to cope with both the French and Owen Glendower in addition to their forces.

Act II

Scene 1

Mistress Nell Quickly in the street tells Fang, a sheriff's officer, and his yeoman, Snare, to detain Falstaff for the debt of one hundred marks he owes her. On meeting Falstaff with his page and Bardolph [not Lord Bardolph of Act I] Fang attempts to arrest him. When the Lord Chief Justice arrives on the scene Mistress Quickly accuses Falstaff of not only non-payment of the debt but breach of promise. The judge orders him to settle with her.

One of the king's men, Gower, comes to deliver a letter to the judge and informs him that the king and Prince Hal are at Basingstoke, having despatched two thousand men to reinforce Lancaster's army. Meanwhile Falstaff manages to wriggle out of arrest by claiming to be "upon hasty employment" for the king; he even succeeds in borrowing a further sum from Mistress Quickly.

Scene 2

In another street Hal confesses to his companion Edward Poins his sadness at his father's sickness, which Poins treats as hypocrisy. They come across Bardolph and his page; Bardolph produces a letter from Falstaff which Poins reads out.

The letter advises Hal to mistrust Poins who, it says, has been maintaining that the prince is to marry his sister Nell. Hal laughs this off and arranges with Poins to disguise themselves as waiters in leather jerkins and aprons in order to see how Falstaff behaves at the *Boar's Head* tavern. He tips Bardolph and the page to secure their silence.

Scene 3

Hotspur's widow, Lady Percy, pleads with her father-in-law Northumberland at Warkworth Castle not to join the Earl Marshal and the Archbishop in the rebellion against the king, pointing out that he never went to his son's aid when he was alive. Northumberland is finally persuaded by his wife to go instead to Scotland to await the outcome of the conflict.

Scene 4

Two waiters at the *Boar's Head* tavern in Eastcheap

are joined by Mistresses Nell Quickly and Doll Tearsheet. As one waiter leaves Falstaff enters and engages in badinage with them. The waiter returns to say that Falstaff's ensign, Pistol, is at the door. Over Nell Quickly's objections Falstaff has Pistol admitted together with Bardolph and his page.

After some brawling Falstaff pricks the drunken Pistol with his sword and Bardolph turns Pistol out. Doll Tearsheet sits on Falstaff's knee to listen to some musicians while Hal and Poins appear at the back in the guise of waiters. Falstaff proceeds to malign both of them, encouraged by Doll Tearsheet with endearments. When they reveal themselves Falstaff cunningly insists that he disparaged the prince to his "wicked" companions only to prevent their attachment to Hal, which would bring him into further disrepute with his father.

Peto, another friend, enters to tell Hal that the king is now at Westminster and that a dozen captains are looking for Falstaff. Hal leaves hurriedly, followed by the others, while the two women lament Falstaff's departure.

Act III

Scene 1

At the palace King Henry IV, unable to sleep, sends a page with letters to fetch the Earls of Warwick and Surrey ("Uneasy lies the head that wears a crown."). When they arrive at one o'clock in the morning Henry refers to the rebellion, reminding them that his predecessor Richard II had forecast that Northumberland would turn against him. Warwick reassures him, saying that the royal forces will easily overcome Northumberland and that Owen Glendower, the Welsh leader, is dead.

Scene 2

Two country Justices of the Peace, Masters Silence and Robert Shallow, meet in a court near Shallow's house in Gloucestershire with a group of recruits including Mouldy, Shadow, Wart, Feeble and Bullcalf with their servants. They reminisce about old friends in London and elsewhere. Corporal Bardolph enters with a friend to announce the arrival of Captain Falstaff. He is followed by Falstaff who asks to review the recruits.

Ralph Mouldy is marked down for service, as are Simon Shadow, Francis Feeble and Peter Bullcalf but Thomas Wart is rejected. Shallow and Falstaff also reminisce before going off to dinner with Master Silence. Meanwhile Bullcalf and Mouldy attempt to bribe Bardolph to release them from service for two pounds each; Feeble, though, is resigned to his fate.

When Falstaff returns with the Justices Bardolph tells him blandly that he has been offered a total of three pounds to free Mouldy and Bullcalf. Falstaff accordingly takes Wart after all, plus Shadow and Feeble, furnishes them with coats and muskets and sends them off with Bardolph. After the Justices have left Falstaff reflects on Shallow's lies and posturings; he determines to fleece him on his way back from the wars.

Act IV

Scene 1

The Archbishop informs Mowbray and Hastings in Gaultree Forest [north of the city of York] that Northumberland has written from Scotland to say that he will not be joining them. A messenger reports that the opposing army of 30,000 men is now a mile to the west of the forest. The Earl of Westmoreland brings greetings from Prince John of Lancaster and an offer from him to hear the rebels' grievances. The Archbishop hands him a schedule of wrongs, including the execution of his brother Stephen. Westmoreland leaves but returns shortly afterwards to invite them to a parley with Lancaster, to take place between the two armies.

Scene 2

Elsewhere in the forest the meeting takes place between Lancaster and Westmoreland on the one hand and the Archbishop, Mowbray and Hastings on the other, with officers and attendants. Lancaster promises that the rebels' grievances will be redressed and suggests that both armies be disbanded. The Archbishop accepts his word and accordingly Hastings instructs a captain to pay off their men. Lancaster despatches Westmoreland to disperse his army, while Hastings goes to dismiss his men similarly.

Westmoreland soon reports that the royal commanders will not leave until personally ordered to do so by the prince, while Hastings returns to say that the rebel forces have promptly scattered in all directions. At this, Lancaster arrests the Archbishop, Hastings and Mowbray as traitors, justifying the treachery by pointing out that he promised, and still promises, redress of their grievances, not freedom from arrest for rebellion.

Scene 3

A rebel knight, Sir John Colevile, surrenders to Falstaff in another part of the forest. When Lancaster, Westmoreland and Sir Wafter Blunt come along Falstaff claims the credit for capturing Colevile. Lancaster puts Colevile in Blunt's charge and sends him to York to be executed. With Blunt and Westmoreland he then prepares to leave for London where his father, the king, is ill, while Falstaff asks to return via Gloucestershire (to fleece Shallow). Left alone, Falstaff compares Lancaster's cold unsociability with Hal's lustiness before leaving with Bardolph.

Scene 4

In the Jerusalem Chamber at Westminster Palace Henry refers to his planned crusade [mentioned in part 1], to be undertaken when the rebellion is crushed and he himself feels stronger. In the presence of Humphrey of Gloucester and the Earl of Warwick he counsels his son Thomas, Duke of Clarence, to be attentive to Prince Hal, who seems to be unready to succeed him on the throne.

Westmoreland brings news of Lancaster's success and Harcourt arrives to report that

Act V, Scene 5

King Henry V, departing with his train from his coronation in West-minster Abbey, sees his old companion Falstaff. He remarks that he does not know this "fool and jester" and banishes him from his presence.

Northumberland and Lord Bardolph have been overthrown by the Sheriff of Yorkshire. The courtiers attempt to cheer the king, who is too weak to enjoy the good news to the full.

Scene 5

Clarence, Gloucester, Warwick and others attend the king who is lying on a bed in his chamber. Hal enters and is enjoined to be quiet while his father settles down to sleep. He remains on watch while the others go out. Seeing the king on the point of death he lifts the crown from his pillow, tries it on and steals out.

Henry awakes and calls the others in. Finding his crown gone he sends Warwick to find the Prince of Wales. Warwick returns to report that he found the prince in the next room, weeping. They leave as Hal re-enters, explaining that he never thought to hear the king speak again. Henry rebukes him at length ("Thy wish was father, Harry, to that thought:").

Hal humbly excuses his conduct and begs his pardon. Henry forgives him and advises him on how to cope with the vicissitudes of the monarchy. When Lancaster and Warwick re-enter he asks to be carried back to Jerusalem (i.e. the Jerusalem Chamber) to die, in accordance with a prophesy which led him to believe that he would die in the Holy Land.

Act V

Scene 1

At home in his hall Justice Shallow presses Falstaff to stay, in the company of Bardolph and his page. He calls his servant, Davy, to fetch William the cook and discusses dinner while Davy brings up other household matters. When he bustles out Falstaff gleefully plans to mimic his simple ways for Hal's amusement.

Scene 2

Back at the palace the Lord Chief Justice hears from Warwick that the king has passed away and Prince Hal is now King Henry V. They are joined by Lancaster, Clarence, Gloucester, Westmoreland and others who are apprehensive of change and remind the Lord Chief Justice that he will now have to "speak Sir John Falstaff fair".

Henry V enters with his entourage and, as expected, assumes a stern air, chiding the Lord Chief Justice for past indignities, including committing him, the "immediate heir of England", to prison. When the Lord Chief Justice responds that he was

bound by duty to the then king, Henry relents and agrees. He confirms him in his post and dedicates his own life to good and wise government, aided by the noble counsel of princes and courtiers.

Scene 3

Shallow, Silence, Falstaff, Bardolph and the page are eating apples and drinking wine in the garden of Shallow's house, served by Davy amid much merriment. Pistol arrives with the news that Prince Hal is now King Henry V. Falstaff, thinking that he will be a royal favourite, arranges to leave immediately; he declares woe to the Lord Chief Justice and promises Shallow any office in the land that he wishes.

Scene 4

Two beadles are dragging Nell Quickly and Doll Tearsheet along a London street. They have been arrested by constables for the death of a man beaten by them and Pistol.

Scene 5

Two grooms strew rushes in the vicinity of Westminster Abbey while a confident Falstaff gathers with Shallow, Pistol, Bardolph and his page to await the emergence of Henry V from his coronation at two o'clock. He again promises preferment for Shallow, from whom he has borrowed a thousand pounds, and on hearing from Pistol that Doll Tearsheet has been imprisoned he promises to free her.

Henry enters with his train, including the Lord Chief Justice, but when Falstaff hails him as "King Hal" he remarks that he does not know this "fool and jester". As the new monarch he has forsaken his previous colleagues; he banishes Falstaff from his presence and passes on.

Shallow is now nervous about his loan but Falstaff quickly assures him that although the king had to take that line in public he would send for him privately that night. However at this point Lancaster returns with the Lord Chief Justice and orders some officers to throw Falstaff and his companions into the Fleet prison. As they are taken away Lancaster refers to the coming campaign in France.

Epilogue

A dancer asks indulgence for the play and promises a better one [Henry V] in which Falstaff will reappear and Henry will woo Katharine of France.

THE LIFE OF
King Henry V

This play, the fourth in Shakespeare's so-called history-cycle, was written in 1599. Like the others in the cycle it is based on the history books by Holinshed and Hall. Other sources include an anonymous play, *The Famous Victories of Henry V*. The action runs on from Part 2 of *King Henry IV* to some point between the battle of Agincourt (25th October, 1415) and Henry's marriage to Katharine of Valois (2nd June, 1420).

Prologue

Chorus asks the audience to overcome the limitations of "this wooden O" (the Globe theatre) and imagine the clash of two mighty monarchies culminating in the battle of Agincourt. ("O! for a Muse of fire, that would ascend The brightest heaven of invention;").

Act I

Scene 1

The Archbishop of Canterbury and the Bishop of Ely are discussing a parliamentary bill in an antechamber of the king's palace. The bill, which had already been debated in the reign of Henry IV (when the present king was Prince Hal), would strip from the Church the wealth of its 'temporal lands', i.e. those that had been left to the church in people's wills.

Canterbury, praising the king's sober reformation on his father's death, mentions that he has offered him a large sum of money from the Church to finance a war with France. The two arrange to press this plan on the king before the arrival of the French ambassador.

Scene 2

King Henry V is in the throne room with his brothers, the Dukes of Gloucester and Bedford, his uncle the Duke of Exeter, the Earls of Warwick and Westmoreland and other counsellors. When Canterbury and Ely enter the king asks the Archbishop whether the Salic Law bars his claim to the French throne. He entreats accuracy since a war may depend on the answer.

Canterbury replies that there is no bar other than the provision that no woman shall be the inheritrix of Salic territory. However that territory is actually Meisen, part of Germany occupied by the French in the time of Charles the Great. He goes into historical detail, showing that the accession of some French kings did pass through the female line, despite the law, and concludes that Henry is justified in reclaiming the French throne. He is supported by Ely and the counsellors.

Henry points out that if he moves on France the Scots will seize the opportunity to invade England. He is told that he need take only a quarter of his forces, leaving the rest to defend England; Henry makes the decision to attack.

An attendant brings in ambassadors from the French Dauphin who ask leave to speak frankly. They tell Henry that his claim to certain French dukedoms, by right of his great-grandfather Edward III, is rejected by the Dauphin who offers him a gift of a small barrel instead. Exeter discovers that it contains tennis balls. Henry angrily threatens vengeance for this mockery and bids his supporters prepare for an expedition to France.

Prologue

Chorus describes how the youth of England are girding themselves for war while the French, quaking with fear, have bribed Richard Earl of Cambridge, Henry Lord Scroop of Masham and Sir Thomas Grey of Northumberland to assassinate the king in Southampton before he embarks for France.

Act II

Scene 1

Two former companions of the king, Corporal Nym and Lieutenant Bardolph, meet in Eastcheap. Nym has fallen out with Ensign Pistol because Pistol has married Mistress Nell Quickly, the hostess of the *Boar's Head* tavern, who was once engaged to Nym. When Pistol comes along with his new wife he and Nym confront each other with threats but are not resolute enough to come to blows.

A serving boy brings news that his master, Sir John Falstaff, is ill; Nell Quickly goes off with the boy to see how he is. Nym and Pistol continue to quarrel until Pistol pays him off a betting debt. Mistress Quickly returns to call them to Falstaff's bedside; the king has treated him badly and he has a high fever.

Scene 2

Exeter, Bedford and Westmoreland discuss the pending apprehension of some traitors in a council-chamber in Southampton. Henry enters with Scroop, Cambridge, Grey and other Lords and attendants, who give him their support for his enterprise. When Henry asks Exeter to release a man who had been imprisoned for speaking against him the three traitors are merciless and urge punishment of the man.

Henry hands them their commissions; however on opening them they find evidence of their treachery. They beg for mercy on their knees but Henry coldly reminds them that they have just that moment been arguing against mercy; he reproaches them for their ingratitude and corruption. Exeter arrests them for high treason; they crave the king's pardon but Henry invokes the death penalty for conspiracy and they are taken away.

Scene 3

Back in London Falstaff has died and Pistol, Nym, Bardolph and Falstaff's boy are preparing to join the army in Southampton. Pistol and Bardolph kiss Nell Quickly farewell and they all set off.

Scene 4

In an apartment in his palace at Rouen Charles VI, King of France, orders Lewis [Louis] the Dauphin, together with the Dukes of Berri and Britaine and Charles Delabreth, the High Constable of France, to prepare defences against the coming English invasion. The Dauphin is inclined to belittle any exploits by the vain and shallow Henry but the king and the Constable [commander-in-chief] know the strength of the English from a previous defeat at Crecy.

A messenger announces the arrival of ambassadors from England. Exeter enters with other lords; he presents Charles with a detailed claim on the French crown and a threat of war if it is refused. Charles undertakes to reply the next day. Exeter goes on to pour scorn and defiance on the Dauphin for his mocking gift of the tennis balls.

Prologue

Chorus invites the audience to picture the English ships sailing across the Channel. He describes the siege of Harfleur by the English forces and relates how an ambassador has brought an offer from the French king of the hand of his daughter Katherine and certain 'petty and unprofitable' dukedoms. The offer has been rejected and the English cannon are bombarding the town.

Act III

Scene 1

Henry urges Exeter, Bedford, Gloucester and their troops to scale the walls of Harfleur, which have been damaged by the artillery ("Once more unto the breach, dear friends, once more; Or close the wall up with our English dead!....Stiffen the sinews, summon up the blood....Cry 'God for Harry! England and Saint George!'").

Scene 2

Bardolph encourages the reluctant Nym, Pistol and the Boy. The three men are driven forward by the Welsh Captain Fluellen, leaving the Boy behind to soliloquise on their thievery and roguishness. Fluellen reappears with the English Captain Gower; they are joined by the Irish Captain Macmorris and the Scottish Captain Jamy [Jamie?]. The four discuss military theory and the progress of the siege until a trumpet call signals a parley.

Scene 3

By the gates of Harfleur Henry threatens the Governor of the town, perched up on the walls, with rape, pillage and general destruction. The Governor admits that assistance from the Dauphin is not forthcoming and therefore surrenders. Henry orders Exeter to hold the town while he withdraws to Calais to attend to the sick and wounded at the approach of winter.

Scene 4

In the palace at Rouen the king's daughter Katharine of Valois is being given an elementary English lesson by Alice, an older lady-in-waiting. Alice's pronunciation is poor and Katherine's even worse but when the princess acquires nine common English nouns Alice sycophantically assures her that her delivery is that of a native English speaker.

Scene 5

Elsewhere in the palace King Charles, the Dauphin, the Duke of Bourbon and the Constable of France note with shame that Henry has already crossed the mouth of the Somme [about half way from Harfleur to Calais] without opposition. The king calls upon them and other nobles to bar Henry's way and take him captive. The Constable is confident that Henry and his small weakened army will surrender. Montjoy, a herald, is sent to negotiate Henry's ransom.

Scene 6

Fluellen meets Gower in the English camp in Picardy and tells him of a battle to secure a bridge over the River Ternoise [about sixty miles from Calais]. Fluellen praises the valour of Ensign Pistol under his commander Exeter. Pistol arrives to ask Fluellen to plead with Exeter for the life of Bardolph, who is to be hanged for stealing an osculatory [carved tablet to be kissed] from a church. Fluellen refuses. After Pistol flounces off Gower recalls that he is a rascally cutpurse and warns Fluellen not to believe his boasts of military prowess.

Henry enters with Gloucester and receives Fluellen's report on the holding of the Ternoise bridge. Hearing of Bardolph's robbery he orders that nothing is to be taken by his troops unless it is paid for.

Montjoy arrives with the French ransom demand. Henry admits that his men are enfeebled by sickness but defiantly states his intention to march on to Calais. He is not seeking battle but will not shun it if offered.

Scene 7

At two o'clock in the morning in the French camp near Agincourt [about half way between Amiens and Calais] the Constable, the Duke of Orleans and the Dauphin impatiently await the dawn in the company

Act III, Scene 1

King Henry V urges the dukes of Exeter, Bedford and Gloucester with
their troops to scale the walls of Harfleur, which have been damaged by
the English artillery. ("Once more unto the breach, dear friends...")

of the master of the crossbows, Lord Rambures. A messenger reports that according to Lord Grandpré the English are encamped just fifteen hundred paces away. The Dauphin boasts about his horse and they wager on how many prisoners they will each take before midday.

Prologue

Chorus paints a word picture of the battlefield by night, with the whispering sentries, the neighing horses and the sounds of the knights' armour being riveted. The French troops play dice but the English sit gloomily by their fires while Henry goes round raising their morale.

Act IV

Scene 1

Before dawn in the English camp Henry greets Bedford and Gloucester; he borrows a cloak from Sir Thomas Erpingham to remain incognito and when he is challenged by Pistol gives his name as Harry le Roy. He overhears Fluellen telling Gower to keep his voice down and is then joined by three soldiers, John Bates, Alexander Court and Michael Williams. Henry disputes Williams' view that the king should pay the demanded ransom and spare his men ("Every subject's duty is the king's; but every subject's soul is his own"). He and Williams exchange gloves, to be worn in their caps after the battle, when Williams promises 'le Roy' a box on the ear.

Henry soliloquises on the responsibilities of a king; his only perquisite is ceremony and that is of no worth. Repose is not gained through "the balm, the sceptre and the ball, The sword, the mace, the crown imperial,". When Erpingham finds him Henry tells him to gather the nobles in his tent. He offers up a prayer before Gloucester comes to collect him.

Scene 2

In the French camp the Dauphin, Orleans, Rambures and the Constable look forward to the battle. The Constable makes an encouraging speech and Grandpré denigrates the miserable English forces.

Scene 3

On the other side the English nobles calculate the odds against them as five to one and Westmoreland wishes they had ten thousand more men. Henry, entering, demurs; the fewer the men, the greater the share of honour. He delivers an inspiring speech; any man who wishes may depart but in years to come "gentlemen in England now a-bed Shall think themselves accurs'd they were not here, And hold their manhood cheap whiles any speaks That fought with us upon St. Crispin's day."

The Earl of Salisbury announces that the French are about to attack and Montjoy again appears to demand a ransom and is again rebuffed. The Duke of York begs to be allowed to lead the vanguard. Henry

agrees and they leave for the battle.

Scene 4

A French soldier is ready to surrender to Pistol on the battlefield but he speaks no English and Pistol has no French. Aided by the Boy as interpreter Pistol spares his life for a ransom of two hundred crowns. As they leave the Boy stays to guard the luggage, reflecting on Pistol's bombast ("The empty vessel makes the greatest sound").

Scene 5

In another part of the battlefield the Dauphin, the Constable, Orleans, Bourbon and Rambures cry out in desperation as the French ranks are broken. Orleans observes that they could still win by weight of numbers, if discipline could be imposed, but Bourbon and the others prefer to sacrifice themselves rather than live in shame.

Scene 6

Elsewhere Henry praises his men and reminds them that there is yet more to do. Exeter describes the deaths of York and Suffolk. As the French consolidate Henry orders all prisoners to be killed.

Scene 7

Fluellen and Gower are outraged to find that the retreating French troops have ransacked the king's tent and killed the boys guarding the luggage. Fluellen embarks on a eulogy to Henry, comparing him with Alexander the Great.

A wrathful Henry enters with Warwick, Gloucester, Exeter and others. He sends a message by a herald to a group of cavalry on a hill telling them to come down and fight or leave the field; if they do neither they will be scattered and any remaining will be killed. Montjoy appears again, not for ransom but to ask leave to identify the French dead and bury them. Henry assents and sends heralds with him to do the same for the English.

Fluellen reminds Henry that his great uncle the Black Prince and his grandfather John of Gaunt fought bravely in France, in commemoration of which Welsh regiments wear leeks in their Monmouth caps (as does Henry on St. David's day, having been born in Monmouth himself).

Henry spots Williams and asks him why he is wearing a glove in his cap. Williams replies that he is looking for the swaggerer who undertook to wear his glove, so that he can box his ears. Henry sends him to fetch his captain, Gower; meanwhile he mischievously gives Fluellen the other glove to wear in his cap, pretending it belonged to the Duke of Alençon and telling him to apprehend anyone who challenges him. He then sends Fluellen also to call Gower, followed by Warwick and Gloucester with instructions to prevent any bloodshed when Williams and Fluellen meet.

Scene 8

In front of Henry's pavilion Williams and Fluellen

find Gower and deliver their messages. Williams sees his glove in Fluellen's cap and strikes him. Fluellen tries to arrest him but they are parted by Warwick and Gloucester. Henry and Exeter arrive as Williams produces his glove and shows that Fluellen's glove is one of the pair. Henry in turn produces his own glove and matches it with the one in Williams' cap. He confesses that he was the soldier who disputed with Williams in the night. Upon Williams' courteous apology Henry tells Exeter to give him the glove filled with crowns as a reward. Fluellen, mollified, offers Williams a shilling.

A herald brings a list of the dead, the great majority being French. Henry forbids any boasting about the victory, ascribing it to God alone.

Prologue

Chorus explains that King Henry has come back to England via Calais and Dover and been given a tumultuous welcome. Sigismund, the Emperor of the Holy Roman Empire, has come to London to arrange peace terms, after which Henry has returned to France again.

Act V

Scene 1

In a guarded court in France Fluellen tells Gower that Pistol has mocked the leek in his cap, which he is still wearing. When Pistol enters he cudgels him, forces him to eat the leek, hands him a groat and leaves. Gower also leaves, telling Pistol that he is a knave to mock an ancient tradition. Left alone, Pistol reveals that Nell Quickly has died of venereal disease; he decides to live as a pimp and pickpocket in England, pretending that his injuries from Fluellen are honourable war wounds.

Scene 2

The two courts assemble in an apartment in the royal palace at Troyes in Champagne. They include Henry, Bedford, Gloucester, Exeter, Warwick and Westmoreland on one side and Charles, his queen Isabel, Katharine, Alice and the Duke of Burgundy on the other with attendant lords and ladies.

Burgundy, as mediator, speaks of disorder in France and the need for peace. Henry insists on his demands but agrees when Charles proposes a joint delegation to work out the terms. All leave to participate except Henry, Alice and Katharine (whose gift in marriage was a principal demand).

Henry woos Katharine as 'a plain soldier', comparing her with an angel and even attempting a little French. In broken English she tells him that if her father agrees she will be content. Although she informs him that it is not the custom for French girls to allow a man to kiss them before they are married Henry manages to kiss her before the others return.

Amid some bantering Westmoreland and Exeter confirm that Charles has accepted the English terms and recognises Henry as the heir to the French throne. Queen Isabel blesses the coming marriage and hopes that France and England may remain similarly allied.

Epilogue

Chorus comments that after these great feats, sadly, Henry dies at the early age of thirty five, leaving England and France to his son Henry VI, at that time a baby less than one year old. In his subsequent reign France will be lost and England will be engulfed in the turmoil of civil war.

King Henry VI, Part 1

In historical chronology this, the fifth play in the 'history-cycle', follows *Henry V*, although it was written some seven years earlier. It opens with the funeral of King Henry V who had died at Bois de Vincennes on 3rd August, 1422, probably of dysentery. Henry VI (who was only one year old at that time) became king of England on September 1st and king of France shortly afterwards. The play ends with Henry's decision, in 1445, to marry Margaret

Act I

Scene 1

The cortège funèbre of Henry V enters Westminster Cathedral to the sound of a dead-march. The mourners include the elderly Duke of Bedford, the Dukes of Gloucester and Exeter, the Earl of Warwick and Beaufort, Bishop of Winchester. They lament the passing of the king and acknowledge Humphrey, Duke of Gloucester as the Protector [regent]; he chides Winchester for lack of piety.

A messenger brings news of the loss of seven French towns including Paris, Rheims and Orleans, through disagreements between the English generals. Bedford, regent of France, listens as a second messenger reports that the Dauphin Charles has been crowned at Rheims, supported by the Bastard of Orleans [Jean, Count of Dunois], Duke Reignier [René] of Anjou, titular king of Naples, and the Duke of Alençon.

A third messenger arrives to report on the battle of Patay on August 10th in which Lord Talbot, falling back from Orleans with six thousand men, was surrounded and attacked by twenty three thousand French. Such was his zeal that he nearly prevailed when Sir John Fastolfe [see introduction to *Henry IV*, Part 1] turned coward and fled, allowing a Walloon to thrust a spear into Talbot's back. Accordingly he was taken prisoner along with Lords Scales and Hungerford.

Bedford swears vengeance and departs to relieve the Earl of Salisbury in France. Gloucester goes to check munitions in the Tower of London and Exeter leaves for Eltham to safeguard the infant king, whom Winchester secretly plans to kidnap.

Scene 2

Near Orleans Charles discusses the siege with Reignier and Alençon and decides to attack the Earl of Salisbury's force. Shortly afterwards he is in retreat, railing against his soldiers for deserting him in battle.

Dunois arrives, bringing with him a "holy maid" who is "ordained to raise this tedious siege". Charles gets Reignier to stand in for him as Dunois ushers in Joan La Pucelle [Joan of Arc]. Joan is not deceived by the substitution. She calls the Dauphin forward and explains confidentially that the Virgin Mary appeared to her in a vision and bade her free her country from calamity. Charles challenges her to a duel and is defeated. The others wonder what the two are talking about as Charles defers to her. She promises them "halcyon days" when she has lifted the siege that night.

Scene 3

Back in England Gloucester arrives at the gate of the Tower with his bluecoated serving-men but the warders will not admit him. From within, the lieutenant Woodville [Mayor of London] tells him that Winchester has forbidden him entry. As the outraged Gloucester is about to break in Henry Beaufort, now Cardinal of Winchester, arrives with his supporters in tawny coats. The two men exchange insults and the Gloucester party attack the Cardinal's party and drive them back.

Woodville emerges with his officers as the scuffle continues. An officer makes a proclamation requiring all to discard their weapons and disperse. Gloucester and Winchester leave the scene, both muttering threats.

Scene 4

On the walls of Orleans the master-gunner instructs his boy to keep watch on a tower to which the English are rumoured to have access. If he sees them the boy is to fetch the master-gunner who will set off an explosive charge.

Lord Salisbury appears on the turrets with Sir William Glansdale, Sir Thomas Gargrave and some men. He greets Lord Talbot, who has been exchanged with a French prisoner, Lord Ponton de Santrailles. Talbot refers to Fastolfe's treachery and describes how he was put on show and taunted in a French market place.

Unseen, the boy returns with a lighted fuse. As the English officers decide to attack the North gate an explosion hurls Salisbury and Gargrave to the ground, mortally wounded. Talbot can do nothing for them. As a thunderstorm begins a messenger comes to tell Talbot that the Dauphin and Joan of Arc have assembled a new force to break the siege. Talbot has the bodies carried to his tent.

Scene 5

Talbot pursues Charles and drives him away from one of the city gates. Joan passes by, beating back some of the English before her. Talbot and Joan return and fight. Joan breaks off, saying "thy hour is not yet come", and goes off with soldiers to victual Orleans. Talbot is ashamed that this 'witch' has overcome his besieging troops and entered the city.

Act II, Scene 4

*In the garden of Temple Hall in London Richard Plantagenet plucks a white rose from
a bush and invites the Earl of Warwick to do the same. The Earl of Somerset picks a
red rose, as does the Earl of Suffolk, symbolically initiating the Wars of the Roses.*

Scene 6

Joan and Charles appear on the walls of Orleans with Reignier, Alençon and soldiers. Charles is lost in admiration of Joan's achievement and declares her a saint. The others call for church bells to be rung and bonfires to be lit to celebrate the victory.

Act II

Scene 1

At the town gates a French sergeant posts two sentries. Talbot, Bedford and the Duke of Burgundy [an ally from the north] approach with soldiers carrying scaling ladders. The three hope to surprise the French, who have been carousing and banqueting. They climb the walls at separate points and burst into the town, yelling "St. George!" and "A Talbot!" The French, out of armour, leap aside.

Dunois, Alençon and Reignier assemble, half-dressed. They are joined by Charles who is impatient with Joan at this setback. Joan suspects poor sentry-keeping and Alençon, as captain of the watch, is blamed. They are scattered by one of Talbot's men.

Scene 2

At dawn inside Orleans Talbot asserts to Bedford, Burgundy and a captain that the town will be sacked to avenge Salisbury's death and he will be honoured with a tomb. They wonder if the Dauphin and Joan have fled.

A messenger arrives with an invitation for Talbot to visit the Countess of Auvergne in her castle. He accepts but the others decline to accompany him. Talbot whispers an order to the captain and leaves.

Scene 3

The Countess of Auvergne gives instructions to a porter in the court of her castle and orders him to bring her the keys when he has complied. After he has left the messenger conducts Talbot in. The Countess derides the mighty 'scourge of France' as a silly dwarf and a shrivelled shrimp. Talbot turns abruptly to leave as the porter returns with the keys.

When the Countess informs Talbot that he is a prisoner he laughs and tells her that she has captured no more than his shadow. He blows a horn. To the sounds of drum and cannon his soldiers force the gates and pour in. The Countess quickly apologises and Talbot forgives her, asking only for food and wine for his men.

Scene 4

William de la Pole, the Earl of Suffolk, has drawn Richard Plantagenet (son of the late Earl of Cambridge) and others out of the Temple hall in London and into the garden to resolve a legal argument between Richard and the Earl of Somerset. He and the Earl of Warwick excuse themselves as having no expertise in law so Richard plucks a white rose from a bush and invites those who side with him to do likewise. Somerset defiantly picks a red rose in the same way. Thus enjoined, Warwick takes a white rose and Suffolk a red one.

Vernon, who is present with a lawyer, suggests that the one with the fewer roses be adjudged the loser. He then picks a white rose. Somerset contemptuously warns him not to prick his finger and inadvertently stain it red. The lawyer offers his opinion that Somerset was legally in the wrong and also picks a white rose.

Somerset accuses Richard of being tainted with his father's execution for treason. They continue to snarl at each other until Somerset leaves with Suffolk. Warwick assures Richard that he will prevail when he is created Duke of York and the four go off to dinner.

Scene 5

Edmund Mortimer, the fifth Earl of March, is carried in a chair by two gaolers into a room in the Tower of London. Grey-haired, wasted and half blind, he hopes that his nephew Richard Plantagenet will come to see him before he dies. Richard, sent for by the gaolers, enters and embraces him. He tells him about the dispute and the factions of the roses and asks him for the truth about his father.

Mortimer reviews the complex recent lineage of the Plantagenets. Richard II was a legitimate king since his father, Edward the Black Prince, was the first-born son of Edward III and predeceased him. However Richard was deposed by Henry Bolingbroke (grandfather of the present infant king Henry VI), whose father was John of Gaunt, Duke of Lancaster, the fourth-born son.

Since Richard II left no heir the Percy family championed Mortimer for the throne because his great-grandfather on his mother's side was Lionel of Antwerp, Duke of Clarence, the third-born son of Edward III (thus taking precedence of John of Gaunt by primogeniture). [The second-born son, William of Hatfield, was not involved, being childless].

To complicate matters, Mortimer's sister Anne, the true heiress, married Richard Plantagenet's father, who was the son of Edmund of Langley, Duke of York, the fifth-born son of Edward III. Mortimer thus considers himself the rightful claimant to the monarchy. Hence although his brother-in-law, Richard's father, was unsuccessful when he tried to install him on the throne, he was no traitor. [Thomas of Woodstock, Duke of Gloucester and William of Windsor were Edward's sixth-born and seventh-born sons].

As Mortimer has no son he appoints Richard his heir. Richard deems his father's execution "nothing less than bloody tyranny" but Mortimer, as he expires, counsels caution since the house of Lancaster is now strongly established. The gaolers remove Mortimer's body as Richard swears vengeance on Somerset.

Act III

Scene 1

King Henry, now a young man, is in the Houses of Parliament with Exeter, Warwick, Somerset, Suffolk, Richard Plantagenet and others. Gloucester offers up a bill but Winchester snatches it and tears it up. Gloucester reviles him, saying that he does not need the written document to remember that the Cardinal twice tried to have him waylaid and assassinated, at London Bridge and the Tower. Winchester retorts that Gloucester wants to be the only person having influence with the king.

Warwick enters the quarrel on Gloucester's side and Somerset on Winchester's side. Richard sympathises with Gloucester but remains silent while Henry beseeches the two to compose their differences. To the sound of a commotion outside Woodville enters to report that the followers of Gloucester and Winchester, having been forbidden by proclamation to carry weapons, have filled their pockets with pebbles and are beating each others' brains out.

The bands of followers burst in, still skirmishing. Gloucester restrains his men, out of respect for the king, and offers his hand to Winchester, who grudgingly responds. The skirmishers depart to have their broken heads attended to.

Warwick submits a scroll to the king creating Richard a princely Duke of York and restoring his inheritance, to Somerset's concealed chagrin. Gloucester advises Henry to be crowned king of France and the court moves out. Exeter is left to ponder the truth of a popular old prophecy that Henry of Monmouth (Henry V) would win all and Henry of Windsor (Henry VI) would lose all.

Scene 2

Joan of Arc approaches Rouen in disguise, accompanied by soldiers dressed as countrymen and carrying sacks. The guard admits them, believing them to be poor peasants. Charles arrives with Dunois, Alençon and their troops. They see Joan's signal of a burning torch and storm in, shouting "A Dauphin!"

Talbot and Burgundy arrive with their forces to meet Bedford, who is ill, being carried out of Rouen on a chair. Joan, Charles, Dunois and Alençon appear on the walls above them. Talbot challenges the men to come down and fight but Joan merely scoffs before the king's party disappears.

Bedford declines Talbot's offer of a bed, wishing to remain on the battlefield like King Arthur. He is left seated alone while Sir John Fastolfe hurries past with a captain, intent on abandoning Gloucester and saving his own life. The two are followed by a party fleeing from the town, including Charles, Joan and Alençon. Bedford expires, content, and is carried off. Talbot and Burgundy return exultant in their success and make arrangements for Bedford's funeral

before leaving to greet Henry in Paris.

Scene 3

Charles gathers with Joan of Arc, Dunois and Alençon on a plain near Rouen. Joan rallies them and proposes to entice the Duke of Burgundy to renounce Talbot and join them. They see Talbot and his men marching to Paris, followed by Burgundy and his men. They detain Burgundy and Joan wins him over by appealing to his patriotism.

Scene 4

In the palace in Paris Talbot kneels in obeisance to Henry in the presence of Gloucester, Winchester, York, Suffolk, Somerset, Warwick, Exeter, Vernon (white rose faction) and Basset (red rose faction). Henry, who has not previously met Talbot, hails his victories and creates him Earl of Shrewsbury. After the court departs Vernon and Basset quarrel; Basset goes to petition the king to permit a duel between them.

Act IV

Scene 1

Winchester crowns Henry in a room of state in the palace, watched by Gloucester, Exeter, York, Suffolk, Somerset, Warwick, Talbot and the Governor of Paris, who swears an oath of fealty and leaves.

Sir John Fastolfe brings in a letter from Burgundy, claiming to have received it while hastening to the king's aid from Calais. Talbot contemptuously tears the knightly garter from his leg, relating the story of his cowardice and flight at Patay. Henry banishes him on pain of death and he goes out.

Gloucester reads Burgundy's letter, which informs them of his defection to Charles, "the rightful King of France". Henry sends Talbot to reason with him. Vernon and Basset enter, asking to be allowed to fight over the honour of their white and red roses respectively. When Henry deplores the triviality of the dispute York and Somerset offer to take up the challenge. Gloucester rebukes all of them and Henry calls on them to desist and as a gesture pins on a red rose, somewhat to York's consternation.

He appoints York regent of France and orders Somerset to unite his cavalry with York's foot soldiers. When he departs for Calais York again holds his tongue, leaving Exeter still brooding on the "jarring discord of nobility".

Scene 2

As Talbot approaches Bordeaux the General of the French garrison appears on the walls. Talbot calls on him to open the gates and acknowledge Henry as king or he will suffer famine, fire and the sword. The General defies him, saying the Dauphin is in the vicinity. Talbot hears the French drums and prepares for battle.

Scene 3

On the Gascony plain a messenger reports to York that Charles' army is marching to Bordeaux to surround Talbot and has been augmented by two forces even larger. York chafes over Somerset's delay in providing cavalry support. Sir William Lucy entreats him to go to Talbot's rescue but York will not move without Somerset's mounted force and predicts, as a consequence, the loss of Poitou, Maine and other provinces. Sir William Lucy sees Henry V's conquests being lost through "sleeping neglection".

Scene 4

Elsewhere in Gascony Somerset tells one of Talbot's captains that it is too late to send the cavalry. He suggests that York has sacrificed Talbot so that he can be supreme. Lucy arrives and emphasises the need to succour Talbot. Somerset demurs but eventually agrees to despatch the horsemen who, however, will take six hours to reach Bordeaux.

Scene 5

At the English camp Talbot urges his young son John to fly from certain death. The boy recoils from the dishonour and suggests that his father save himself instead. In the end they decide to stay together and see the battle out.

Scene 6

In the thick of the fight Talbot rescues his son and again urges him to flee. John again refuses and they continue the fight side by side.

Scene 7

A little later Talbot, wounded, is being led along by a servant. Soldiers bring in the body of John, who has died in hand-to-hand fighting after protecting his father from attack. He embraces the body and dies.

Charles, Joan of Arc, Alençon, Burgundy and Dunois come upon the corpses and praise the valour of the Talbots. Lucy arrives, preceded by a French herald. Joan belittles the Talbots' exploits but Lucy collects their bodies, remarking that "from their ashes shall be rear'd A phoenix that shall make all France afeard".

Act V

Scene 1

The emperor and the pope having called for peace between England and France, the Earl of Armagnac has offered his only daughter to Henry together with a large dowry. In his palace in London Henry accepts and makes ready, with Gloucester and Exeter, to receive the French ambassadors. They enter with a legate [papal delegate] and Winchester (now Cardinal Beaufort, to Exeter's misgivings). Henry presents them with a jewel and instructs Gloucester to see that they are conducted safely to Dover. The court then retires.

Winchester privately promises the legate a sum of money to be given to the pope for his cardinalship and gloats that now he is not outranked by Gloucester.

Scene 2

On the plains of Anjou Charles comments to Burgundy, Alenflon, and Joan of Arc that the Parisians are rebelling. A spy reports that the two English armies have coalesced and are preparing for battle.

Scene 3

Outside Angers Joan of Arc calls upon the spirits for aid. Some fiends appear briefly, shaking their heads sorrowfully but not speaking. She interprets this as a bad omen for France. During the battle York and Joan fight hand to hand and Joan is captured. She curses both him and Charles as she is led away.

Suffolk encounters Reignier's daughter Margaret and is captivated by her beauty. When she asks what ransom he requires he tells her that she is to be queen of England as Henry's bride. A parley is sounded and Reignier appears on the walls. Suffolk asks his consent to the royal marriage and Reignier descends to give it. Suffolk bids them farewell, still bewitched by Margaret.

Scene 4

At the Duke of York's camp in Anjou Joan of Arc is arraigned before York and Warwick with her father, a shepherd. Claiming royal descent and celestial grace she denies her father who departs in a bitter rage. When York and Warwick condemn her to be burned at the stake she claims to be pregnant by Alençon, though a virgin. When this excites no pity she names Reignier as the father but the two men wave her away. Cardinal Beaufort announces the imminent arrival of the Dauphin to discuss a peace treaty while York angrily deplores this outcome of many heroic battles.

Charles enters with Alençon, Dunois and Reignier and enquires the nature of the peace terms. Beaufort (Winchester) answers, as York is choking with fury. He tells Charles that he will be Henry's viceroy and pay tribute to him. Charles retorts that he already possesses half of France outright and sees no reason to accept the viceroyalty of the whole. To avoid further slaughter Alençon urges him confidentially to accept the terms, which he can always repudiate later. Charles glumly assents and the French swear fealty to Henry.

Scene 5

Back in London Suffolk rhapsodises about Margaret to the king. Gloucester reminds Henry that he is already engaged to the Earl of Armagnac's daughter. Suffolk argues that the daughter of the king of Naples is a more suitable bride for the king of England; the Armagnac dowry is irrelevant.

Henry is swayed. He sends Suffolk back to France to collect Margaret while Suffolk tells himself that Margaret may rule Henry but he will rule her, the king and the whole realm.

King Henry VI, Part 2

The original title of this, the sixth play in the history-cycle was *The First Part of the Contention of the two Famous Houses of York and Lancaster with the Death of the Good Duke Humphrey*. It follows on immediately from Part 1, covering a period of ten years from the arrival of Margaret of Anjou in London (1445) to the first battle of St. Albans (1455). [The 'contention' was the Wars of the Roses, begun symbolically in the Temple garden in part 1, Act II, Scene 4].

Act I

Scene 1

King Henry VI enters a room of state in the palace in London by one door accompanied by the Duke of Gloucester, Cardinal Beaufort [the bishop of Winchester in part 1] and the Earls of Salisbury and Warwick. Queen Margaret is led in through another door by the Earl of Suffolk, accompanied by the Dukes of York, Somerset and Buckingham.

Suffolk reports that, as commanded, he has married Princess Margaret of Anjou in Tours as Henry's proxy and now presents her as his queen. Henry greets Margaret warmly and the courtiers acclaim her. Gloucester reads out the articles of the concomitant peace treaty. He is shocked by the clause ceding the duchy of Anjou and the county of Maine to Margaret's father, the Duke of Anjou and titular king of Naples, Sicily and Jerusalem. Henry, however, is pleased with the treaty. He elevates the Earl of Suffolk to a dukedom and releases the Duke of York from the regency of France, before leaving with Suffolk and his new queen.

Gloucester is scandalised by the loss of Anjou and Maine, so hardly won, and Margaret's lack of a dowry; in addition Suffolk has added his costs for transporting her to England! He refuses to be placated by Beaufort and strides out. Beaufort then reminds the other peers that the hostile Gloucester is heir apparent to the crown. They see no reason why Gloucester should continue to be the Protector, now that the king is of age, and Beaufort goes to reason with him. Buckingham and Somerset follow.

Salisbury, remarking that "Pride went before, ambition follows him", draws attention to Beaufort's insolence and the aspirations of Buckingham and Somerset. He and Warwick agree to curb them as they leave, to York's secret satisfaction. In a soliloquy York expresses his resentment at the loss of 'his' territories in France and resolves to toady to Gloucester for the time being. However when an opportunity occurs he will pre-empt Suffolk and seize the throne, brandishing the white rose emblem in triumph.

Scene 2

Gloucester, at home, gloomily tells his wife Eleanor about a dream he has had. In it his staff of office was broken in two, probably by Beaufort, and the heads of Suffolk and Somerset were placed on the ends. Dame Eleanor responds with a dream of her own, in which she was enthroned in Westminster Cathedral while Henry and Margaret crowned her. He gently chides her for her presumption.

A messenger comes to invite them to join the king at St. Albans for some hawking. As Gloucester follows the messenger out Eleanor calls in a priest, John Hume. He reports that he has conferred with Margery Jourdain, a witch, and Roger Bolingbroke, a magician, who will raise a spirit from the nether world to answer her questions. After she has paid him and left Hume reveals that he has already been hired by Suffolk and Beaufort to put false ideas into her head.

Scene 3

In the palace a group of petitioners approaches Suffolk and Queen Margaret. One petitioner mistakes Suffolk for Gloucester and submits a petition against John Goodman, one of Beaufort's men, for impounding his property and his wife. A second petition is against Suffolk himself, for enclosing the common land of Melford [ten miles south of Bury St. Edmunds].

Peter, an armourer's apprentice, presents a petition against his master, Thomas Horner, for asserting that York was the rightful heir to the crown. Suffolk orders some servants to apprehend Peter and send a pursuivant for Horner. Margaret tears up the other petitions, telling the men to present them to Gloucester.

When the petitioners have gone Margaret expresses her concern that such matters are being decided by Gloucester as the Protector while Henry merely meditates and says his rosary, more like a pope than a king. She mistrusts the power of the other peers and is especially irritated by Gloucester's wife Eleanor who sweeps through the court like a queen, parading her wealth. Suffolk promises support, assuring her that he has set a trap for Dame Eleanor.

Henry enters surrounded by peers wrangling over the regency of France. Margaret and the others reprove Gloucester for usurping the king's powers as Warwick and Beaufort quarrel and Suffolk grumbles. Gloucester withdraws in dudgeon. Margaret drops her fan and boxes the ears of a lady who is slow in retrieving it, affecting surprise when it turns out to be the Duchess of Gloucester. Eleanor, ready to scratch her eyes out, vituperates and leaves.

Gloucester returns from a turn in the quadrangle and expresses support for York as the

Act I, Scene 4

The Duchess of Gloucester and a priest, John Hume, watch from a window in her house as the prostrate witch, Margery Jourdain, conjures up Asmodeus, a spirit. Another priest, John Southwell, records the spirit's predictions in a book.

French regent, to Suffolk's annoyance. York fears that Somerset will withhold the necessary money and provisions. Servants bring in Peter and Thomas Horner, who denies having uttered the traitorous words about York's right to the crown. Henry turns to Gloucester who suggests that Somerset be made regent and that Peter and Horner settle their dispute in single combat.

Scene 4

Bolingbroke arranges for Margery Jourdain to be prostrate in Gloucester's garden while John Southwell, a priest, reads a book. Hume brings the duchess to an upper window to watch them form a circle and conjure up a spirit [possibly Asmodeus] with thunder and lightning.

The spirit tells Margery that Gloucester will be deposed by Henry but will outlive him, only to die a violent death. Suffolk will die by water; furthermore Somerset should avoid castles and remain in the plains. Southwell writes the predictions in his book as the spirit descends from view.

York and Buckingham dash in with guards and arrest the duchess, Hume and the magician's troupe. York reads Southwell's notes and sends Buckingham to overtake the king and Gloucester on their way to St. Albans.

Act II

Scene 1

At St. Albans the king's party, including the queen, Gloucester, Beaufort and Suffolk, have been watching the falconers. Beaufort and Gloucester bicker and privately arrange to meet on the east side of the grove for a duel. A man appears crying out that a blind man called Saunder Simpcox has just miraculously recovered his sight at St. Albans shrine. The mayor of St. Albans and his councillors arrive with Simpcox, carried in a chair by two people, followed by his wife and a crowd of townsmen.

Simpcox tells the king that he was born at Berwick and has been blind since birth. He was called to the shrine in his sleep by St. Alban. Gloucester is sceptical when he says that he is also lame, through falling from a tree which he climbed to pick damsons for his wife. Under questioning Simpcox recognises Gloucester's red cloak and black gown but cannot identify him or the others.

Gloucester calls him a lying knave since if he were blind from birth he could just as well have named the eminent personages present as well as the colours of their clothes. Saying that he will perform another miracle he asks the mayor to summon a beadle with a whip. He calls for a stool and tells Simpcox to jump over it; Simpcox replies that he cannot stand alone. However when the beadle arrives and gives him a cut with the whip he leaps over the stool and runs away, followed by the people shouting "A miracle!" Gloucester tells the departing mayor to have the impostor and his wife whipped through every market town back to Berwick.

Buckingham arrives and gives an account of Eleanor and the witchcraft rites. Beaufort chortles; Gloucester is dismayed and offers to banish his wife if the story is true.

Scene 2

In his garden York canvasses the support of Salisbury and Warwick for his claim on the crown. He goes through his lineage [see part 1, Act II, Scene 5]; they agree that his argument is valid and acclaim him as king. He cautions them to wait until Beaufort and the others have pulled Gloucester down and promises Warwick that he will be his first minister.

Scene 3

In a hall of justice the king sentences Margery Jourdain to be burned in Smithfield and Southwell, Hume and Bolingbroke to be strangled on the gallows. He banishes the Duchess of Gloucester to live with Sir John Stanley in the Isle of Man, after three days of penance. Encouraged by the queen he relieves Gloucester of his staff of office, saying that he will henceforth be his own protector. The downcast Gloucester leaves.

York announces the contest between the armourer and his apprentice. From one side Horner enters, drunk; from the other Peter enters, giving his name as 'Thump' and supported by apprentices Robin, Will and Tom, all drinking. The two fight with sandbags tied to staves and Peter fells Horner, to the king's satisfaction.

Scene 4

Gloucester waits for his banished wife in the street at ten o'clock. Accompanied by Stanley, a sheriff and other officers she comes along barefoot and carrying a taper, dressed in a white sheet with papers pinned to the back. She rails at her fate and warns Gloucester to beware of York, Beaufort and the others. Armed in innocence he entreats her to be patient.

A herald comes to summon Gloucester to the parliament at Bury on the first of the month while Eleanor prepares to sail for the Isle of Man.

Act III

Scene 1

Henry is presiding over a session of parliament in the abbey at Bury St. Edmunds with the queen, Beaufort, Suffolk, York and Buckingham in attendance. Margaret remarks that Gloucester has become haughty and should be removed from the Council. The others join in the condemnation. Somerset enters to report that France is lost (to York's disappointment).

Gloucester arrives with apologies for his lateness. He is promptly arrested by Suffolk for high treason, being accused by York of taking French bribes, pocketing the soldiers' pay and devising strange tortures for petty offenders. Gloucester denies everything and charges the others with malicious conspiracy. He is taken away under guard and Henry, who believes in him, then departs in sorrow. Margaret wants Gloucester executed and the others, having only a flimsy case against him, signify agreement.

A messenger arrives to report that Englishmen have been put to the sword in a rebellion in Ireland. York suggests that Somerset be sent there as regent but Beaufort assigns York to lead an expedition against the Irish. York asks Suffolk to give him troops at Bristol within fourteen days. After the others have gone he gloats that at last he has an army; while he is in Ireland his rebel accomplice Jack Cade, a tailor of Ashford, will assume the name of John Mortimer and foment trouble in Kent. York will then be able to return and seize the throne.

Scene 2

In Bury St. Edmunds palace two murderers confirm to Suffolk that they have killed Gloucester and disappear. To the sound of trumpets Henry enters with Margaret, Beaufort, Somerset and other lords. He sends Suffolk to fetch Gloucester for trial and arranges the others in their places. Suffolk returns to report that Gloucester is dead in his bed; Henry faints in horror. When he recovers Margaret reproaches him for setting his remorse for Gloucester higher than his regard for herself and Suffolk.

Warwick and Salisbury come with the news that the Commons has heard of Gloucester's assassination by Suffolk and Beaufort and is in a commotion. While Salisbury retires to calm them Henry sends Warwick to investigate the death and prays to God that it was not murder. Warwick brings Gloucester's body in on a bed; he points to the signs of a violent struggle and implies that Suffolk and Beaufort were responsible. He and Suffolk exchange insults as Beaufort and Somerset leave. Finally they go off to fight it out while Henry comments, "Thrice is he arm'd that hath his quarrel just,".

Warwick and Suffolk soon return with swords drawn. Suffolk accuses Warwick of setting the men of Bury on him. Salisbury re-enters with the report that unless Suffolk is executed or banished the Commons will put him to a lingering death. The members of the Commons are heard shouting for an answer. Henry thanks them for "their tender loving care" and gives Suffolk three days to leave the kingdom for ever. He then leaves with Warwick.

Margaret weeps and kisses Suffolk's hand, lamenting that two courtiers have now gone. Vaux brings news that Beaufort is on the point of death, gasping and clutching the air. Margaret dolefully bids Suffolk to go to France but to stay in touch.

Scene 3

Beaufort is attended by Henry, Salisbury and Warwick in his bedroom in London. He raves guiltily about Gloucester's death before expiring, to Henry's compassionate exhortations.

Act IV

Scene 1

The captain of a pinnace lands on the seashore near Dover from a longboat, with officers and prisoners. He hands over a prisoner to the master and another to the master's mate for ransoms of one thousand crowns each. He then hands the banished Suffolk, disguised, to Walter Whitmore who lost an eye in seizing the prize and threatens to kill him in revenge.

Suffolk recollects a prophecy that he would die 'by water' [referred to by the spirit in Act 1, Scene 4]. He reveals his identity and tells Whitmore that he is not destined to be slain by him. The captain reviles him for the loss of the French territories and for Gloucester's murder; he orders Whitmore to strike off his head against the side of the boat. Whitmore complies and one of the prisoners who has been spared prepares to take the body to the king.

Scene 2

Two of Jack Cade's followers, George Bevis and John Holland, wait for him on Blackheath. He arrives with other working men including a tanner from Wingham [east of Canterbury], Dick the butcher, Smith the weaver and a sawyer. Cade aspires to be king in an overweening speech, to much ribald heckling. Emmanuel, a clerk of Chatham, is brought forward and condemned to be hanged for knowing how to write(!). A man called Michael comes to warn Cade that the Staffords are approaching with the king's forces.

Sir Humphrey Stafford and his brother William arrive with soldiers and call upon Cade and the others to disperse. Cade claims to be the son of a bricklayer who was one of a pair of twins stolen by a beggarwoman from Edmund Mortimer (the Earl of March). William suspects that York has coached Cade in this story but Cade cheerfully admits he invented it himself. When Dick swears to have Lord Say's head, for selling the dukedom of Maine, Stafford impatiently orders a herald to proclaim Cade's men traitors.

Scene 3

The two forces meet and fight elsewhere on Blackheath [on the SE outskirts of London] and both the Staffords are killed. Cade dons Stafford's armour and proposes to drag the bodies to London at his horse's heels.

Scene 4

Henry reads Cade's supplication in his palace in London in the company of Buckingham and Lord Say. To one side Margaret grieves over Suffolk's head.

A messenger reports that the rebels have reached Southwark [in central London, on the south bank of the Thames]. Cade is proclaiming himself Lord Mortimer and intends to crown himself at Westminster. Buckingham advises Henry to withdraw to Killingworth [Kenilworth, near Coventry] until the rebellion is suppressed. Lord Say decides to hide in London. As the king and queen make ready to leave a second messenger reports that Cade has taken London Bridge and is attracting some local support.

Scene 5

On the walls of the Tower of London, near the bridge, Lord Scales prepares to aid the Lord Mayor and sends Matthew Goffe to Smithfield to raise another force.

Scene 6

Cade reaches Cannon Street [in the City, on the north bank] and orders London Bridge to be set ablaze. A soldier who fails to address him as Lord Mortimer is put to death.

Scene 7

Cade's force arrives at Smithfield [near St. Paul's] and routs the king's force, killing their leader Matthew Goffe. Cade incites the multitude to arson and pillage.

George Bevis brings in Lord Say and Cade hurls absurd and ignorant charges at him. Lord Say defends his record and pleads ill health. The relentless Cade orders him and his son-in-law, Sir James Cromer, to be beheaded. The mob rushes off and returns with the heads on two poles.

Scene 8

Cade and the rabble gather at the White Hart in Southwark, having yielded ground to a force under Buckingham and Lord Clifford of Cumberland. They tell Cade that all who go home in peace will have a free pardon; the fickle crowd welcome the idea. Cade regains their support in a fiery speech but Clifford sways them back again by recalling the achievements of Henry V their behalf. As Cade makes off Buckingham offers a thousand crowns for his head.

Scene 9

Henry mopes on Kenilworth Castle terrace with Margaret and Somerset. Buckingham and Clifford come to report that Jack Cade has fled and point to a number of his followers who are assembled below the terrace with halters round their necks. Henry expresses his gratitude and praise.

A messenger reports that York has landed from Ireland and is leading an army to overthrow the traitor Somerset. Henry relapses into gloom again. He despatches Buckingham to reason with York and

commits Somerset to the Tower for his own safety.

Scene 10

After five days' flight the famished Cade climbs a brick wall to look for some salad in a Kentish garden. The owner, Alexander Iden, is strolling quietly with five servants. However when Cade threatens him he overcomes him in a sword fight. Discovering whom he has killed Iden has the body cast on a dunghill and plans to take the head to the king.

Act V

Scene 1

York and his Irish army approach the king's camp in Kent between Dartford and Blackheath. Buckingham meets him and informs him that Somerset has been immured in the Tower. York tells his men to disperse and report to St. George's field the next day for their pay.

Henry comes up, followed by Iden carrying Cade's head. Henry knights him on the spot and gives him a reward of one thousand crowns. Margaret arrives with Somerset, to York's surprise. He accuses Henry of a breach of faith and is accused by Somerset in turn of capital treason.

York calls for his sons, Edward and Richard Plantagenet, with their forces; Margaret orders Buckingham to summon Lord Clifford and his son with their forces similarly. York proclaims himself the legitimate sovereign and calls up Warwick and Salisbury with their men, while Henry recalls Buckingham. Clifford thinks that York has gone mad and Henry laments the treachery of Salisbury and Warwick. The two factions defy each other.

Scene 2

Warwick calls on Lord Clifford to face him at St. Albans. When he appears York arrives and pre-empts Warwick; he fights with Clifford and kills him. Young Clifford comes to carry his father's body away.

Richard fights with Somerset and kills him. Henry vacillates but is persuaded to fly by Margaret and young Clifford.

Scene 3

In the country near St. Albans York is looking for Salisbury. Richard tells his father that he has three times defended him and led him to safety on his horse but Salisbury fought on. Salisbury appears and thanks Richard while York calls Warwick to help him pursue the king to London.

King Henry VI, Part 3

The seventh play in the history-cycle was originally entitled *The True Tragedy of Richard, Duke of York, and the Good King Henry the Sixth*. The action follows immediately on from Part 2, encompassing the Wars of the Roses (between the Plantagenet houses of York and Lancaster) from 1455 and ending with Henry's murder on May 21st, 1471. The historical events are rearranged and compressed, as usual.

Act I

Scene 1

Some Yorkist soldiers break into the Parliament House followed by Richard Plantagenet Duke of York, his sons Edward Earl of March and the humpbacked Richard, the Duke of Norfolk, the Marquess of Montague and the Earl of Warwick wearing white roses in their hats. York recalls the end of the battle of St. Albans, when the king slipped away and various lords were killed in a counter-attack. Edward and Montague display their bloodstained swords and Richard throws down the Duke of Somerset's head. The soldiers withdraw as York is led by Warwick to the throne and takes his seat.

A fanfare signals the arrival of King Henry VI, Lord Clifford, the Earls of Northumberland and Westmoreland and the Duke of Exeter, all with red roses in their hats. Henry glares at York but counsels patience when his followers are eager to assail Warwick's group. He approaches the throne and orders York to kneel to him as his sovereign. York retorts that he is the sovereign and Warwick tells Henry to be content as the Duke of Lancaster.

Threats are exchanged and the familiar argument over the Plantagenet succession ensues [see Act II, Scene 5 of part 1 and Act II, Scene 2 of part 2]. Exeter wavers, Clifford is defiant and the soldiers reappear at a signal from Warwick. Finally it is agreed that Henry will remain monarch for life, after which York will succeed to the throne. Northumberland, Westmoreland and Clifford are scandalised by the arrangement, which disinherits the Prince of Wales, and go to inform the queen.

York descends from the throne and the lords acclaim the reconciliation. York and his sons depart; Norfolk leaves for his seat and Montague for the sea while Warwick decides to remain in London with his troops.

Exeter steals away, seeing the wrathful Queen Margaret approaching with Edward, Prince of Wales. Henry tries to do the same but is too slow. Margaret reviles him for allowing his son to be disinherited and the "savage duke" to become his heir, telling him that he has preferred his life to his honour. She pronounces a divorce, asserting that the three northern peers have forsworn him and will now follow her, and sweeps out with Edward. The forlorn Henry asks Exeter to carry some pleading letters to the three.

Scene 2

With Montague, Edward and Richard accost their father York in Sandal Castle, near Wakefield. They urge him to seize the throne despite his sworn agreement to let Henry reign for life. He is persuaded; he tells Montague to incite Warwick, Richard to inform Norfolk and Edward to get Lord Cobham to raise the Kentishmen.

A messenger reports that Queen Margaret and the northern lords are close at hand with twenty thousand men and intend to besiege the castle. York changes his plans; Richard and Edward are to stay while Montague is to go to London to warn Warwick and Cobham to strengthen their forces and not to trust Henry. His uncles Sir John and Sir Hugh Mortimer come to let York know that they will oppose the queen with five thousand men.

Scene 3

York's young son, Edmund Earl of Rutland, is fleeing with his tutor across the battlefield between Sandal Castle and Wakefield. Clifford finds him, has the tutor removed by his soldiers and condemns the youngster to die, since his father slew Clifford's father. He curses the entire house of York and stabs Edmund to death.

Scene 4

Elsewhere on the field York has seen his sons fight heroically but his uncles have been killed and his men are in retreat. Queen Margaret appears with Clifford, Northumberland, the Prince of Wales and their men. They call upon York to yield but he defies them. Clifford attacks him with his sword but is restrained by Northumberland, at Margaret's command.

They take hold of York and stand him on a molehill while Margaret shows him a handkerchief stained with Edmund's blood and mocks him by putting a paper crown on his head. York despises her and the piteous death of Edmund. Clifford stabs him and Margaret does the same, ordering that his head be set over the city gates "So York may overlook the town of York".

Act II

Scene 1

Edward and Richard march with their forces over a plain near Mortimer's Cross [five miles north west of

Leominster in Herefordshire] discussing the battle of Wakefield and wondering what has happened to York. They see three suns coalesce in the dawn sky and Richard decides to adopt them as the Plantagenet emblem.

A messenger who witnessed York's assassination describes the event; the brothers are overcome with grief and Edward realises that he is now the Duke. They meet Warwick and Montague with their men and hear more bad news. Warwick tells them that when he heard of York's death, ten days before, he gathered his soldiers and marched with the king to intercept the queen's force at St. Albans. However in this second battle despite his best efforts his men were defeated.

He and Norfolk, now six miles off, have come to find them, together with their brother George Plantagenet from Burgundy, while Henry has gone to join Margaret. They all resolve to turn from mourning to revenge. A second messenger brings word from Norfolk that he needs to confer with them as the queen is approaching with a powerful force.

Scene 2

Henry is saddened to see York's head over the gates of York when he arrives with Margaret, the Prince of Wales, Clifford and Northumberland, fearing that "things ill got had ever bad success". Clifford and Margaret try to embolden him and he dubs the Prince a knight.

A messenger reports that Warwick is approaching with thirty thousand men. Clifford suggests that Henry leave the conduct of the battle to Margaret and depart but he decides to stay. Edward marches in with George, Richard, Warwick, Norfolk, Montague and their troops. He demands the crown from Henry but the king refuses, pointing out that Edward's father broke his oath and rose against him. Warwick supports the demand but is scorned by Margaret for his flight from the second battle of St. Albans. After further insults from the three brothers the factions leave.

Scene 3

Warwick is discovered resting wearily on the battlefield of Towton [between Leeds and York] by Edward and George who are in retreat. They are followed by Richard who tells Warwick that his brother has been killed by Clifford's lance. Warwick gives them new courage and they return to the fray.

Scene 4

Richard meets Clifford in single combat. Warwick comes upon them and Clifford flees.

Scene 5

Elsewhere Henry, having been sent from the field by Margaret and Clifford, sits on a hillock musing on the ebb and flow of the conflict. He is distraught to see a son who has unwittingly killed his father and then a father who has killed his son in the civil conflict.

Queen Margaret, with the Prince of Wales and Exeter, finds him and urges him to fly towards Berwick to escape Warwick and the swiftly advancing Yorkists.

Scene 6

Clifford is wounded and falls in a faint. Edward, George, Richard, Montague and Warwick appear; they hear a groan and Richard discovers that Clifford has just died. Now that the battle is over Warwick orders York's head to be removed from the gates of York and replaced by Clifford's head. He proposes a triumphal march to London for Edward's coronation, after which he will go to Brittany to seek the hand of the king's sister, Lady Bona, for Edward. Edward declares that he will create Richard Duke of Gloucester and George Duke of Clarence.

Act III

Scene 1

Two gamekeepers carrying crossbows prepare to take cover by a chase in the north of England. King Henry comes by in disguise carrying a prayer-book, having returned from hiding in Scotland. He debates with himself whether, in France, Warwick will gain the king's sister for Edward or Margaret will gain his aid for himself. The gamekeepers recognise and apprehend him despite his appeals to them as his erstwhile subjects.

Scene 2

Lady Elizabeth Grey petitions Edward, now King Edward IV, in his palace in London, to restore to her and her three children the lands which were seized when her husband Sir John Grey was killed at the second battle of St. Albans. Gloucester and Clarence withdraw as Edward promises her the lands if he may have her love. When it transpires that he is referring to more than the love of a loyal subject Lady Grey virtuously refuses. Edward is impressed by her wit and modesty and offers to make her his queen. "'Tis better said than done," she responds, regarding herself as unfit for the royal state.

A nobleman enters to report that Henry has been brought in, a prisoner. Edward orders him to be conveyed to the Tower and leaves with the others to interrogate his captor. The misshapen Gloucester soliloquises on his own evil schemes to seize the crown [implemented in *Richard III*]. ("Why, I can smile, and murder while I smile,").

Scene 3

In the palace in France King Lewis [Louis XI] with Lady Bona and Admiral Bourbon receive ex-queen Margaret of Anjou, the former Prince of Wales and the Earl of Oxford. Lewis stands and offers Margaret a seat beside him, insisting when she confesses that she is no longer queen of England; she recounts her story and seeks his aid.

Warwick enters and asks for Lady Bona's hand in marriage to King Edward. Margaret warns Lewis against the union and an argument follows. Lewis takes Warwick aside and asks if Edward is the lawful king and truly loves Lady Bona. Being reassured he declares that his sister shall marry Edward and that a treaty of friendship shall be drawn up to set against her dowry. Margaret decries the "impudent and shameless Warwick".

A courier enters with letters for Lewis from Edward, for Warwick from Montague and for Margaret. Lewis and Warwick frown as they read about Edward's marriage to Lady Grey, while Margaret smiles. Lewis is insulted. Warwick disavows Edward and swears allegiance to Henry; Margaret forgives him and welcomes him to the Lancastrian cause.

Lewis slyly instructs the courier to tell Edward that he is sending some masquers to celebrate his wedding, while the others also send hostile messages. He arranges to supply Warwick and Oxford with five thousand men to invade England and unseat Edward. Margaret and Wales will follow with more men, to be carried by the royal fleet under Admiral Bourbon's command. As a pledge of loyalty Warwick offers to marry his elder daughter to the prince.

Act IV

Scene 1

King Edward and Lady Grey, now Queen Elizabeth, enter a room in the palace in London with the Earl of Pembroke, Lord Hastings and Lord Stafford to find Gloucester, Clarence, Montague and the Duke of Somerset. Clarence tells Edward that his disdain of the French king's sister has made an enemy of Lewis; Gloucester adds that Warwick has been dishonoured by the same action. They also blame Edward for arranging other unwise marriages.

The messenger from France arrives with the various messages and announces that Prince Edward is to marry Warwick's daughter. At the news Clarence hurries off to seek the hand of Warwick's younger daughter, followed by Somerset. Edward is disappointed by these defections but despatches Pembroke and Stafford to conscript more men. Montague, Hastings and Gloucester vow to support Edward.

Scene 2

Warwick and Oxford have reached Warwickshire with the French contingent. Warwick greets Clarence and Somerset and tells them of his plan to take Edward's forces by surprise.

Scene 3

Two watchmen gossip as they guard the tent housing Edward and Hastings in a camp near the town of Warwick. Warwick appears with Clarence, Oxford, Somerset and their men. The party fall on the watchmen and drive them off, yelling battle cries. Gloucester gives chase to Hastings and Warwick's men bring Edward out, sitting in a chair in his gown.

Warwick removes Edward's crown and orders Somerset to conduct him to the archbishop of York for safekeeping. He and Oxford prepare to march to London to release Henry from the Tower of London.

Scene 4

In the palace Queen Elizabeth informs her brother, Lord Rivers, of Edward's capture. Being pregnant she plans to seek sanctuary for the sake of Edward's unborn child.

Scene 5

Gloucester draws Lord Hastings and Sir William Stanley into a thicket in a park near Middleham Castle [in Wensleydale, Yorkshire] and informs them of his plan to rescue the king from the archbishop's clutches. When Edward comes up with a huntsman he tells him that a horse is waiting at the corner of the park; he is to ride to Lynn [King's Lynn on the Wash] and thence take ship for Flanders. Edward and the huntsman lose no time in escaping.

Scene 6

King Henry has been released from the Tower by Warwick, Oxford, Clarence, Somerset, Montague and young Henry Earl of Richmond. He thanks the lieutenant of the Tower for his treatment of him and praises God and Warwick for his freedom. He resigns the government to Warwick who chooses Clarence for protector. Henry asks them to ensure that Margaret and the Prince of Wales be returned to France without delay.

A courier comes to report that with Warwick's connivance Edward has escaped and is on his way to Burgundy. When Henry and the others have left, Somerset and Oxford arrange to send young Richmond to Brittany until the strife is past.

Scene 7

Edward has returned from overseas and is with Gloucester and Hastings outside York. They knock at the gates and the mayor and aldermen appear on the walls. Edward requests entry, if not as king then as Duke of York. The mayor descends and hands him the keys.

Sir John Montgomery arrives with his force, ready to serve his king, Edward. When Edward tells him that for the time being he is only Duke of York, not king, he makes ready to march away again. Hastings and Gloucester persuade Edward to allow a soldier to proclaim him "Edward the Fourth, by the grace of God King of England and France and Lord of Ireland". Montgomery accordingly stays and they all arrange to join up with Warwick and his men.

Scene 8

As Edward marches south with his army, including Dutch and German soldiers, a conference is held in the palace in London. Warwick undertakes to muster troops from Warwickshire, Clarence is to do the same in Kent and East Anglia, Montague in Buckingham, Northampton and Leicestershire and Oxford in Oxfordshire. They depart on their missions.

Act V, Scene 7

King Edward IV is enthroned in his palace.He prepares to kiss the baby Prince of Wales in the arms of his mother, Queen Elizabeth, as his ducal brothers Clarence and the misshapen Gloucester look on together with Lord Hastings.

75

Henry and Exeter, left behind, are surprised by a troop of soldiers led by Edward and Gloucester. Henry is seized and taken away to the Tower while the others leave to confront Warwick at Coventry.

Act V

Scene 1

Two messengers report to Warwick and the mayor of Coventry on the walls of the city. They tell them that Oxford is approaching via Dunsmore [south of Aylesbury] and Montague has a powerful force at Daintry [Daventry, south of Rugby]. Sir John Somerville adds that Clarence is at Southam and will arrive in two hours.

The sound of a drum is heard and Warwick is shocked to see Edward appearing with Gloucester and his army. Edward calls on the turncoat Warwick to kneel to him as king; Warwick defies him. The Lancastrian supporters Oxford, Montague, Somerset and Clarence march in with their respective forces. The first three enter the city but Clarence throws down his red rose, recants his defection from Edward [Act IV, Scene 1] and declares his support for his brother. Warwick spurns him as a traitor and challenges Edward to meet him in battle at Barnet [north of London at that time].

Scene 2

On the battlefield near Barnet Edward lays down the wounded Warwick and goes to look for Montague as his next victim. Warwick resigns himself to defeat and death. Before he expires Oxford and Somerset come to tell him that Montague has been killed but the queen has landed from France with a strong force.

Scene 3

In another part of the field King Edward, with his brothers Clarence and Gloucester, claims victory but hears that Oxford and Somerset have joined the queen whose army, thirty thousand strong, is advancing. He decides to oppose them at Tewkesbury.

Scene 4

Queen Margaret rallies the Prince of Wales, Somerset and Oxford on the plain near Tewkesbury [in the Vale of Gloucester]. The prince is encouraged to fight on, despite the loss of Warwick and Montague. At a distance Edward similarly spurs his followers on.

Scene 5

Elsewhere in the field King Edward, Clarence and Gloucester have taken Margaret, Oxford and Somerset prisoner. Edward orders Oxford to be taken to Hames Castle and Somerset to be beheaded. The Prince of Wales is brought in. Not being meek like his father Henry he defies the brothers and brands them usurpers. Margaret swoons in horror as they all stab him to death.

When she recovers Margaret curses them while Gloucester slips away to hurry to the Tower in London. She invites the other two brothers to put an end to her life but Edward orders her to be forcibly removed.

Scene 6

Gloucester comes upon Henry sitting in a room in the Tower reading a book. He sends the Lieutenant, Sir Robert Brakenbury, away. Henry, knowing why he has come, curses his birth, his deformity, his cruelty and his murderous deeds. Gloucester kills him and stabs the dead body as he swears bitterly to eliminate Clarence next.

Scene 7

King Edward IV is enthroned in the palace, attended by Queen Elizabeth holding the infant prince, Clarence, Gloucester, Hastings and others. Edward reviews all the nobles who have paid with their lives for opposing the house of York. He kisses the baby Prince of Wales and invites the others to do likewise; Gloucester mutters darkly that his kiss is that of Judas.

Edward hears from Clarence that the Duke of Anjou has pawned Sicily and Jerusalem to the king of France to pay the ransom of his daughter Margaret. Edward sends her back to France and orders celebrations "For here, I hope, begins our lasting joy."

THE FAMOUS HISTORY OF THE LIFE OF
King Henry VIII

The Globe theatre burned down (for the first time) on June 29th, 1613 during a performance of the play, possibly under its alternative title, *All Is True*. The fire was apparently caused by one of the cannon discharged in Act I, Scene 4, an ember from which flew up into the thatch. It seems that the authorship of the play was shared with John Fletcher, as was the case in *The Two Noble Kinsmen* and another play, now lost. The action runs from the Field of the Cloth of Gold (1520) to the christening of Princess Elizabeth (1523).

Prologue

The audience is warned not to expect a comedy; for a shilling they will "find truth" in a serious two-hour play [i.e. two hours without the intervals between acts].

Act I

Scene 1

The Duke of Norfolk meets the Lord High Constable, Edward Bohun Duke of Buckingham, and Lord Abergavenny in an anteroom in the palace in London. Buckingham regrets that through illness he was not with Norfolk at the glittering tournament near Guisnes organised by the portly Cardinal Wolsey, at which Henry VIII and Francis I of France outshone each other in pomp and feats of strength. Norfolk cautions the other two when they criticise the cardinal's vanity and presumption.

Cardinal Wolsey passes through, exchanging disdainful glances with Buckingham; he is accompanied by guards, preceded by the bearer of the Chancellor's purse and followed by two secretaries with papers. Buckingham knows that Wolsey has received secret payments from the Emperor Charles V to break up potential Anglo-French amity. Suspecting that Wolsey is on his way to the king, he plans to follow and denounce him but is restrained by Norfolk.

Brandon enters with a sergeant-at-arms and orders him to arrest Buckingham on a charge of high treason and conduct him to the Tower. Abergavenny is also to go to the Tower pending the king's decision on his disposal. Brandon mentions that the arrest warrant includes Lord Montacute, Buckingham's chaplain John de la Car, his chancellor Gilbert Peck and a Carthusian monk Nicholas Hopkins. Buckingham realises that his spy has been suborned by Wolsey.

Scene 2

The king leans on Wolsey's shoulder in the council chamber, attended by Sir Thomas Lovell and other lords and officers. Henry thanks Wolsey for his vigilance and calls for Buckingham's agent to be arraigned. Queen Katharine is ushered in by the Dukes of Norfolk and Suffolk. She kneels, is raised and kissed by the king and placed by his side.

Katharine informs Henry that his subjects have grievances, principally against Wolsey but also against him. Norfolk supports her, saying that the tailors have stopped ordering from the fullers and weavers because of excessive taxation.

Henry, knowing nothing of a tax, asks Wolsey to explain. When he prevaricates Katharine tells Henry that his people are being subjected to a capital levy of one sixth of their wealth to pay for the wars in France. Henry, displeased, instructs Wolsey to remit the tax and pardon those who have rebelled against it. Wolsey quietly tells his secretary to write to all the shires saying that the tax is to be revoked as a result of his own intercession with the king.

Buckingham's agent is brought in. He reports that Buckingham repeatedly told Abergavenny that should the king die without children he would gain the royal sceptre; furthermore on the king's death the cardinal and Lovell would lose their heads. Wolsey confirms this, stating that Buckingham told him that Hopkins had prophesied to John de la Car that Buckingham would one day govern England. The agent goes on to say that Buckingham even contemplated killing the king if he had committed him to the Tower for taking on Sir William Blomer, a royal servant.

Henry orders Buckingham to stand trial for treason.

Scene 3

In another room in the palace the Lord Chamberlain and Lord Sands deplore the French customs and dress that are in vogue in the court. Lovell joins them, mentioning a proclamation against the new ways and inviting them to a sumptuous supper at Wolsey's house.

Scene 4

A small canopied table for the cardinal and a longer table for the guests are set out in the presence-chamber of York Place [later Whitehall]. Oboes are playing. The queen's maid of honour, Anne Bullen [Anne Boleyn], enters by one door with guests and Sir Henry Guildford enters by another. The group is joined by the Lord Chamberlain, Sands and Lovell. The Lord Chamberlain arranges the guests and Wolsey enters and seats himself at his table.

As Wolsey toasts his guests the sound of gunfire, drums and trumpets is heard. A servant goes to enquire, returning to report that a "noble troop of strangers" has landed from a barge in the Thames. The Lord Chamberlain is deputed to receive them while the others clear the room.

The Chamberlain ushers in the king and others,

masked and dressed like French shepherds. They acknowledge the cardinal as they pass in front of him, while the Chamberlain explains that the visitors speak no English. They take partners for dancing, the king choosing Anne Bullen. Wolsey identifies Henry, who then unmasks, and all pass into another room for the banquet.

Act II

Scene 1

In a Westminster street a gentleman tells a friend that at Buckingham's trial Peck, Hopkins, de la Car and his agent all testified against him and he was found guilty of high treason. The two agree that this was brought about by Wolsey's machinations. Buckingham comes along, preceded by tipstaves [sheriff's officers], and accompanied by halberdiers and an executioner with an axe. He is followed by Lovell, Sands, Sir Nicholas Vaux and a number of commoners.

Buckingham addresses the crowd, pardoning his accusers and urging them not to glory in his downfall. At least he has had a trial, unlike his father who was similarly betrayed by a servant when he rose against the usurper Richard [see *Richard III*, Act V, Scene 1]. He warns them against fickle friends and moves on to his execution.

The gentlemen gossip about a greater "ensuing evil", namely the estrangement of Henry and Katharine. This has been brought about partly at the instigation of the papal legate Cardinal Campeius [Campeggio] and Wolsey who is seeking revenge for not being granted the archbishopric of Toledo.

Scene 2

The Lord Chamberlain is reading a letter in an antechamber in the palace. It informs him that some horses which he had sent for have been appropriated by one of Wolsey's men. When Norfolk and Suffolk enter he tells them that Henry is troubled by gloomy thoughts. Wolsey has disturbed Henry's conscience by suggesting that it was a mortal sin to have married his deceased brother's wife [previously justified by Pope Clement VII on the grounds that the marriage of Katharine and Arthur had not been consummated].

The Lord Chamberlain leaves as the two dukes open a closet door to find the king reading pensively. Henry is annoyed at the interruption; when Wolsey brings Campeius in he dismisses the dukes. Wolsey introduces Campeius and is sent to fetch Dr. Stephen Gardiner, the bishop of Winchester and the king's secretary. While Henry and Gardiner converse Campeius warns Wolsey that he is being blamed for getting rid of Dr. Pace, Gardiner's predecessor. Henry gives Gardiner a message for the queen and proposes to convene an ecclesiastical court at Blackfriars to pronounce on his marriage.

Scene 3

In the queen's apartments an old lady scoffs when Anne Bullen tells her that she would not be a queen, like the pitiable Katharine, or even a duchess for all the world. The Lord Chamberlain appears and tells Anne that the king has created her Marchioness of Pembroke with an income of a thousand pounds a year. When he leaves the old lady twits Anne for hypocritically accepting the honour.

Scene 4

A procession enters a hall in Blackfriars. First come two vergers with short silver wands, then two scribes in academic gowns, the Archbishop of Canterbury, the bishops of Lincoln, Ely, Rochester and St. Asaph, the bearer of the Purse with the great seal and cardinal's hat, two priests with silver crosses, a bare-headed gentleman usher and a sergeant-at-arms carrying a silver mace, two men carrying great silver pillars, two cardinals, two noblemen with the sword and mace and finally the king and queen followed by the Crier and other attendants. The king takes his seat under the cloth of state with the queen seated apart. The cardinals sit as judges with the bishops, scribes and lords on either side.

The Crier calls upon Henry and Katharine to come into the court. Henry responds but Katharine kneels at his feet, protesting that her marriage was judged lawful by his father and by hers, King Ferdinand of Spain, and his council. Since then she has been a true and humble wife for twenty years. She turns on Wolsey, pronouncing him a malicious foe and troublemaker. When he retorts that he is acting for the consistory of Rome she rejects him as a judge, appeals directly to the pope and departs with her attendants.

Henry praises Katharine's piety and obedience; he also exculpates Wolsey from stirring up trouble. He avers that the marriage question was originally raised by the Bishop of Bayonne when he came to arrange a marriage between Princess Mary and the Duke of Orleans. His own conscience being troubled he then approached the Bishops of Lincoln and Canterbury to call a conclave. When Campeius calls for an adjournment, the queen's presence being necessary, Henry perceives that he is bent on procrastination.

Act III

Scene 1

The queen and her ladies listen to a song in her apartments in the palace at Bridewell ("Orpheus with his lute made trees.....Bow themselves, when he did sing:"). Wolsey and Campeius, announced by a gentleman, enter and ask to speak privately to Katharine. She tells them there is nothing that her attendants cannot hear — and in English, not Latin.

The two urge Katharine to put herself in the hands of the king, since if she undergoes an examination she will find herself disgraced. Katharine is not deceived; she informs them that she may have lost Henry's love but she will not lose her royal dignity and status for no reason.

Scene 2

In the antechamber to the king's apartment the Earl of Surrey tells Norfolk, Suffolk and the Lord Chamberlain that Wolsey has at last forfeited Henry's confidence. His letter to the Vatican advising the pope to delay granting a royal divorce, because the king was "tangled in affection" with Anne Bullen, miscarried and was seen by the king. Cardinal Campeius had already left for Rome to further Wolsey's scheme. Meanwhile Dr. Thomas Cranmer, backed by the European universities, has sanctioned the divorce (after which Katharine will be known as 'princess dowager') and is preparing for a second royal marriage and coronation.

Wolsey appears with his servant Cromwell, who confirms that Henry has seen the contents of a packet that he gave him and leaves. As the peers watch, Wolsey fulminates against Cranmer and mutters to himself that the king must marry the Duchess of Alençon (the French king's sister) and not a "spleeny Lutheran" like Anne Bullen.

Reading a list, Henry enters with Lovell. Henry is not surprised when Norfolk tells him that Wolsey appears agitated since he is holding the damning letter and an inventory of the cardinal's valuables and household possessions. Lovell calls Wolsey over. Henry reminds Wolsey that he has made him his prime man of the state and the object of his bounty. Wolsey fawningly agrees. Henry coldly hands him the packet and goes off to breakfast with the others. Wolsey scans the contents and realises that he is undone.

The four peers return. Norfolk orders him to give up the great seal and to confine himself in Asher House (Gardiner's place) until further notice. Wolsey arrogantly questions their authority. Surrey accuses Wolsey of having sent him to Ireland while he got rid of Buckingham, of using "I and the king" without warrant when writing to Rome and other countries, of carrying the great seal into Flanders and of concluding a treaty with Ferrara without the king's consent. Finally Suffolk, on Henry's behalf, orders all his lands, goods and chattels to be forfeited.

Left alone, Wolsey muses on his sudden fall from favour. When Cromwell reappears with the news that Sir Thomas More has been appointed Chancellor in his place he declares himself at peace and resigned to his fate. Cromwell goes on to say that Cranmer has been installed as Archbishop of Canterbury and Lady Anne (Bullen), who has been secretly married to Henry, has appeared openly with him in chapel. Wolsey warns Cromwell not to be betrayed by ambition, as he was, but to serve the king.

Act IV

Scene 1

The two men are again in the street in Westminster, waiting to see Anne Boleyn return from her coronation. One tells the other that Cranmer and other dignitaries held a late court at Dunstable, six miles south of Ampthill where Katharine was staying, and annulled her marriage. She is now lying ill at Kimbolton Castle [a further twenty miles north].

The coronation procession passes by, to the sound of trumpets. It consists of two judges, More the Lord Chancellor preceded by the purse and mace, some choristers singing, the Mayor of London bearing his mace, Garter in a coat of arms wearing a gilt copper crown, the Marquess of Dorset wearing a gold circlet and bearing a sceptre of gold, the Earl of Surrey wearing a collar of esses and carrying a rod of silver with the dove, the Duke of Suffolk as High Steward in robe and coronet bearing a long white wand, the Duke of Norfolk as Earl Marshal with his rod of office, coronet and collar of esses, the Queen, crowned with pearls and flanked by the bishops Stokesly of London and Gardiner of Winchester under a canopy borne by four barons of the Cinque-ports, the Duchess of Norfolk in a gold circlet wrought with flowers holding the queen's train and Countesses and other ladies in plain gold tiaras.

The gentlemen comment on the personages and are joined by a third man who has been in the Abbey. He describes how Anne was crowned with Edward the Confessor's crown and other emblems while the choir sang the Te Deum. With the fall of Wolsey York Place has been renamed Whitehall and Thomas Cromwell has been made master of the jewel house and a member of the Privy Council.

Scene 2

At Kimbolton the ailing Katharine is helped to a chair by Griffith, a gentleman usher, and Patience, a lady-in-waiting. Griffith reports that the Earl of Northumberland arrested Wolsey at York. Wolsey fell ill, sought shelter in Leicester Abbey and died three days later. Griffith reminds Katharine that for all his deceitful presumption Wolsey endowed two seats of learning (at Ipswich and Oxford), one of which has already achieved fame.

As musicians play Katharine falls asleep. In a vision six figures appear in white robes and golden masks, garlanded with bay; they bow to her and dance. Two hold a garland over her head while the other four curtsey; the movement is repeated twice by the others in sequence. She stirs in her sleep and raises her hands to heaven.

On waking she tells her companions that the spirits of peace have bidden her to a celestial banquet. They fear that she is sinking. A messenger announces a gentleman sent from the king. He brings in Capucius, an ambassador from Emperor Charles V, who conveys Henry's best wishes. Katharine hands him a letter for the king, commending Henry's young daughter to his care and asking him to look after Katharine's serving men and women. She departs in dignity to her death bed.

Act V

Scene 1

At one o'clock in the morning Gardiner, accompanied by a page with a torch, encounters Lovell in a gallery at the palace. Lovell speaks of fears that the queen may die in childbirth. Gardiner

Act V Scene 5

At the gates of the palace Archbishop Cranmer kneels as King Henry VIII and his retinue await the procession in which the Duchess of Norfolk brings the newly-christened baby (the future Queen Elizabeth I).

doesn't care, as long as the baby lives; in fact he would be happy if Cranmer and Cromwell disappeared as well. As he and the page leave, Henry comes in with Suffolk, with whom he has been playing cards. He asks after the queen and bids Suffolk goodnight.

Sir Anthony Denny brings in Cranmer, who kneels to Henry; Denny and Lovell are dismissed. Henry informs Cranmer with regret that he will have to appear before the Council later that morning to answer certain grievous complaints. Giving Cranmer a ring he warns him that his many enemies will produce perjured evidence and urges him not to rely on honesty but to defend himself vigorously.

As Cranmer leaves an old lady comes to tell Henry that Anne has been delivered of a baby girl. Henry wanted a boy; nevertheless he calls Lovell to give the old woman a hundred marks and hurries off to see the queen.

Scene 2

Cranmer arrives in the lobby of the Council chamber and is detained by the doorkeeper among the pages and pursuivants. The king's physician, Dr. Butts, passes through and then appears with the king at an upper window. He points out to Henry the indignity being done to Cranmer by being made to wait outside the chamber.

Scene 3

The Lord Chancellor, More, takes his place near the upper end of a table in the Council chamber, leaving one seat vacant above him. Suffolk, Norfolk, Surrey, the Lord Chamberlain and Gardiner take their seats, with Cromwell at the lower end as secretary and the keeper at the door. Cranmer, who has been waiting half an hour, is summoned.

More, supported by Gardiner, informs the archbishop of reports that he and his chaplains have been spreading heresies. Cranmer demands to face his accusers. Suffolk and Gardiner point out that as a member of the Council he cannot be accused directly; however the king wishes him to be committed to the Tower as a private citizen against whom charges may be brought. Cranmer reproves Gardiner who brands Cranmer a dissenter; when Cromwell objects Gardiner includes him in the accusation.

More allays the argument and calls the guard to conduct Cranmer to the Tower. However he and the others are taken aback when Cranmer produces the king's ring. At that moment Henry enters, frowning, and takes his seat. He waves aside Gardiner's flattering welcome and rebukes them all for forcing Cranmer to wait at the door like a footman. Having expressed his approbation of Cranmer he asks him directly to baptise the new princess and be her godfather, the other godparents being the Duchess of Norfolk and the Marchioness of Dorset. At the king's behest Gardiner signifies his support.

Scene 4

A noisy mob have crowded into the palace yard to see the nobility returning from the royal christening. A porter and his assistant attempt to quell the tumult of the mob, backed by the Lord Chamberlain.

Scene 5

A procession arrives at the palace comprising trumpeters, two aldermen, the Lord Mayor, Garter, Cranmer, Norfolk, Suffolk, two noblemen with standing-bowls for the christening gifts, the Duchess of Norfolk carrying the baby under a canopy borne by four noblemen with a lady holding her train, the two godmothers and other ladies. The king and his retinue are greeted by Cranmer, kneeling. He names the child Elizabeth and Henry kisses her.

Cranmer predicts that the royal infant "promises upon this land a thousand thousand blessings" and eulogises the future Queen Elizabeth I at length.

Epilogue

The women in the audience are invited to applaud the play, although it cannot please everyone; the men will then surely join in.

THE LIFE AND DEATH OF
King John

This play, all in verse, appears to owe much of its narrative to *The Troublesome Reign of King John of England*, an old play of the Queen's men based on Holinshed's *Chronicles* and John Foxe's *Book of Martyrs*. The dialogue, however, is original. The action runs from an interview at Le Goulet on March 25th, 1202, to John's death on October 19th, 1216.

Act I

Scene 1

A French ambassador, Chatillon, is received by King John, his mother Queen Elinor and the Earls of Pembroke, Essex and Salisbury. Addressing the king as "borrow'd Majesty", to Elinor's annoyance, he presents a demand from King Philip of France for Britain and various French provinces to be handed over to John's nephew Arthur Plantagenet, Prince of Brittany. John rejects the demand and Chatillon threatens war; he is led out by Pembroke. Elinor ascribes the demand to the ambitions of her widowed daughter-in-law Constance, Arthur's mother.

A sheriff enters briefly and whispers to Essex, who asks the king to listen to a strange controversy. The sheriff returns with Robert Faulconbridge and his bastard brother Philip. Robert is the son and heir of Sir Robert Faulconbridge of Northamptonshire, through his death-bed will. However Philip, a soldier decorated by John's older brother Richard I (Coeur-de-Lion), claims the inheritance as the eldest son. Robert resists the claim, believing that Philip was fathered by Richard I during Sir Robert's absence as ambassador in Germany.

John tells Robert that Philip's claim is legitimate [by the primogeniture law of the time] since he is his first-born son of his mother after her marriage, the supposed identity of the father being irrelevant. Robert asks if his father's will then has no force.

Elinor puts it to Philip that he might prefer being Richard Coeur-de-Lion's son, even with no estate, to being the squire of Faulconbridge with five hundred pounds a year. Upon reflection he agrees, renounces his claim and offers to follow Elinor to France. John thereupon dubs him Sir Richard Plantagenet and calls on the others to speed to France. Left alone, Philip delights in his knighthood and imagines how he will converse with his inferiors.

His mother, Lady Faulconbridge, comes looking for Robert with her servant James Gurney. He is dismissed while Philip tells her what has happened. She confesses her seduction by Richard I, to Philip's satisfaction.

Act II

Scene 1

Lymoges, Duke of Austria, meets King Philip of France accompanied by Lewis [Louis], the Dauphin, and Constance with her son Arthur outside the walls of Angers with their respective forces. The king greets Lymoges who assures Arthur that he will not go back home until Arthur has been crowned king of England, Ireland, Anjou, Touraine and Maine. He and Philip prepare to attack the town but Constance suggests that they await the return of Chatillon from England.

Chatillon arrives and bids them turn their armies against the English whose forces are close behind him headed by Queen Elinor. King John arrives with Elinor, her niece Lady Blanch of Spain, the newly knighted Sir Richard, lords and soldiers. King Philip tells him that Arthur should be on the throne by virtue of his descent from Constance's husband Geoffrey, the second-born son of Henry II [thus taking precedence over John, Henry's third-born son]. Elinor and Constance squabble over the line of succession.

Philip calls on some leading citizens of Angers to state whether they recognise John's title or Arthur's. John reminds them that he is their lawful king who will protect them from the French cannon. King Philip tells them that if they acknowledge Arthur he will remove his guns. The first citizen avers that they are the King of England's subjects. However they require proof of kingship before swearing allegiance.

At this, everyone leaves as the two kings marshal their troops and battle is joined. After a while a French herald approaches and calls for the gates to be opened for Arthur of Brittany. He is followed by an English herald who calls for the bells to be rung to welcome King John. However the citizens cannot make out which side has won and the gates remain closed.

The two kings re-enter, both claiming victory, to no avail. Sir Richard suggests that they combine to attack the town and resume their quarrel later. They agree that John shall attack from the west, Lymoges from the north and Philip from the south. (Sir Richard sniggers at the thought that the Austrians and the French will be shooting towards each other). The first citizen hastily proposes that Lewis and Lady Blanch be joined in matrimony instead; the town will then be open to all, with no further death or destruction.

Elinor confidentially urges John to support the idea. He offers thirty thousand marks plus the French territories (with the exception of Angers itself) as Blanch's dowry. Blanch and the Dauphin being agreeable, the wedding is to be solemnised in St. Mary's chapel in the town.

Philip fears the wrath of Constance at this compromise but John reassures him that he will create Arthur Earl of Richmond as compensation. They enter the town leaving Sir Richard to soliloquise on the way in which the kings have reached an accommodation, which he would never have done.

Act III

Scene 1

In the French king's tent Constance and Arthur cannot believe it when they hear of the agreement from the Earl of Salisbury. Constance rages and seats herself on the ground. The kings enter with Lewis, Blanch, Elinor, Sir Richard, Lymoges and their attendants. Constance rails at them and Sir Richard takes the opportunity to taunt Lymoges.

Pope Innocent's legate, Cardinal Pandulph of Milan, comes to ask John why he is keeping the Archbishop of Canterbury, Stephen Langton, out of his holy see. John rejoins that no Italian priest shall "tithe or toll" in his dominions. Pandulph informs him that he will stand cursed and excommunicated unless he submits to Rome and bids Philip not to ally himself with John.

Philip pleads with Pandulph but the cardinal is unbending . Lewis urges him to war while Blanch implores him not to mar their wedding day with more slaughter. Eventually Philip yields to the cardinal's injunction and the two parties leave to prepare for further conflict.

Scene 2

Sir Richard carries Lymoges' severed head over the plain near Angers. Encountering John he tells him that he has rescued Elinor. John instructs Hubert de Burgh to take charge of Arthur, whom he has taken prisoner.

Scene 3

Elsewhere on the plain John despatches Sir Richard to England to dun the abbots for campaign money while Elinor takes Arthur to one side. John declares his warm feelings for Hubert de Burgh and hints that he intends to reward him. He then suggests darkly that Hubert do away with Arthur.

Scene 4

In his tent Philip contemplates the scattered fleet, the loss of Angers, the capture of Arthur and the shame of defeat. Constance enters tearing her hair and passionately bewailing Arthur's capture to him, Pandulph and Lewis. She leaves, followed by Philip who fears that she will do herself some mischief.

Pandulph calmly points out to the Dauphin that to remain secure John cannot allow Arthur to live. However when Arthur is executed the English will turn from John in disgust and he, Lewis, will be able to claim Arthur's inheritance through the right of Blanch, now his wife. Pandulph proposes that a small band of Frenchmen go to England to recruit the disaffected.

Act IV

Scene 1

At Northampton Castle Hubert de Burgh instructs two attendants to conceal themselves; when he stamps his foot they are to rush in and bind Arthur to a chair. Arthur comes in and awakens Hubert's pity with his innocent chatter. Hubert shows him a warrant under which he is commanded to put Arthur's eyes out with hot irons. Arthur professes his affection for Hubert and reminds him of the time when he soothed away his headache but Hubert duly stamps and the attendants enter with cords and irons for the brazier.

Arthur reproachfully bids Hubert dismiss the attendants, saying that he will sit still, unbound, and suffer the torture. Finally he begs him to spare his eyes and cut his tongue out instead while the irons remain cold. Hubert is moved. He spares Arthur and tells him that he will send a false report of his death to John, at considerable risk to himself.

Scene 2

King John seats himself on the throne, "once again crown'd", in a room of state and seeks the approbation of Pembroke, Salisbury and other lords. Salisbury observes that he was already the sovereign and that "To gild refined gold, to paint the lily.....is wasteful and ridiculous excess".

As Pembroke requests Arthur's release Hubert enters and takes John to one side. Pembroke knows about Hubert's warrant and fears that he has already carried it out. The king changes colour and informs the court that Arthur is dead. Salisbury and Pembroke denounce the foul deed and leave in disgust.

A messenger enters to report that Lady Constance is said to have died in a frenzy and that Queen Elinor also died three days later on April 1st. Furthermore the Dauphin has landed in England with an army. Sir Richard enters with Peter, a prophet. He tells John that while collecting money from the clergy he encountered Peter in Pontefract prophesying to the people that before next Ascension day at noon John would give up his crown. When Peter confirms the prediction John angrily orders Hubert to take him away to prison and have him hanged at noon on the day in question.

Sir Richard relates how he met Lord Bigot and Lord Salisbury seeking Arthur's grave and blaming the king. John sends him and the messenger to recall them rapidly. Hubert returns to report strange omens and agitation among the people at the rumours of Arthur's death. When John blames him for precipitating the unrest Hubert shows him the warrant with his own seal on it. John waves it aside, saying that he had only toyed with the notion of Arthur's disposal; had Hubert demurred or shaken his head he would have dropped the idea.

As John is beset with foreign enemies Hubert takes pity on him and reveals that Arthur is in fact

Act IV, Scene 3

Lord Salisbury draws his sword and accuses Hubert de Burgh of the murder of Arthur Plantagenet, Prince of Brittany. In fact Arthur has leapt from the walls of Northampton Castle to his death on the rocks below.

still alive. John asks his forgiveness for his remarks and hurries him off to convey the news to the incensed peers.

Scene 3

Arthur tries to escape from Northampton Castle disguised as a cabin boy. He leaps down from the high wall but falls on the rocks and is dashed to death. Nearby Salisbury tells Pembroke and Bigot that he will meet the Dauphin at St. Edmundsbury [Bury St. Edmunds] in response to a letter from Pandulph brought by Count Melun. Sir Richard appears and requests them to attend the king but they refuse.

They come upon Arthur's body and assume that Hubert was responsible. Hubert himself arrives with the message that Arthur lives and the king has sent for them. Salisbury draws his sword and accuses Hubert of murder. Hubert protests that he left the prince alive and well only an hour before; he is defended by Sir Richard. The lords depart for Bury in disgust. Sir Richard is still suspicious of Hubert; he tells him to take up Arthur's corpse and follow him to the king.

Act V

Scene 1

Back at the castle John, as a convert, hands his crown to Pandulph who returns it to him, with papal authority, and agrees to persuade the Pope to get the French to lay down their arms. It being Ascension day John recollects that Peter of Pontefract prophesied that before noon he would give up his crown.

Sir Richard comes to report that Kent has yielded to the French, only Dover Castle still holding out. The Dauphin and his forces have reached London and the nobles have gone to offer him their support. John, who had hoped to win them over, learns of Arthur's death and is despondent. Sir Richard decries John's rapprochement with Pandulph and attempts to inspire him to dauntless defence of the realm.

Scene 2

At the French camp near Bury Salisbury grieves at having to take up arms against his own countrymen but swears fealty to Lewis in the presence of Pembroke, Bigot, Melun and the troops. Pandulph arrives to report that as John is reconciled with Rome there is no need for war but Lewis is determined to fight on and win England as his right, through his wife Blanch.

A trumpet sounds the arrival of Sir Richard.

Hearing that the Dauphin is bent on war he conveys King John's defiance and pours scorn on the English peers for abetting Lewis.

Scene 3

John, who is feverish, confers with Hubert on the field of battle. A messenger from Sir Richard comes to ask John which way he intends to go. John tells him he is making for Swinstead Abbey [fifteen miles west of Spalding]. The messenger adds the good news that three of the Dauphin's supply ships have been wrecked on the Goodwin Sands and the French are falling back.

Scene 4

Elsewhere Salisbury, Pembroke and Bigot are surprised that although the ailing King John has left the field Sir Richard and his men are holding on. Count Melun is led in, wounded. He advises them to fly to John and cast themselves on his mercy because if the French win the Dauphin has sworn to behead all of them. He asks to be carried from the field to die peacefully.

Scene 5

Lewis, in the French camp, believes that as sunset approaches he is on the verge of victory. However a messenger reports that Melun has died, the English lords have defected to John and the French ships have foundered on the Goodwins.

Scene 6

Near Swinstead Abbey Hubert and Sir Richard greet each other warily. Hubert tells him that the king has been poisoned by a monk. Although he can scarcely speak he has pardoned the returned lords at the request of his son, Prince Henry, who is tending him with them.

Scene 7

Prince Henry is walking in the abbey orchard with Salisbury and Bigot. They are joined by Pembroke who says that the king wishes to be brought into the open air. Bigot goes and fetches King John, who is carried by attendants in a chair.

John is burning up with fever and anticipating death. Sir Richard arrives with the news that Lewis is approaching while much of his own force has been lost in the Washes. The king dies and Salisbury acknowledges the prince as King Henry III. Sir Richard is still ready to confront the Dauphin but Salisbury informs him that Cardinal Pandulph has brought a peace offer. They prepare for John's funeral at Worcester as Sir Richard and the others affirm their loyalty to the new king.

King Lear

The play is based on fragments of Celtic myth preserved by the bishop of St. Asaph, Geoffrey of Monmouth, in his *Historia Britonum* (1139). Shakespeare acquired the material from Holinshed and from Spenser's *Faerie Queene*, his primary source being *The True Chronicle History of King Leir* (sic) (1605). Act III, Scene 1 is sometimes omitted in performance.

Act I

Scene 1

In a room of state in the palace of Lear, king of ancient Britain, the Earl of Gloucester introduces his bastard son, Edmund, to the Earl of Kent. King Lear enters accompanied by his three daughters, Goneril with her husband the Duke of Albany, Regan with her husband the Duke of Cornwall and unmarried Cordelia, the youngest. He commands Gloucester to summon the King of France and the Duke of Burgundy, Cordelia's suitors; Gloucester goes off to do so, taking Edmund with him.

Producing a map Lear tells his daughters that he intends to lay down the burdens of government. He has divided his kingdom into three parts and proposes to confer the largest part on the daughter who loves him the most. He asks the eldest, Goneril, to speak first.

Goneril affirms that she loves him "dearer than eye-sight" and "no less than life"; she is allotted a substantial portion of the kingdom. Regan follows suit with even more extravagant professions of love and receives her portion. Cordelia, scorning to outdo the others, tells Lear that her love cannot be put into words; in any case when she marries half of her love will be bestowed on her husband.

Lear angrily cuts her off and divides her inheritance between her sisters. He hands a coronet to Cornwall and Albany and invests them with regal power, informing them that he and a retinue of one hundred knights will henceforth live with each of them in alternate months. When the Earl of Kent attempts to reason with the king he is peremptorily given five days to leave the kingdom for good; if he is found there after ten days he will be executed.

As Kent departs Gloucester returns with the king of France, the Duke of Burgundy and attendants. The duke, learning that Cordelia is now a pauper, declines her hand. The French king, however, takes her for his queen, saying that "She is herself a dowry." The members of the court depart as Cordelia bids a tearful farewell to her sisters. Left alone, they express their apprehension of Lear's volatility and of his plans.

Scene 2

The illegitimate Edmund, clutching a letter, is meditating in the hall of the Earl of Gloucester's castle. He resents the fact that Gloucester's land will not come to him and plans to seize his inheritance from Edgar, his legitimate brother. On his father's approach he stuffs the letter into his pocket but Gloucester sees it and demands to read it. The letter, signed 'Edgar', complains that old men withhold their fortunes from their sons until they are too old to enjoy them and hints at a conspiracy against Gloucester. Gloucester is horrified at Edgar's apparent villainy and instructs Edmund to find him.

After Gloucester has left Edgar comes along. Edmund tells him of his father's severe displeasure and suggests that he arm himself and lie low in Edmund's lodgings for a time.

Scene 3

In the Duke of Albany's palace Lear's knights have been troublesome and Lear has struck a gentlemen for rebuking his jester. Goneril tells her steward, Oswald, to give the king sullen service so that he will go to stay with her sister.

Scene 4

The loyal Earl of Kent has not gone into exile; he reappears in the palace hall in disguise. He is found but unrecognised by Lear, who is attended by knights and others, receives a tip and is engaged as a serving man. Lear calls for dinner and sends for his jester. When Oswald, Goneril's steward, displays insolence, as instructed by his mistress, Kent assists Lear to cuff him and hustle him out, thus earning Lear's gratitude. The equally loyal jester diverts the king with quips and jokes.

Goneril comes to tell Lear that his quarrelsome knights are turning the palace into a riotous tavern; she begs him to dismiss half of them before she does so herself. When her apologetic husband Albany arrives Lear, in dudgeon, calls for his horses to be saddled so that he and his entourage can go to stay with Regan instead ("How sharper than a serpent's tooth it is To have a thankless child!"). After Lear, followed by his jester, has swept out, Goneril sends Oswald ahead of him with a letter warning her sister of the impending visit.

Scene 5

In the palace courtyard Lear in his turn sends Kent with a disarming letter to Regan. He is remorseful over his treatment of Goneril but the jester diverts him with riddles.

Act II

Scene 1

Curan, a courtier, approaches Edmund in a court of the Earl of Gloucester's castle to tell him that the Duke of Cornwall and Regan will be with his father that night. Upon Curan's departure Edgar enters. Edmund pretends that Edgar has made an enemy of Cornwall and bids him hide from him as well as from Gloucester.

After a scared Edgar hurries off to comply, Edmund cuts his own arm lightly. Then when Gloucester comes by with his servants Edmund's story is that Edgar was trying to enlist him in killing their father and that Edgar wounded him in the arm when he demurred. Gloucester sends his servants to hunt for the "murderous coward" Edgar and promises to bestow his lands on Edmund instead.

A flourish of trumpets heralds the arrival of Cornwall, Regan and their party. Regan informs Gloucester that she and her husband have come visiting in order to avoid being at home when Lear and his train arrive there; she asks Gloucester's advice on how to answer the letters from Goneril and Lear.

Scene 2

Oswald encounters Kent (whom he does not recognise in his disguise) near Gloucester's castle. Kent insults him for "a lily-liver'd, action-taking knave" and beats him with his sword. Edmund parts them as Cornwall, Regan, Gloucester and servants come up. They continue to quarrel as Cornwall seeks to discover the cause of the commotion; eventually, losing patience, he claps Kent in the stocks. When the others leave Gloucester offers to intercede but Kent is content to lie for a while in the stocks and have a chance to read a letter from Cordelia. Afterwards he drops off to sleep.

Scene 3

Edgar, having escaped his hunters by hiding in a hollow tree, resolves to avoid detection by becoming a ragged grimy beggar.

Scene 4

Lear, his jester and a gentleman, having found Regan's palace deserted, arrive at Gloucester's castle to find Kent asleep in the stocks. Lear's affront at this insult to one of his serving men turns to outrage when he learns from Gloucester that he is being refused admission to the castle. Gloucester fetches Cornwall and Regan with their servants. While Kent is released from the stocks Lear begs Regan to take him in, telling her how unkind Goneril has been to him. He is dumbfounded when she remarks that her sister was justified and suggests that he return to her.

Oswald appears, announcing Goneril's arrival. The sisters greet each other and Regan tells Lear that she is out of provisions; if he will return to Goneril (with only fifty knights) she herself will consent to have him at the end of the month. When he resentfully refuses she observes that in any case if he came to her she would allow him only twenty five knights. Lear turns back to Goneril but she queries his need for any knights at all, since there are plenty of servants at her palace.

Lear strides away across the heath, with bitter cries of revenge for such ingratitude. He has no shelter and a storm is brewing but, to Gloucester's misgivings, nobody tries to stop him.

Act III

Scene 1

Kent meets a gentleman wandering over the heath. Giving him a ring for identification he despatches him to Dover to meet Cordelia who will land from France.

Scene 2

Elsewhere on the heath Lear and his jester defy the tempest, which in his eyes is less pernicious than his daughters ("Blow, winds, and crack your cheeks!....I am a man More sinn'd against than sinning"). As he raves more wildly Kent appears and tells him of a nearby hovel where he can shelter. The jester sings "He that has a little tiny wit, With hey, ho, the wind and the rain, Must make content with his fortunes fit, Though the rain it raineth every day." [The verse is almost identical with Feste's song at the end of *Twelfth Night*].

Scene 3

In his castle Gloucester tells Edmund how he has been turned out of his own home by Regan, for taking the king's part. He alludes to vengeance, already afoot, and prepares to join the king. He asks Edmund to tell Cornwall that he has gone to bed, to cover his absence, but Edmund plans to reveal everything to Cornwall.

Scene 4

Lear, Kent and the jester arrive at the hovel. Lear tries to forget the ingratitude of his daughters ("O! that way madness lies:") and sends his jester before him into the hovel. The jester emerges in a panic, having encountered a 'spirit'; it is Edgar, in the guise of a madman. Lear wonders wildly if he too has been driven to distraction by his daughters.

Gloucester arrives with a flaming torch. He does not recognise Edgar, who addresses him as "thou fiend". Despite Lear's wish to stay and discuss 'philosophy' with the babbling Edgar, Gloucester and Kent manage to conduct him to a farmhouse adjoining the castle.

Scene 5

Inside the castle Edmund has betrayed Gloucester to Cornwall and has shown him a letter which reveals Gloucester to be an agent of the French.

Scene 6

In the farmhouse, while Gloucester scouts for news, Edgar continues to feign madness and Lear becomes deranged. He sets Edgar and the jester on either side of him like three magistrates and proceeds to 'try' two stools, representing his daughters, for treason. Edgar weeps at Lear's crazed manner.

Gloucester returns, having learned of the plot against the king, and tells Kent to take Lear to Dover. They depart, leaving Edgar to reflect on his own lesser woes.

Scene 7

Cornwall orders the castle servants to find the traitor Gloucester. He sends Goneril hurrying to tell her husband Albany that the French army has landed. Oswald reports that Gloucester is conveying Lear to Dover, along with some thirty five knights. Cornwall tells him and Edmund to accompany Goneril on her mission.

The servants re-enter with the captive Gloucester and bind him to a chair. Regan pulls his beard while she and Cornwall question him fiercely. When Gloucester declares his pity for the harsh treatment of King Lear Cornwall viciously puts one of his eyes out. Horrified by this barbarity, a senior servant protests, fights with Cornwall and succeeds in wounding him. Regan promptly grabs his sword and slays the servant, whereupon the injured Cornwall blinds Gloucester's other eye. The shocked servants turn against the evil Cornwall; they lead the blood-soaked Gloucester away to bind his wounds with flax and egg-white.

Act IV

Scene 1

Out on the heath Edgar, still posing as a lunatic, sees the blind Gloucester coming along, led by an old man. Gloucester, not recognising his son, hands him his purse and asks him to guide him to the white cliffs of Dover.

Scene 2

Goneril and Edmund arrive at Albany's palace. They are met by Oswald, who had gone ahead, with the news that Albany welcomes the French invasion and does not believe reports of Gloucester's treachery. Goneril hastily sends Edmund back to her brother-in-law Cornwall with this information, kissing him and giving him a favour to wear.

Albany appears and castigates Goneril for her cruelty to her father. A messenger brings news that Cornwall has died of the injury inflicted by the servant. Albany, hearing the details of the terrible blinding of Gloucester, swears to avenge him.

Scene 3

Kent is informed by a gentleman in the invaders' camp near Dover that the French king has returned to France, leaving a marshal in command. He is further told that Cordelia is grief-stricken at her father's fate.

Scene 4

In a nearby tent Cordelia bewails Lear's madness, sends soldiers to find him and asks a doctor if he can be cured. A messenger enters to tell her that the British forces are marching towards Dover.

Scene 5

The widowed Regan questions Oswald in Gloucester's castle but he refuses to let her read a letter from Goneril to Edmund. Regan now favours Edmund and, suspecting that Goneril is taken with him also, tells Oswald to let Goneril know that she and Edmund have an understanding. At the same time she coldly suggests that Oswald should finish Gloucester off if he should come across him.

Scene 6

Gloucester and Edgar are making their way towards the cliff top at Dover; Edgar leads the sightless Gloucester to a low knoll, describing the dizzy height and the beach below and asking if he cannot hear the sound of the sea. From his words Gloucester, apparently on the cliff edge, detects that his companion is not truly mad; he dismisses him and, renouncing the world, pitches forward. However he survives his tumble and is helped up by Edgar, still unrecognised, who tells him that the gods have miraculously saved him. In remorse Gloucester resolves to live and bear his affliction.

Lear appears, decked with weeds and babbling crazily. Gloucester, knowing his voice, kneels to kiss his hand. At first Lear takes him for blind Cupid, the god of love, but eventually recognises him.

He raves on about killing his sons-in-law when a party of men come to apprehend him, speaking of his "most dear daughter". They are part of Cordelia's search party but Lear flees from them under the impression that they come from Regan or Goneril.

Oswald comes on the scene and endeavours to run Gloucester through, as Regan had suggested. Edgar fights him off and kills him. As Oswald expires he entrusts Goneril's letter to Edgar. From it Edgar is appalled to find that Goneril is urging Edmund to kill her husband Albany.

Scene 7

In her tent Cordelia expresses her gratitude to Kent, who asks to remain in his servant's disguise a little longer. The doctor suggests that the king be roused from his slumbers; the servants carry him in, in a chair, and Cordelia kisses him awake. At first Lear mistakes her for a heavenly spirit but when he recognises her he is overcome with joy and regains a semblance of sanity.

Act V

Scene 1

At the British camp near Dover Regan's jealousy leads to an argument with Edmund. Albany appears with Goneril; they urge unity against the French. Edgar slips in as they move off and detains Albany; he hands him the letter passed to him by Oswald but before Albany has time to read it Edmund comes back to report that the enemy is in sight. They go to prepare for the battle.

Act V, Scene 3

At the British camp near Dover King Lear, crazed with grief, carries the body of his youngest daughter, Cordelia, who has been hanged by order of the dying bastard, Edmund. The loyal Earl of Kent kneels to Lear.

Scene 2

The French forces are defeated on the battlefield and Lear and Cordelia are taken prisoner.

Scene 3

Afterwards at the British camp Edmund orders Lear and Cordelia to be taken away to prison, surreptitiously handing a note to the captain of the guard. Albany enters, having read Goneril's letter to Edmund. When Edmund refuses to hand over Lear and Cordelia Albany arrests him "on capital treason", denouncing Goneril at the same time. Albany and Edmund formally challenge each other while Regan collapses and is helped out.

A trumpet sounds and a herald proclaims that any volunteer to fight a duel with Edmund should come forward at the third trumpet call. Edgar steps forward, still in disguise; the duel is fought and Edmund falls wounded. Goneril goes to his aid but backs away when Albany produces the damning letter. As Edmund grows weaker Edgar reveals his true identity ("The wheel has come full circle; I am here."). He is now the Earl of Gloucester, his father having died of grief at the capture of King Lear.

A gentleman carrying a bloodstained knife rushes in to say that Regan's collapse was due to poison administered by Goneril. She has died of it and Goneril has committed suicide with the knife. Kent comes in to say goodnight to Lear, reminding everyone of the king's existence. The dying Edmund remorsefully reveals that his note to the captain of the escort was a death-warrant; he gives his sword to Edgar who dashes off to use it as a token of reprieve. Edmund is carried away.

Shortly afterwards a grieving Lear enters with Cordelia's body in his arms, followed by Edgar and others. The reprieve was too late; although Lear escaped death himself and managed to kill Cordelia's executioner she had already been hanged. The loyal Kent reveals himself to Lear and an officer reports that Edmund has succumbed to his wounds. Lear, again out of his mind with grief, dies weeping over Cordelia's corpse.

Love's Labour's Lost

This early play is experimental. The original title may have been *Love's Labour Won*, although this has also been ascribed to *All's Well That Ends Well*. There is evidence of revision by the author prior to the 1598 quarto. The play is set in Navarre and the characters appear to be suggested by Henry of Navarre and his followers, whose names have been adapted. The King is based on Shakespeare's early mentor, the Earl of Southampton. Armado is taken to be a caricature of Don Antonio Pérez, Philip II's ex-Secretary of State, while Rosaline and Berowne are held to be representations of the Dark Lady and Shakespeare himself.

Act I

Scene 1

Ferdinand, the King of Navarre, is walking in his park with three attendant lords, Berowne, Longaville and Captain Dumaine. He reminds them that they have sworn to live with him ascetically for three years in accordance with statutes which require them to study, to fast and to sleep only three hours a night. Further, no woman is to come within a mile of the court. Berowne demurs, pointing out that Ferdinand will have to receive the French king's daughter to discuss the surrender of Aquitaine; however he signs the schedule.

Antony Dull, a third-borough constable, brings a letter from Don Adriano de Armado, a fantastical Spaniard who serves, in effect, as court minstrel. He is accompanied by Costard, a jester. The letter informs the king, in high-flown language, that Armado has seen Costard in the park with a comely wench, Jaquenetta, contrary to the royal edict. Ferdinand condemns Costard to a week's fast on bran and water, while Berowne observes glumly that such statutes "will prove an idle scorn".

Scene 2

Elsewhere in the park Armado is talking to his page, Moth. Armado reflects that although he too has promised to study for three years with the king he is in love with the comely Jaquenetta. Dull brings in Jaquenetta and Costard, advising Armado that the king wishes him to be responsible for Costard while he fasts. Moth is ordered to take Costard off to prison while Armado makes plans to woo Jaquenetta.

Act II

Scene 1

The princess of France and her retinue are found near a pavilion in the park. After she despatches Boyet, one of her attendant lords, to ascertain if Ferdinand will receive her despite his ascetic vows, she asks her ladies about Ferdinand's attendants. Maria, of Falconbridge, describes Longaville while Katherine, of Alençon, speaks of Dumaine and Rosaline praises Berowne.

Boyet returns to say that Ferdinand will meet the princess but that she must remain outside the house. The ladies don masks as Ferdinand and his train arrive; he accepts a letter from the princess while Berowne and Rosaline dally. The letter states that the French king has paid one hundred thousand crowns, being half the sum disbursed by Ferdinand's father Charles in his wars, and demands repayment.

Ferdinand tells the princess that the money has not been received but that if her father will pay it he will give up his surety rights in Aquitaine. The princess maintains that the amount has already been paid; Boyet offers to produce receipts from Charles' officers when the packet of relevant papers arrives the next day.

The king agrees to wait for the papers. On his departure Berowne and Rosaline continue their flirtation. Dumaine and Longaville enquire the identities of the other ladies. When they have left the ladies unmask and Boyet makes advances to Maria.

Act III

Scene 1

Armado and Moth continue to converse in the park, with much raillery and wordplay. Moth goes off to release Costard and returns with him. Armado tells Costard that he will set him at liberty if he will carry a letter to Jaquenetta, for a fee. Having agreed, Costard is then approached by Berowne who wants him, for one shilling, to hand a missive to Rosaline when she accompanies the princess on a hunt in the park that afternoon. Costard departs and Berowne muses on his lovelorn state.

Act IV

Scene 1

The princess and her retinue stroll in the park. A forester indicates a bush which can be used to conceal her royal highness when she looses an arrow at the deer. Costard arrives with the letter which he insists is from Berowne to Rosaline. The princess commands Boyet to read the letter; it turns out to be the one from Armado to Jaquenetta, in his usual extravagant language.

When the princess and her attendants have departed, Boyet attempts to find out from Rosaline who her suitor is; she parries his questions. When Katharine and Rosaline have left Costard exchanges pleasantries with Boyet and Maria.

Act IV, Scene 2

While constable Antony Dull looks on, the curate Sir Nathaniel discusses with the schoolmaster Holofernes the age of the deer shot by the princess. Jaquenetta hands him a letter, supposedly from Don Adriano de Armado.

Scene 2

Sir Nathaniel, a curate, is discussing with Holofernes, a schoolmaster, the age of the deer that has been shot by the princess. Constable Dull, who is with them, maintains that it was a pricket [fallow deer buck in its second year] and Holofernes improvises a poem on the subject, heavy with alliteration ("The preyful princess pierc'd and prick'd a pretty pleasing pricket;").

Costard arrives with Jaquenetta who hands Nathaniel a letter to read which she believes to be from Armado. Nathaniel reads out some passionate verse which he finds is addressed to Rosaline by Berowne. Holofernes tells her to hand it to the king. After she and Costard depart Holofernes proceeds to invite Nathaniel and Dull to dinner, promising them better verses.

Scene 3

Berowne appears, reading a paper; on seeing Ferdinand he climbs into a tree. The king comes along declaiming a love poem from a paper but on seeing Longaville he hides. Longaville enters, reads out a poem and hides in his turn on the approach of Dumaine. Dumaine likewise reads out a poem of love.

Ferdinand and Longaville reveal themselves and Ferdinand chides the others for breaking their chaste vows with their 'guilty rhymes'. Berowne descends from the tree and observes that the king is as guilty of backsliding as the others, while he himself remains pure.

Costard arrives with Jaquenetta, who hands the king a letter 'from Armado' and asks that it be read since Nathaniel considers it treasonable. Berowne, being requested to read the letter, hastily tears it up but Dumaine picks up the pieces and discovers that it is from Berowne himself. When Costard and Jaquenetta have left Berowne delivers a long speech extolling the virtues of love. They all agree to abandon asceticism and entertain their respective lady loves.

Act V

Scene 1

Holofernes, Nathaniel and Dull reflect on their excellent dinner. Armado, Moth and Costard join them; Armado asks Nathaniel and Holofernes to help him give some show or pageant before the king. They arrange to present *The Nine Worthies*.

Scene 2

In front of the princess' pavilion Katharine, Rosaline, Maria and the princess show each other the favours that they have received. Rosaline and the princess have received verses, Katharine has a glove from Dumaine and Maria some pearls from Longaville. Boyet enters and tells them that he has overheard the king and his companions gleefully planning to approach them disguised as Muscovites. The princess instructs the ladies to don masks and not to dance with, or even respond to, the men.

At the sound of a trumpet a troupe of blackamoors enters with the king and his lords in Russian dress. Moth delivers a prologue, the ladies turning their backs. The king, through Boyet as intermediary, pleads with the masked Rosaline, supposing her to be the princess. Despite his claims that they have come many miles to 'tread a measure' with the ladies they refuse to dance when the music plays.

The king takes Rosaline to one side while Berowne does the same with the princess. Dumaine and Maria similarly converse together, Maria being taken to be Katharine, as do Katharine and Longaville. As none of the men makes any progress they all withdraw. The ladies compare notes and Boyet tells them that the men will soon return, in their own identities. The ladies resolve to tease them by telling them about some Muscovites who had made fools of themselves; they retire to the pavilion.

The king and his lords return and Boyet fetches the princess and her ladies, who have interchanged their favours. They taunt the men with the words of love that each spoke to the wrong lady. Costard comes to enquire if they are ready for *The Three Worthies* (each presenting three characters). Armado brings in a programme; the king sees that Armado is to represent Hector of Troy, Costard is to play Pompey the Great, Nathaniel Alexander, Moth Hercules and Holofernes Judas Maccabeus. Berowne and Dumaine tease Holofernes, pretending to take him for Judas Iscariot.

Costard, as Pompey, makes a speech. He is followed by Nathaniel, as Alexander, who is heckled by Berowne and Costard. Holofernes, as Judas, and Moth, as Hercules, appear and are accosted by Berowne and Dumaine. Armado, as Hector, is interrupted by Longaville and Dumaine while Costard informs him that Jaquenetta is two months pregnant by him.

Monsieur Marcade, a messenger, brings the princess news of her father's death; she grieves and prepares to depart while the Worthies are dismissed. The princess tells Ferdinand that if he will undertake to live in a hermitage for one year she will retire to a house of mourning. After that she will consent to marry him. Berowne is similarly condemned by Rosaline to spend a year attending the sick while Dumaine is banished for a year by Katharine and Longaville by Maria.

Armado agrees to wait no less than three years for Jaquenetta and offers to present the end of the show which was cut short. The Worthies accordingly re-enter and give a dialogue between Spring, in praise of the cuckoo, and Winter, in praise of the owl. ("When icicles hang by the wall, And Dick the shepherd blows his nail.....Then nightly sings the staring owl, Tu-who; Tu-whit, tu-who — a merry note, while greasy Joan doth keel the pot.")

Macbeth

Shakespeare may have gained his knowledge of Scottish history from Raphael Holinshed's *Chronicle*. The witch lore probably comes from *Discoverie of Witchcraft* published by Reginald Scot in 1594 and from King James I's *Demonologie*. The drama has acquired a reputation for ill-luck in the theatre, in which it is superstitiously referred to as "the Scottish play".

Act I

Scene 1

Three witches gather on a desert heath in a thunderstorm and arrange to meet Macbeth, a general of the King's army. ("When shall we three meet again In thunder, lightning or in rain?").

Scene 2

In a camp near Forres [on the Moray firth, about 25 miles from Inverness] King Duncan of Scotland listens to the tale of a wounded sergeant in the company of Malcolm and Donalbain, his sons, and Lennox, a nobleman. The sergeant relates how heroic Macbeth slew Macdonald and put to flight his Irish foot-soldiers from the western isles. However Sweno, the king of Norway, aided by Scottish rebels, seized his chance to renew the assault on the King's forces under the command of Macbeth and Banquo, another general.

As the sergeant goes to receive attention the Thane [king's companion] of Ross enters to report that in Fife the Norwegian king, together with the Thane of Cawdor who was traitorously supporting him, has been defeated and is suing for peace. Duncan is delighted at the news; he orders that the Thane of Cawdor be executed and sends Ross and Angus to greet Macbeth and confer the Cawdor title on him.

Scene 3

The three witches on the heath chortle over the evil spells that they have cast on various people. Macbeth and his fellow officer Banquo pass by on their way to Forres. The witches hail Macbeth as Thane of Glamis and of Cawdor and also as a future king. Macbeth knows that he is the Thane of Glamis but is puzzled by the other acclamations. The witches greet Banquo as lesser than Macbeth, and greater — not so happy, yet much happier. They inform him that his heirs will be kings although he himself will not; they vanish before they can be questioned.

Ross and Angus meet the generals and tell Macbeth that he is indeed the new Thane of Cawdor. Macbeth is startled at the witches' accuracy; a wild surmise crosses his mind that he may become king by getting rid of Duncan. The four move off towards the king's palace at Forres.

Scene 4

In the palace King Duncan is told that the treasonous Thane of Cawdor repented before his execution ("Nothing in his life Became him like the leaving it;"). The four noblemen enter and Macbeth swears loyalty to the king. Duncan welcomes them and announces that his elder son, Malcolm, is to be Prince of Cumberland and heir to the throne. Macbeth, on hearing that Duncan intends to come to his castle at Inverness, departs to warn his wife of the royal visit. He muses darkly on the new obstacle presented by Malcolm.

Scene 5

In Inverness castle Lady Macbeth reads a letter from her husband describing the encounter with the three witches and their predictions. She feels that Macbeth is not sufficiently resolute to turn the situation to his advantage and resolves to urge him on ("Yet do I fear thy nature; It is too full o' the milk of human kindness To catch the nearest way;").

A messenger arrives to tell Lady Macbeth that Duncan will be arriving that night. At first she is taken aback but she quickly recognises a golden opportunity to assassinate the king. When Macbeth turns up she tells him to leave everything to her.

Scene 6

Outside the castle Duncan has arrived with his sons Malcolm and Donalbain together with Banquo, Lennox, Ross, Angus and also Macduff, another nobleman. Lady Macbeth welcomes them, playing the perfect hostess.

Scene 7

In the castle the servants are arranging torches, dishes and musical instruments. Macbeth tries to steel himself to quick action ("If it were done when 'tis done, then 'twere well It were done quickly;"). However he dreads the murderous deed, recalling that Duncan is a kinsman as well as his guest and his king. He tells Lady Macbeth that he will go no further.

She scorns him for his cowardice, for "letting 'I dare not' wait upon 'I would', Like the poor cat i' the adage." She tells him that when the weary Duncan falls asleep she will ply his two chamberlains with wine until they fall into a drunken stupor. Macbeth marvels at her mettle and falls in with her plan, suggesting that the daggers of the two sleepers be used, in order to incriminate them.

Act II

Scene 1

Elsewhere in the castle General Banquo, unable to sleep, is pacing up and down with his son Fleance.

Before going off to bed he meets Macbeth with a servant and tells him that he has had a dream of the three 'weird sisters' [the witches].

Macbeth sends his servant to Lady Macbeth to ask her to ring a bell when his drink is ready. Alone, he has a disturbing vision ("Is this a dagger which I see before me, The handle toward my hand?") In a macabre speech he draws his own dagger as the bell sounds. ("Hear it not, Duncan; for it is a knell That summons thee to heaven or to hell.")

Scene 2

Lady Macbeth, having drugged the grooms' drinks, is waiting for Macbeth's return from Duncan's chamber. He enters, fearful of every noise, to tell her that he has done the dreadful deed but that two of the guests gave him a shock when they awoke, said their prayers and settled down again. He imagined a voice crying, "Sleep no more! Macbeth does murder sleep".

Lady Macbeth tells him to pull himself together, wash the blood from his hands and take the gory daggers back so that the grooms will be accused of the murder. Macbeth is too unnerved, so Lady Macbeth goes to do it herself. Loud knocking at the gate is heard as Lady Macbeth returns to take Macbeth to their bedchamber.

Scene 3

The castle porter has also taken some drink; he grumbles as he slowly opens the gate to admit Macduff and Lennox, who have come to wake the king. After some backchat between Macduff and the porter Macbeth enters in his nightgown to say that the king has not yet risen; Macduff goes off to awaken him while Lennox comments on the wildness of the night.

A horror-stricken Macduff comes back to report Duncan's murder. While Macbeth and Lennox go to confirm his story he rouses the whole castle by ringing the bell. Banquo arrives with Lady Macbeth, who laments that such a dreadful thing could have happened in their house. Macbeth and Lennox return, followed by Malcolm and Donalbain.

Macbeth confesses that he has just killed the two grooms in a fit of fury, as they are the apparent culprits. Lady Macbeth faints at this new horror. Amid the confusion Malcolm and Donalbain perceive that as the king's heirs they are now in danger; Malcolm decides to go to England and Donalbain to Ireland for the time being.

Scene 4

Outside the castle Ross is in conversation with an old man for whom the murder is the worst event in his life. Macduff comes along to tell them that the flight of Malcolm and Donalbain has aroused suspicions that the two of them got the grooms to murder Duncan. In their guilty absence, therefore, the succession passes to Macbeth, who has already gone to Scone [north of Perth] to be invested. Ross decides to attend but Macduff leaves for Fife.

Act III

Scene 1

At the palace in Forres Banquo reveals his suspicion that Macbeth himself was the murderer. Macbeth and Lady Macbeth enter as king and queen, with Ross, Lennox and other attendants. Macbeth invites Banquo to attend a solemn supper at seven o'clock that evening. He questions Banquo closely on how he and Fleance plan to spend the afternoon and learns that they will be out riding.

He determines to get rid of Banquo ("To be thus is nothing; But to be safely thus.") and despatches an attendant to bring in two men who are at the gate. The attendant is then dismissed and Macbeth reminds the men of a conversation the previous day. He instructs them to kill both Banquo and Fleance that evening, away from the palace.

Scene 2

In another room Lady Macbeth, concerned about Macbeth's state of mind, sends a servant to fetch him to her. Macbeth reflects that "Duncan is in his grave; After life's fitful fever he sleeps well;" but warns her that "We have scotch'd the snake, not kill'd it:" He refers to a 'deed of dreadful note' that will occur that night but does not reveal that Banquo's murder has been arranged; on the contrary he asks her to be particularly pleasant to Banquo at supper.

Scene 3

In the park at sunset a third murderer has joined the first two, on Macbeth's orders. They ambush Banquo and Fleance; Banquo is hacked to death but Fleance manages to escape in the gloom when his torch is extinguished.

Scene 4

At the banquet in the palace the new king and queen bid their guests be seated. The first murderer appears at the door and surreptitiously tells Macbeth that he has cut Banquo's throat but that Fleance got away. Macbeth is again in despair ("But now I am cabin'd, cribb'd, confin'd, bound in To saucy doubts and fears.")

As Macbeth returns to his place the ghost of Banquo enters and occupies his seat. Macbeth is appalled, startling the guests who cannot see Banquo. Lady Macbeth calms them and quietly tells Macbeth again to pull himself together. When the ghost vanishes Macbeth manages to get a grip on himself; he even proposes a toast to the absent Banquo. At that moment the ghost re-appears, reducing Macbeth to quivering terror. Lady Macbeth hustles the guests out ("Stand not upon the order of your going, But go at once.") When they have gone a shaken Macbeth insists on going back to see the weird sisters.

Scene 5

On the heath the three witches meet their goddess Hecate, who rebukes them for meddling in

Macbeth's affairs without involving her. They arrange to meet 'at the pit of Acheron' [a river in the infernal regions] in the morning.

Scene 6

Lennox is mulling over the recent strange events with another lord in the palace. He praises Macbeth for killing Duncan's grooms, believing that Malcolm, Donalbain and Fleance were all guilty of patricide. He reveals that Macduff has exasperated Macbeth by going to the English court of King Edward (to which Malcolm fled) to seek help in raising an army in Northumberland against the Scots.

Act IV

Scene 1

The three witches circle a boiling cauldron in a cavern, adding ghastly ingredients to the brew ("Double, double toil and trouble; Fire burn and cauldron bubble.") They are joined by Hecate, who commends their spells, and greeted by Macbeth ("How now, you secret, black, and midnight hags!")

In response to Macbeth's demands the witches conjure up three apparitions. The first is an armed head which adjures him to beware of Macduff. The second is a bloody child which tells him that "none of woman born Shall harm Macbeth." The third is a crowned child with a tree in its hand. It prophesies that Macbeth shall never be vanquished until great Birnam wood comes to high Dunsinane hill.

Macbeth is reassured by the predictions, since trees cannot move about and he is apparently safe from any man born of woman. However he presses the witches to know if Banquo's descendants will reign in the kingdom as they had said on the heath. In a further apparition eight kings pass by, the last carrying a mirror that shows even more. They are followed by the bloodstained ghost of Banquo who points to them, confirming them as his. The witches dance with Hecate and vanish, leaving Macbeth aghast.

Lennox appears to tell Macbeth about Macduff's flight to England. In a fury Macbeth decides to capture Macduff's castle in Fife and put his wife and children to the sword.

Scene 2

In her castle Lady Macduff wonders aloud to Ross why her husband has fled to England, leaving her unguarded. Ross defends Macduff before departing. Lady Macduff is left to tell her son that his father is a traitor and has abandoned him. A messenger enters to entreat Lady Macduff to flee from danger. However before she can do so the murderers break in, stab the boy and pursue Lady Macduff out of the room.

Scene 3

Prince Malcolm and Macduff confer in front of King Edward's palace in England. Malcolm, fearing that Macduff is a spy for the tyrant Macbeth, tests him by depicting himself as a voluptuous and avaricious villain. A shocked Macduff mourns for Scotland under such a king. Reassured, Malcolm confesses his stratagem.

A doctor appears to tell them that King Edward will be coming out shortly to heal the sick with his miraculous powers. He is followed by Ross who at first dissembles but then gives Macduff the dreadful news of the slaughter of his wife, children and servants. Macduff swears that he will kill the evil Macbeth; he arranges with Malcolm to go north with Siward, the Earl of Northumberland, and ten thousand men.

Act V

Scene 1

In Dunsinane Castle [midway between Perth and Dundee] a gentlewoman-in-waiting tells a doctor that her mistress has been sleepwalking since Macbeth's departure. They watch as Lady Macbeth comes by with a taper; her eyes are open but she is asleep. She rubs her hands together ("Out, damned spot! out, I say!") trying to wash Duncan's blood off ("all the perfumes of Arabia will not sweeten this little hand"). She mentions Lady Macduff and Banquo in her laments before going off to bed.

Scene 2

Angus and Lennox approach Dunsinane with their army, accompanied by two other Scottish noblemen, Menteith and Caithness. Menteith and Angus have arranged to meet the English forces, led by Malcolm and Siward, near Birnam wood. Siward's son is with them but not Malcolm's brother Donalbain.

Scene 3

Within the castle a white-faced servant comes to tell Macbeth that the English force has arrived, ten thousand strong. Macbeth rages at his fears, relying on the witches' prophesies. He calls Seyton, an officer, to help him don his armour, and urges the doctor to do what he can for the deranged Lady Macbeth.

Scene 4

The English army arrives at Birnam wood with drums and colours. Malcolm tells the soldiers to camouflage themselves with tree branches. They march on, holding the branches.

Scene 5

Back in Dunsinane Macbeth considers his castle impregnable. When Seyton comes to tell him that Lady Macbeth has committed suicide he meditates on the emptiness of life ("Out, out, brief candle! Life's but a walking shadow, a poor player That struts and frets his hour upon the stage, And then is heard no more; it is a tale Told by an idiot, full of sound and fury, Signifying nothing.")

Act V, Scene 1

A doctor and a gentlewoman-in-waiting watch from concealment as Lady Macbeth sleepwalks with a taper in Dunsinane Castle, vainly trying to wash King Duncan's blood from her hands.

A fearful messenger enters to inform him that while on watch he saw Birnam wood begin to move towards Dunsinane. An astounded Macbeth determines to take his men and confront the enemy in the field, prediction or no.

Scene 6

On the plain in front of the castle Malcolm orders the soldiers to throw down their leafy screens. He commands Siward and his son to lead while he and Macduff organise the rest of the army.

Scene 7

On the field of battle Macbeth encounters young Siward and slays him in a sword fight. Elsewhere, Macduff searches for Macbeth, while Malcolm and Earl Siward prepare to enter the castle. Macbeth, meeting Macduff, taunts him with his supposed invincibility and they fight. Macbeth despairs when he learns that Macduff was prematurely delivered by Caesarian section and is therefore not truly 'of woman born' but he defiantly fights on ("Lay on, Macduff, And damn'd be him that first cries 'Hold, enough!'").

In another part of the plain Ross tells Siward that his son has died a hero's death. Macduff joins them, carrying Macbeth's severed head. Malcolm is hailed as King of Scotland; he proclaims the thanes Scotland's first earls and invites everyone to see him crowned at Scone.

Measure for Measure

This play is thought to have been produced when the theatres were reopened in 1604 after the plague. The plot is based on a story used by George Whetstone both in his play *Promos and Cassandra* (1578) and in his *Heptameron of Civil Discourses* (1582). It had already been borrowed by Whetstone from Giraldi Cinthio's *Hecatommithi* (1566).

Act I

Scene 1

In an apartment in his palace Vincentio, the Duke of Vienna, informs an elderly counsellor called Escalus that he is to be away for a while. Escalus agrees with him that Angelo should be appointed Lord Deputy in his absence. Angelo is sent for and given the commission, with Escalus as his aide.

Scene 2

Lucio, a dandy, is gossiping with two friends in the street. They are joined by Mistress Overdone, a procuress, who tells them that a young gentleman called Claudio has been arrested and condemned to death for making his fiancée, Juliet, pregnant. Lucio and his friends go off to learn more while Mistress Overdone's tapster, Pompey, comes to tell her that all the brothels are to be closed. The suburban ones, like hers, are to be pulled down, those in the city having been bought up for redevelopment by a wise burgher.

The two retire as the Provost and his officers come by with Juliet and the captive Claudio. They meet Lucio and his companions, returning. Claudio takes Lucio aside, pointing out that Juliet and he would have been married long ago but for the withholding of her dowry. He asks Lucio to get his sister Isabella, who is about to enter a convent, to intercede with Angelo for him.

Scene 3

Duke Vincentio confides to Friar Thomas in a monastery that he needs to borrow a monk's habit. He has let it be known that he is travelling to Poland but in fact he plans to stay and mingle with the Viennese disguised as a friar to see if Angelo will enforce laws that have been unenforced and flouted for fourteen years.

Scene 4

Sister Francis receives the novitiate Isabella at her nunnery. By the rules of the order she withdraws when Lucio comes to find Claudio's sister. Isabella introduces herself and Lucio informs her that her brother is in prison under sentence of death for impregnating her one-time schoolfriend Juliet. He begs her to seek clemency from Angelo.

Act II

Scene 1

In the hall of his house Angelo holds forth to Escalus together with a judge, the Provost and other law officers. He insists on the rigour of the law and orders the Provost to have Claudio executed at nine o'clock the next morning. As the Provost leaves, a simple-witted constable called Elbow enters with Pompey and Froth, a foolish hanger-on. Muddling his words Elbow charges Froth and Pompey with ill-defined offences against his wife.

Pompey launches into an involved refutation and Angelo leaves, exasperated. After further confusing evidence Escalus dismisses Froth. He suspects Pompey of being a pimp and advises him to make himself scarce and not appear before him again. He tells Elbow in kindly tones to find a replacement for himself and concludes by inviting the judge to dinner.

Scene 2

The Provost has been waiting in another room for Angelo to confirm the dire sentence on Claudio. As Angelo does so Isabella and Lucio are shown in. Isabella pleads vainly for her brother's life to be spared. Angelo scoffs, "Condemn the fault, and not the actor of it?"

She turns away disconsolately but is urged by Lucio to renew her entreaty. Her pleading, abetted by Lucio, then becomes imperiously passionate ("but man, proud man, dressed in a little brief authority....like an angry ape, Plays such fantastic tricks before high heaven As make the angels weep;"). Angelo finally relents to the extent of bidding her return for his decision the following morning. After she has left with Lucio and the Provost, Angelo admits to himself that he is lustfully tempted by her beauty and virtue.

Scene 3

Vincentio, dressed as Friar Lodowick, arrives at the prison and asks the Provost to let him minister to the inmates. The pregnant Juliet appears and confesses to the friar that she is as guilty as the unfortunate Claudio.

Scene 4

Isabella comes to visit Angelo at his house, as arranged, and innocently offers to do anything to save her brother's life. Angelo slyly asks if she would submit herself to someone with the power to lift the sentence. When she refuses he makes it clear that she is to yield to him in order to obtain Claudio's pardon. Isabella contemptuously retorts that she will make his vile proposal public but he assures her that no-one will believe her. In despair Isabella determines to let her brother know, at the least.

Act II Scene 2

Isabella pleads with Angelo, the Lord Deputy of Vienna, for the life of her brother Claudio, urged on by Lucio, a dandified friend. The Provost listens as the lustful Angelo slyly bids her return the following morning.

Act III

Scene 1

In the prison Vincentio, as a friar, counsels Claudio in the presence of the Provost. When Isabella comes to visit Claudio Vincentio gets the Provost to conceal him where he can overhear their conversation. Isabella tells Claudio that he can be freed if she surrenders her virginity to the devilish Angelo. At first Claudio is resolute but as he contemplates the terrors of execution he suggests to Isabella that if she could thus bring herself to save him it would not be accounted a sin. She is ashamed of him and scornfully prepares to leave.

Having heard everything Vincentio re-enters and asks her to wait for a moment. He suggests to Claudio that Angelo's proposal was advanced only to test Isabella's virtue and sends him and the Provost away.

Vincentio then puts a plan to Isabella that will involve Mariana, who is betrothed to Angelo but has not wed him because her soldier brother Frederick was lost at sea with her entire dowry. Vincentio advises Isabella to consent to meet Angelo in some dark and secluded place. He will then arrange for Mariana to turn up in her stead. Isabella agrees to check the arrangements with Vincentio at St. Luke's, where Mariana resides, after she has spoken to Angelo.

Scene 2

Constable Elbow has re-arrested Pompey and they encounter the friar (Vincentio). Pompey tries unsuccessfully to get Lucio to bail him before Elbow hauls him off to prison. Lucio grumbles to Vincentio about Angelo's severity and hopes that the Duke will soon return despite his many faults. The Provost and his men come past with Mistress Overdone, who is also under arrest, and Escalus, to whom she appeals. Escalus dismisses her and pauses to comment to Vincentio on Angelo's harshness and the Duke's previous temperance.

Act IV

Scene 1

A boy sings a song to Mariana at the moated grange of St. Luke's. Vincentio arrives in his friar's habit followed by Isabella; Mariana retires. Isabella reports that Angelo has been hooked. He has given her two keys, one to a vineyard gate and the other to gain access to his garden by a door from the vineyard, and has told her twice how to get there. She is to visit him in the middle of the night, leaving a servant at the gate. Vincentio calls Mariana to hear the details of the assignation from Isabella. Mariana is told to say, "Remember now my brother" when she takes her leave of Angelo.

Scene 2

At the prison the Provost tells Pompey that he can earn remission if he will act as assistant to Abhorson, the executioner, when he beheads Claudio and Barnadine, another prisoner. Pompey accepts the offer and goes off with Abhorson to learn the tricks of the trade.

The Provost shows Claudio the death warrant before admitting the friar (Vincentio), who hints that a countermand is on its way. Sure enough, a messenger arrives shortly but to Vincentio's dismay Angelo has double-crossed Isabella. The message instructs the Provost to have Claudio executed at four o'clock (and Barnadine also in the afternoon). Moreover he is to send Claudio's head to Angelo by five o'clock, as proof.

Vincentio learns that Barnadine is a Bohemian drunkard who freely admits his guilt. He shows the Provost the Duke's seal and orders him to execute Barnadine and send his head to Angelo instead of Claudio's, shaved to disguise its identity. Claudio is to be reprieved for four days.

Scene 3

Pompey finds himself at home in the prison since many of the inmates are old customers of Mistress Overdone. Abhorson enters and the two of them call Barnadine to meet his Maker, with heavy humour. The 'friar' Vincentio tries to console him but the unrepentant Barnadine goes back to his cell with the others.

The Provost informs Vincentio that a pirate called Ragozine, who resembles Claudio slightly, has died in the prison that morning of a fever. With relief, they arrange to send Ragozine's head to Angelo and to keep Claudio and Barnadine secretly immured.

Vincentio prepares to write letters apprising Angelo of his sudden return and appointing a consecrated fountain outside the city wall as a rendezvous. When Isabella comes in he tells her that Claudio has already been executed. He goes on to say that the Duke will return on the morrow and that she must go with Friar Peter to meet the Duke, although he himself will not be there. Lucio enters, greets Isabella and walks off with Vincentio, regaling him with more scandal about the Duke.

Scene 4

At home with Escalus, Angelo is puzzled by the Duke's letters, especially the one requiring a proclamation, one hour before his arrival, that any petitions for redress of injustice should be brought out at that time. He tries to reassure himself that Isabella will not advertise her shame in public.

Scene 5

Outside the city Vincentio in his ducal clothes gives Friar Peter instructions and greets Varrius, a friend.

Scene 6

Isabella and Mariana confer near the city gate and agree to go along with Vincentio's arrangements. Friar Peter calls them to welcome the Duke.

Act V

Scene 1

Mariana, veiled, and Isabella are seated with Friar Peter in a stand at the city gate. The Duke and Varrius approach with a group of lords, to be met by Angelo with Escalus, Lucio, the Provost and other officers and citizens. They exchange greetings.

Isabella, prodded by Friar Peter, kneels before Vincentio and implores justice. She denounces Angelo as an adulterous thief and murderer while he tries to persuade Vincentio that she is deranged. Isabella goes through her story, supported by Lucio who is told not to interrupt.

Vincentio, affecting disbelief, asks who put her up to the allegation and is informed that it was Friar Lodowick (Vincentio's assumed identity). Lucio remarks that Lodowick is a scurvy fellow. Friar Peter, however, supports Lodowick, declaring himself spokesman for the friar, who has a fever.

As Isabella is carried off to prison under guard Mariana comes forward and tells Vincentio that Isabella's accusation of fornication is directed at her 'husband'. She then unveils and reveals that it was she who met Angelo in his garden by night. The Duke again pretends to disbelieve the story; he appoints Angelo to hear the case and calls for Lodowick to be fetched, fever or no. He then leaves Escalus to examine the witnesses.

Escalus has Isabella recalled; she is brought back, followed by Vincentio, dressed once again as Friar Lodowick, and the Provost. Under questioning, Lodowick denies inciting the women to slander Angelo and, as a supposed looker-on, refers to the corruption and lawlessness of the Viennese.

He is challenged by Lucio and is about to be marched off to prison when he throws off his habit, to the consternation of Lucio, who tries to sneak away, and Angelo, who confesses his guilt abjectly. Vincentio tells him to marry Mariana instantly. The two go off with the Provost and Friar Peter while Vincentio forgives Escalus and pardons Isabella.

Angelo and Mariana re-enter with the Provost, having been married by Friar Peter, only to hear the Duke condemn Angelo to death ("Measure still for Measure" for the death of Claudio). The ladies seek mercy in vain.

Vincentio then turns on the Provost and fires him for executing Claudio without a warrant at the unusual hour of four in the morning. The Provost protests that he has in fact saved two lives and brings in Barnadine, Juliet (now with her baby in her arms) and Claudio, muffled. The Duke pardons Barnadine, restores the unmuffled Claudio to Juliet and pardons Angelo. Lucio is commanded to marry a woman he has wronged. Finally Duke Vincentio offers his hand and heart to the virtuous and chaste Isabella.

The Merchant of Venice

This play may have been inspired by the alleged poison plots of Roderigo Lopez, Queen Elizabeth's Jewish physician. He was executed in 1594, two years before the play is thought to have been written. The story lines in it are to be found in Italian novelle; Marlowe's *The Jew of Malta* was a possible influence. The action takes place in Venice and nearby Belmont.

Act I

Scene 1

In a Venice street, the eponymous merchant Antonio feels unaccountably sad. His friends Salarino and Salanio suggest that he is in love or is worried about the merchandise which he has in four ships coming from Mexico, England and elsewhere, but Antonio rebuts their speculation. His close friend Bassanio comes along with two other friends, Lorenzo and Gratiano. After some further comments on Antonio's sadness the friends go on their way leaving Bassanio alone with him.

Bassanio wants to pay court to Portia, a beautiful heiress who has many suitors. However he is heavily in debt, principally to Antonio himself. He tells how, as a schoolboy, if he lost an arrow he would loose off another in the same direction and watch its flight as it fell, hoping thus to find both. He asks Antonio if he will 'shoot another arrow', i.e. make him another loan. Antonio explains that his wealth is tied up in his ships but he offers to borrow some money on his own account for Bassanio.

Scene 2

Portia, the heiress, is confiding in her lady-in-waiting Nerissa in her house in Belmont. She bemoans the fact that she cannot choose a husband for herself, being bound by the conditions of her deceased father's will. Her suitors include a Neapolitan prince who talks of nothing but horses, the County Palatine who is always frowning, a French lord Monsieur Le Bon, young Baron Falconbridge from England who cannot speak Italian or French, a Scottish lord and the Duke of Saxony's nephew who is a drunkard.

Under the will the successful suitor must choose one of three caskets; if it contains Portia's picture he may have her hand in marriage. Nerissa reminds Portia of the handsome Venetian Bassanio, who visited her when her father was alive. A servant announces that the unsuccessful suitors are leaving and that a messenger is heralding the arrival of yet another, the Prince of Morocco.

Scene 3

Bassanio has found a rich Jewish moneylender, Shylock, in a square in Venice, and is seeking to borrow three thousand ducats for three months, for which Antonio will be the surety. Shylock is not keen on the proposal because Antonio is a Christian and has abused him and spat on him on the Rialto [a main thoroughfare in Venice]. Moreover Antonio sometimes lends out money for nothing, thus damaging the moneylenders' business. However he greets Antonio with false warmth and agrees to obtain the money from Tubal, a wealthy Hebrew, describing how in the Bible Jacob took some lambs instead of interest on a loan.

Shylock cunningly proposes that instead of interest Antonio shall forfeit a pound of his flesh, to be cut off by Shylock, if the loan is not repaid on the due date. Antonio remarks coldly that "The devil can cite Scripture for his purpose". Bassanio is horror-struck but Antonio, who expects his ships to bring him wealth in two months' time, agrees and arranges to meet Shylock at the notary's, to draw up the bond.

Act II

Scene 1

The Prince of Morocco and his followers have arrived at Portia's house in Belmont to go through the casket ritual. He hopes that he will not be rejected because of his dark skin. Portia reminds him that if he chooses the wrong casket he must never court another woman.

Scene 2

Back in Venice Launcelot Gobbo, Shylock's servant, is racked by a mental debate between a fiend who tempts him to leave the miserly Shylock and his conscience which bids him stay. He is about to go when Old Gobbo, his blind father, comes with a present of a dish of doves for Shylock. Launcelot mischievously tells Gobbo that his son is dead but then relents, identifies himself ("it is a wise father that knows his own child") and suggests that the present be given to Bassanio instead.

Bassanio passes by with his servant Leonardo and other followers. Launcelot and Old Gobbo importune him and he agrees to take Launcelot into his service. Gratiano appears and begs Bassanio to take him to Belmont when he goes to woo Portia. Bassanio fears that he is too wild and loud-voiced; nevertheless he kindly agrees to take him.

Scene 3

In Shylock's house Jessica, his daughter, is sorry to see Launcelot go but wishes him well and instructs him to give a letter to her lover Lorenzo, who is Bassanio's guest at supper. She intends to become a Christian and marry Lorenzo.

Scene 4

Launcelot finds Lorenzo in the street discussing a

masque with Gratiano, Salarino and Salanio. He hands Lorenzo Jessica's letter, which directs him to rescue her from her father's house. She will be dressed as a page and will bring gold and jewels.

Scene 5

In front of his house Shylock calls Jessica to him and tells her that he is going out to supper. He is uneasy, having dreamed of moneybags. He instructs Jessica to lock up the house and not to look out at "Christian fools with varnish'd faces" in the masque.

Scene 6

After Shylock's departure Gratiano and Salarino in masks come to wait for Lorenzo. When he joins them Jessica greets him from an upper window and throws down a casket of jewels. She then appears at street level, dressed as a page, and goes off with Lorenzo and Salarino.

Antonio comes to tell Gratiano that the masque has been cancelled; the wind has risen and Gratiano hastens to join Bassanio on the ship to Belmont.

Scene 7

The Prince of Morocco prepares to choose a casket in Portia's house at Belmont. He rejects the lead and silver caskets and chooses the gold casket because its inscription: 'Who chooseth me shall gain what many men desire' seems to point to Portia. On unlocking it, however, he finds a skull with a message beginning "All that glisters is not gold;" Disappointed, he departs.

Scene 8

Salarino and Salanio are chatting in a Venice street. The talk is that Bassanio and Gratiano have set sail for Belmont while Lorenzo and Jessica have eloped in a gondola. Shylock is in a frenzy at losing his daughter and so much money; he is mocked by the urchins. It is rumoured that a Venetian ship has foundered in the English Channel.

Scene 9

Back in Portia's house the Prince of Arragon has come to try his luck. A conceited man, he chooses the silver casket by its inscription: 'Who chooseth me shall get as much as he deserves.' However when he unlocks it he finds a picture of an idiot with a message; "There be fools alive, I wis, Silver'd o'er; and so was this."

He departs in dudgeon and a servant reports that a young Venetian (Gratiano) is at the gate to signal the arrival of Bassanio.

Act III

Scene 1

In Venice Salarino tells Salanio that one of Antonio's ships has been wrecked on the Goodwin Sands [see also *King John*, Act V, Scene 3]. Shylock comes along and accuses Salarino of knowing about his

daughter's elopement. However he is cheered by the news of the shipwreck; he vows to have Antonio's flesh. When Salarino asks what is the good of that he replies, "To bait fish withal: if it will feed nothing else, it will feed my revenge."

A servant tells Antonio's friends that Antonio wishes to see them at his house. As they go off Tubal comes to tell Shylock that he cannot find Jessica, who has spent eighty ducats in one night in Genoa. Shylock is aghast but is consoled when he hears that Antonio has lost another ship coming from Tripoli.

Scene 2

Bassanio gathers with Gratiano, Nerissa and Portia in the Belmont house to choose his casket. Portia is forbidden to help with the choice but she makes her feelings clear. Some musicians sing a song while Bassanio picks the lead casket, the inscription on which is 'Who chooseth me must give and hazard all he hath:' He is delighted to find Portia's portrait inside, with a message that ends, "Turn you where your lady is And claim her with a loving kiss."

Portia humbly pledges herself to him with a ring (which he is never to lose or give away), together with her mansion, servants and possessions. To Bassanio's further delight Nerissa announces that she and Gratiano love each other and are to be married.

Lorenzo, Jessica and Salanio come in with a letter from Antonio; Bassanio reads it and turns pale. It seems that Antonio's other ships, from Lisbon, India and the Barbary Coast, have also foundered — not that it matters because the embittered Shylock would rather have Antonio's flesh than twenty times the sum owed. Since Antonio will obviously die in settling the bond he declares all debts cleared between Bassanio and himself. Bassanio, appalled, is quickly married to Portia in the chapel and rushes off to try to save his friend.

Scene 3

In Venice Antonio has been arrested. Shylock will not listen to any pleas and tells the gaoler to guard Antonio and bring him before the Duke of Venice the next day.

Scene 4

Portia, Nerissa, Lorenzo, Jessica and Balthazar, one of Portia's servants, confer in Belmont. Portia asks Lorenzo and Jessica to look after the house while she and Nerissa retire to a nearby monastery to await the men's return. However when they are out of earshot she tells Balthazar to carry a letter to her cousin, Dr. Bellario, in Padua and bring the reply with all speed. Then she and Nerissa arrange to dress as young male lawyers and travel in her coach to Venice.

Scene 5

Launcelot and Jessica commiserate with each other in the garden ("the sins of the father are to be laid upon the children;"). Lorenzo comes to call them to dinner.

Act IV, Scene 1

In the Venetian Court of Justice Portia, as Dr. Balthazar, checks Shylock as he prepares to take his pound of flesh from Antonio. If he sheds one drop of Christian blood his lands and goods will be confiscated by the state of Venice.

Act IV

Scene 1

The Duke of Venice is sitting in the Court of Justice with Antonio, Bassanio, Gratiano, Salarino, Salanio and various officials. The Duke arraigns Antonio and calls Shylock in. He pleads with him not to proceed but Shylock is adamant. Bassanio offers him six thousand ducats (from Portia) but he insists on his pound of flesh.

The Duke is informed that a messenger has arrived with letters from Dr. Bellario. Nerissa enters dressed as a lawyer's clerk. Meanwhile Shylock is sharpening his knife, to Gratiano's comment ("Not on thy sole, but on thy soul, harsh Jew, Thou mak'st thy knife keen:").

The clerk of the court reads out Dr. Bellario's letter. It says that although the writer is sick he is sending a young Roman, Dr. Balthazar (not the servant of that name), to convey his opinion and adjudicate in Antonio's case. Portia enters dressed as a doctor of laws and is taken for the Roman jurist.

Portia, as the presiding judge, informs Antonio that the terms of the bond are lawful and therefore Shylock must be merciful ("The quality of mercy is not strain'd, It droppeth as the gentle rain from heaven....") but he is still unmoved. Bassanio again offers more than the amount of the debt but Portia will not bend the law. Shylock exults, "A Daniel come to judgement! yea, a Daniel!"

Portia, urged on by Shylock, tells Antonio to prepare his bosom for the knife. She suggests that Shylock have a surgeon standing by to dress Antonio's wounds but Shylock retorts that he cannot find that requirement in the bond. Antonio makes a farewell speech. Portia is not amused to hear Bassanio assure him that he would sacrifice his wife and life itself to save him, if he could.

However just as Shylock makes ready to cut his pound of flesh Portia restrains him. In taking it, she says, he is not to shed "One drop of Christian blood" or his lands and goods will be confiscated by the state of Venice. Shylock, disgusted, is reluctantly willing to accept three times the value of the bond and let the Christian go.

Portia is relentless, however. She now tells Shylock to take his cut of flesh but if it is found to weigh more or less than an exact pound, even by a twentieth of a scruple, he is to die and his possessions are to be confiscated. Gratiano chortles, "Now, infidel, I have thee on the hip." Shylock is defeated; he abandons any hope of earning interest and is ready to go from the court with or without his principal of three thousand ducats.

But Portia has not finished with him. She draws his attention to a Venetian law under which if an alien seeks the life of any citizen that citizen may seize half of his goods, the other half going to the state, while his life is subject to the Duke's mercy. The Duke remits Shylock's potential life sentence and agrees that Antonio may take half of his goods, the other half going to Lorenzo and Jessica upon his death. The Jew must also become a Christian. Shylock shudders and leaves the court a broken man.

Portia, in her legal habit, declines to accept a fee but when pressed by Bassanio asks for remembrances, these being Antonio's gloves and Bassanio's wedding ring. Bassanio, remembering his vow not to lose it or give it away, offers her any other ring but she stalks off coldly. At Antonio's insistence he reluctantly sends Gratiano after her with the ring.

Scene 2

Portia and Nerissa are overtaken by Gratiano in the street outside and he hands her Bassanio's ring. Seeing this, Nerissa decides to see if she can get Gratiano to give her his ring, which he had sworn to keep for ever.

Act V

Scene 1

Lorenzo talks of the beauty of the night to Jessica as they stroll down the avenue of Portia's house. Stephano, one of the servants, comes to tell them that his mistress is returning with a confessor and her maid. Launcelot enters to say that Bassanio is also coming. As musicians play, Lorenzo beguiles Jessica ("How sweet the moonlight sleeps upon this bank!").

Portia and Nerissa then arrive to see a candle burning in the hall ("So shines a good deed in a naughty world."). Lorenzo hears Portia's voice and is told to keep quiet about their recent absence. Bassanio, Antonio, Gratiano and their followers now arrive, to be welcomed by Portia. Gratiano keeps telling Nerissa that he gave his ring to the judge's clerk; she professes not to believe him. He protests that Bassanio, too, gave his ring away — to the judge.

Portia and Nerissa chide them both but Portia, on hearing Bassanio's oath of loyalty, returns the ring, to his amazement. They explain that Portia was the judge and Nerissa the clerk. Furthermore Portia produces a letter that informs Antonio that three of his ships have arrived safely in port, after all. Since Lorenzo and Jessica have Shylock's deed of gift everything ends happily.

The Merry Wives of Windsor

In the preface to *The Comical Gallant* John Dennis reports that this play was written (in only a fortnight) at the behest of Elizabeth I. Apparently the queen wanted something in which Sir John Falstaff was in love, following his introduction in the two parts of *Henry IV* and his failure to appear in *Henry V*, as promised in the epilogue to the second part.

Act I

Scene 1

In front of Thomas Page's house in Windsor, Robert Shallow, a country Justice of the Peace [see Part 2 of *Henry IV*, Act III, Scene 2] is assured by his cousin Abraham Slender and a Welsh parson, Sir Hugh Evans, that his complaint of disparagement by Sir John Falstaff will be resolved. Evans turns the conversation to Page's daughter Anne who will come into an inheritance of seven hundred pounds from her grandfather when she is seventeen. He suggests that her marriage to Slender be arranged.

Page comes out of the house, exchanging greetings with Shallow and Evans and then with Falstaff and his followers, Bardolph, Nym and Pistol. Shallow accuses Falstaff of beating his men, killing his deer and breaking into his lodge. Slender joins in, accusing Falstaff's friends of making him drunk in the *Garter* tavern and picking his pockets of seven groats and two shovel-boards [i.e. shove-ha'penny boards]. Evans suggests that the matter be decided by a panel of himself, Page and the host of the *Garter* while the three rogues deny the charge.

Mistresses Alice Ford and Margaret Page enter with Anne who brings some wine and leaves, followed by the women and the Falstaff party. Page invites the visitors to dine on hot venison pasty and follows the others indoors.

Slender's servant Simple enters as Shallow and Evans press the weak-minded Slender to fall in love with Anne and marry her. He consents to marry but does not promise to be in love at first. Anne returns to call them in to dinner; Shallow and Evans respond, leaving her with Slender, who sends Simple in also. Slender does not know how to woo her. He bashfully maintains that he is not hungry and asks about the sounds of bear-baiting which can be heard. Finally Page returns and persuades him to the table.

Scene 2

Evans gives Simple a letter for Mistress Nell Quickly, a maid-of-all-work at the house of Dr. Caius, a French physician (not the hostess of the *Boar's Head* encountered in Act II of *Henry IV*, part 1). The letter requests her to intercede with Anne on Slender's behalf.

Scene 3

Falstaff is at dinner in the *Garter* tavern with Bardolph, Nym, Pistol, Robin his page and the innkeeper. Falstaff says that he will have to dispense with some of his entourage, who are costing him too much. The innkeeper agrees to employ Bardolph as a tapster and takes him out to show him his duties.

Falstaff tells Pistol that he intends to make love to Mistress Ford, who "has all the rule of her husband's purse." On his way out Falstaff gives Robin letters to Mrs. Ford and also Mrs. Page who he believes had been looking at him lasciviously. Pistol and Nym resolve to inform Messrs. Ford and Page respectively of Falstaff's schemes.

Scene 4

In Dr. Caius' house Nell Quickly and Simple order John Rugby, a servant, to keep watch for the doctor from the window. Mrs. Quickly asks Simple to describe his master, Slender, and assures him she will do her best on his behalf. Rugby warns them that Dr. Caius is back and she hides Simple in a closet.

Dr. Caius enters and bids her bring a green box from the closet. Her relief that he did not go himself is shattered when he looks for some simples [medicinal herbs] in the closet and finds Simple, who interrupts Mrs. Quickly's excuses to reveal his errand. While the irate doctor scribbles a challenge to Evans (with the innkeeper as referee) Mrs. Quickly explains to Simple that Evans is also in love with Anne Page.

Simple departs with the challenge, followed out by Dr. Caius and Rugby. Fenton, a young gentleman, enters and asks Mrs. Quickly if he has any chance of winning Anne. She accepts some money to advance his cause while mentioning drily that Anne has remarked on the wart above his eye ("Well, thereby hangs a tale.").

Act II

Scene 1

Back at Page's house a scandalised Mrs. Page reads Falstaff's love letter. Mrs. Ford brings along a similar letter and the two women conspire to lead him on till he has pawned his horses to the innkeeper. They retire as Frank Ford arrives with Page, Pistol and Nym. Pistol warns Ford about Falstaff and leaves. Nym does the same with Page. The women greet their husbands; when Mrs. Quickly arrives to visit Anne Mrs. Page takes her and Mrs. Ford inside.

The innkeeper and Shallow come to tell the two men that Evans and Dr. Caius are to fight a duel. Ford takes the innkeeper aside and asks to be introduced to Falstaff as Mr. Brook. They all go off to watch the duel.

Scene 2

In the *Garter* tavern Pistol takes Falstaff's refusal of a loan airily ("Why, then the world's mine oyster, Which I with sword will open."). Robin announces Mrs. Quickly who introduces herself and tells him confidentially that the estimable Mrs. Ford thanks him for his letter and says that he may come to 'see the picture' between ten and eleven when her husband will be out. The virtuous Mrs. Page, whose husband is seldom out, also sends her commendations and asks Falstaff to send Robin to her as a go-between.

When Mrs. Quickly and Pistol have left, Bardolph enters with a cup of wine from a Mr. Brook downstairs. He escorts 'Brook' in (Ford, in disguise) and leaves him with Falstaff. 'Brook' exchanges compliments with Falstaff and tells him that he has for years hopelessly pursued the strait-laced Alice Ford, with whom he is infatuated. He gives him twenty pounds and begs him to pay lavish court to Mrs. Ford for him. Falstaff confides to him that he is to see her between ten and eleven when her jealous knave of a rich husband is away from home. Left alone, the outraged 'Brook' fulminates at Falstaff's villainy and his wife's falsity.

Scene 3

Dr. Caius and Rugby wait for Evans in a field near Windsor. The innkeeper, as referee, arrives with Shallow, Slender and Page. Shallow urges Dr. Caius to accompany him home. The innkeeper, aside, despatches the other three to Frogmore [on the Thames, near Windsor] where Evans is waiting; he then offers to conduct Dr. Caius and Rugby to Frogmore so that the doctor can court Anne Page.

Act III

Scene 1

In another field near Frogmore Evans sends Simple to look for Dr. Caius, who is late; melancholy with nerves, he sings to keep his spirits up. Simple returns, followed by Page, Shallow and Slender. Page tells him that Dr. Caius is on the way, armed and dangerous. Dr. Caius then arrives with the innkeeper and Rugby. After some heated remarks the innkeeper calls on the 'soul-curer and body-curer' to put away their arms and confesses that he directed them to different meeting places. After he leaves, Evans and Dr. Caius agree together to be revenged on him for the trick he played on them.

Scene 2

Ford meets Mrs. Page in a Windsor street, on her way to visit his wife. She is accompanied by Robin who has been borrowed from Falstaff by her husband. They pass on while Ford deplores Page's foolishness and plans to expose Falstaff's machinations.

He encounters Page, Shallow, Slender, the innkeeper, Evans, Dr. Caius and Rugby and invites them to have dinner and see 'a monster'. The cousins, Shallow and Slender, decline, being on their way to dine with Anne. Page favours Slender as a suitor for her but says that his wife prefers Dr. Caius; the innkeeper finds no support when he recommends Fenton. Rugby is sent home and the innkeeper goes off to drink with Falstaff; Evans and Dr. Caius accept Ford's invitation.

Scene 3

Two servants, John and Robert, bring a basket into Ford's house. While Mrs. Page listens Mrs. Ford tells them to wait in the alehouse and, when called, to carry the basket to the laundresses by the Thames and empty it into a muddy ditch. Robin enters briefly to report that Falstaff has entered by the back door looking for Mrs. Ford. Mrs. Page checks that Robin has kept her secret and then conceals herself.

Falstaff comes in and professes his love for Mrs. Ford, with extravagant compliments. When Robin's voice is heard announcing the arrival of a breathless Mrs. Page Falstaff hides behind the arras. Mrs. Page re-enters with Robin and tells Mrs. Ford in a carrying voice that her husband is on his way with police officers to search for a man believed to be with her. Falstaff emerges in a panic; telling him there is no time to get him out of the house they cram him into the basket and cover him with dirty linen.

John and Robert are called in and carry the basket away as Ford, Page, Dr. Caius and Evans arrive. Ford locks the outer door and takes the other men upstairs to search for the suspect while the two wives gloat over their prank and plan to involve Mrs. Quickly in another deception the following morning.

The men come down empty-handed. Ford surmises that Falstaff had only been bragging and asks his wife's forgiveness for his suspicions. As they leave for a stroll in the park Page invites them to breakfast the following morning, followed by some hawking.

Scene 4

In Page's house, with Mrs. Quickly in the room, Anne advises Fenton to seek her father's favour despite Page's declared belief that Fenton is only pursuing Anne for the sake of his wealth. Shallow comes in with Slender and asks Mrs. Quickly to break up the lovers' chat and get Anne to listen to Slender; however he finds that he has to do most of the talking as Slender is too witless.

Page and his wife enter and attempt to deter Fenton. While Page invites Shallow and Slender into another room Fenton seeks the approval of Mrs. Page who takes Anne out to ascertain her preference. Mrs. Quickly bustles off on a further errand to Falstaff.

Scene 5

Falstaff sends Bardolph for a quart of Spanish wine in the *Garter* tavern, reflecting ruefully that he might have drowned in the river when he was tipped unceremoniously out of the basket. Bardolph returns, bringing Mrs. Quickly with him. She conveys Mrs. Ford's regrets over the incident and her invitation to visit her again between eight and nine when her husband is off hawking with Page.

She goes out as 'Brook' (Ford) enters. Falstaff tells him about his escapade in the laundry basket, despite which he is off to see Mrs. Ford again. As before, 'Brook' is incensed and vows to catch Falstaff this time.

Act IV

Scene 1

Mrs. Page is taking her son William to school. They meet Mrs. Quickly in the street, followed by Evans. At Mrs. Page's prompting Evans catechises William, to the accompaniment of comically ignorant interjections from Mrs. Quickly.

Scene 2

Falstaff has arrived at Mrs. Ford's, only to be bundled into another room when Mrs. Page arrives. She raises her voice to tell Mrs. Ford that her husband has learned how Falstaff escaped previously and is again coming down the street with a group of friends. Falstaff hastily re-enters, ready to hide in the baking oven or up the chimney but not in the linen basket again. Mrs. Ford provides him with a gown belonging to her "maid's aunt, the fat woman of Brainford". He goes out to put it on, while Mrs. Ford gets the servants to carry the basket to the street door.

Ford arrives with Page, Shallow, Dr. Caius and Evans. He glowers at his wife, commands the servants to put the basket down and empties it. When it turns out to contain only dirty laundry he prepares to search the house, as before. Mrs. Ford calls down Mrs. Page and 'Mother Prat of Brainford'. Ford castigates 'Mother Prat' (Falstaff) as a disreputable witch and cudgels her until she flees. The men leave while the two wives consider that as Falstaff has been taught a lesson they can now tell their husbands the whole story.

Scene 3

Bardolph informs the innkeeper that three Germans who have been staying at the tavern want horses in order to meet a duke at court. The innkeeper goes to deal with the Germans, who have not paid their bills for a week.

Scene 4

Back at Ford's house the explanations have been given and Ford has apologised for doubting his wife. Page suggests to him, their wives and Evans that they play a further trick on Falstaff. Mrs. Page refers to the legend of Herne the hunter and proposes that Falstaff be lured to an old oak tree disguised as Herne with huge horns on his head. She and Mrs. Ford will meet him but will be frightened off by a horde of fairies and goblins who will be her children and their friends suitably dressed with lighted tapers on their heads.

Evans offers to rehearse the children and play his tabor [small drum]. Anne Page is to be queen of the fairies. While buying the white silk for her robe Page means to have Slender abduct her and marry her at Eton; however Mrs. Page plans to provide Anne with a green cloak, still intent on seeing that Dr. Caius becomes her husband.

Scene 5

Simple has been sent by his master Slender to the *Garter* tavern. He is reluctant to knock at Falstaff's door, having seen an old fat woman entering his room. Falstaff is called down by the innkeeper and tells Simple that Mother Prat has gone. Simple was to ask her if Nym still had the chain that he wheedled from Slender; the wily Falstaff says that the same man cheated Slender. Simple was also to ask about Anne Page: was it Slender's fortune "to have her or no"? Falstaff bids him tell his master that it was indeed his fortune "to have her or no". Simple departs, satisfied with his mission.

Bardolph arrives to say that the three Germans dumped him in the mire beyond Eton and galloped off on the innkeeper's horses. The innkeeper hopes that they have gone to meet the duke but Evans comes in briefly to report that the three have cheated other innkeepers of horses and money in Reading, Maidenhead and Colebrook.

Dr. Caius looks in to confirm that no German duke is expected at court. The doleful innkeeper and Bardolph set off on a hue and cry after the thieves.

Falstaff admits that he too has been duped and beaten. Mrs. Quickly arrives with a letter to say that Mrs. Ford has also suffered a beating. She and Falstaff go to his room to study the letter.

Scene 6

In another room Fenton offers the innkeeper a hundred pounds in gold for his help. He has a letter from Anne which gives details of the planned escapade at Herne's Oak. His beloved Anne has agreed with her father to run away with Slender and has also agreed with her mother to marry Dr. Caius at the deanery. However as the fairy queen she will be dressed in white with a green cloak and masked, which will enable her to slip away with Fenton. The innkeeper agrees to have a vicar waiting at the church between twelve and one, to marry them.

Act V

Scene 1

Mrs. Quickly leaves Falstaff's room at the tavern, having secured his agreement to attend the goings-on at Herne's Oak. When Ford arrives, still as 'Brook', Falstaff tells him about his sufferings as Mother Prat. He assures 'Brook' that he will be revenged on Ford and will deliver Mrs. Ford to him.

Scene 2

Page waits in Windsor Park with Slender, who has

Act V, Scene 5

*At midnight in Windsor Park Falstaff falls prostrate under Herne's Oak.
Sir Hugh Evens (as a satyr), Pistol (as a hobgoblin) and Anne Page (as the
fairly queen) singe him with tapers as the children dance round them.*

arranged with Anne to use the passwords 'mum' and 'budget'. Shallow reminds him that she will be wearing white.

Scene 3

The two wives, in a street in Windsor, impress on Dr. Caius that Anne will be wearing green and will go with him when he takes her hand. They chortle over their plans and hurry off to the oak tree.

Scene 4

Evans assembles his fairies in Windsor Park.

Scene 5

Elsewhere in the park Falstaff, wearing the head of a deer with antlers, listens to the chimes of midnight as the two wives approach. He embraces Mrs. Ford and welcomes Mrs. Page. At that moment Evans appears dressed as a satyr with Pistol as a hobgoblin, Anne as the fairy queen and William and other children as fairies; the women run off.

Falstaff quickly lies face down, believing that it is fatal to speak to, or even look at, a fairy. Evans, Pistol and Anne singe him with their tapers and the fairies circle round, singing and pinching him. Caius appears and grabs a fairy dressed in green and Slender takes one dressed in white while Fenton makes off with the fairy queen. A noise of hunting is heard; the fairies disperse and Falstaff takes off his deer's head and rises.

Page, Ford and their wives enter, seize Falstaff and mock him. Mrs. Page asks him how he likes merry Windsor wives. Pointing to the antlered head Ford asks him who the cuckold is now. His wife regrets that Falstaff cannot be her lover but laughs, "I will always count you my deer."

Evans exhorts him to serve God and abandon his desires as Falstaff realises what an ass he has been. Ford even suggests that he will be taken to Windsor to repay the twenty pounds that 'Mr. Brook' gave him to procure Mrs. Ford for him. Eventually they all forgive Falstaff and Page invites him to drink a posset [milk curdled with wine] at his house, to celebrate the fact that he has outwitted his wife (i.e. by marrying their daughter to Slender rather than Dr. Caius).

A mournful Slender enters and describes how he exchanged the words 'mum' and 'budget' with a fairy figure in white but when he took her to Eton to be married he discovered that she was the post-master's lubberly son. In passing, Dr. Caius reveals that he took a figure in green and experienced the same shock and disappointment.

Finally Fenton brings his new wife Anne in and everyone accepts the situation. As a parting shot Ford notes with mocking approval that Falstaff has succeeded in keeping his word to 'Brook', since that night he (Ford) would indeed lie with Mrs. Ford.

A Midsummer-Night's Dream

It has been suggested that this masque-like play was originally intended for some courtly wedding or entertainment rather than for the public stage. The narrative is based on *The Knight's Tale* by Chaucer and on the fairy folklore of Western Europe. The setting is Athens and the woods near the city; the play takes the form of a fairy tale with a concluding epithalamium.

Act I

Scene 1

In his palace in Athens the Duke, Theseus, is looking forward to his marriage to Hippolyta, Queen of the Amazons, in four days' time on the night of the new moon, May 1st. He sends the Master of the Revels, Philostrate, to promote merrymaking among the Athenian youth.

Hermia enters with her father, Egeus, and two suitors, Lysander and Demetrius. Egeus complains that although Demetrius has his consent to marry Hermia, Lysander has stolen her heart with smooth words and love-tokens. He asks the Duke to be allowed to exercise the ancient legal privilege of Athens, by which a father can marry his daughter to whomever he chooses.

Theseus tells Hermia to comply with the law; if not she will be either executed or banished to a nunnery for life. He gives her four days, i.e. till his wedding, to decide. Lysander points out that Demetrius has previously wooed Nedar's daughter, Helena, a school friend of Hermia's, and that Helena is infatuated with him; Theseus, however, will not relent.

Left alone, Lysander consoles Hermia ("The course of true love never did run smooth;") and devises a plan which involves their running away to his widow aunt who lives seven leagues [21 miles] from Athens, in an area where Athenian law does not apply. The two arrange to meet the next night in a wood one league outside the city.

Helena, a taller girl, enters and reproaches Hermia for attracting Demetrius. To reassure her Hermia unwisely reveals the plan to escape with Lysander. When they have left Helena decides to betray the lovers to Demetrius and thus earn his gratitude.

Scene 2

As part of the celebrations Peter Quince, a carpenter, has assembled some friends in his house to devise an 'interlude' for the duke and duchess on their wedding night. They include Nick Bottom, a weaver, Francis Flute, a bellows-mender, Robin Starveling, a tailor and Tom Snout, a tinker. Quince informs the others that they will be presenting "the most lamentable comedy, and most cruel death of Pyramus and Thisby" (sic). [This is an old Babylonian love story related by Ovid in his *Metamorphoses*].

Bottom and Flute are to play the tragic lovers Pyramus and Thisbe. Flute objects to being cast as a woman, as he has a beard coming, but is over-ruled. Starveling and Quince himself are cast as Thisbe's mother and father. Snout is to play Pyramus' father while Snug is to be the lion. On hearing this Bottom wants to play the lion, promising not to frighten the ladies out of their wits ("I will roar you as gently as any sucking dove:") but is also dissuaded. The tradesmen agree to learn their lines and meet at the duke's oak, a mile outside the city, to rehearse privately.

Act II

Scene 1

Puck (Robin Goodfellow, a mischievous hobgoblin) and a fairy meet in the woods. Puck warns the fairy that Oberon, King of the Fairies, is frightening the elves with his wrath because Titania, his Queen, has taken into her train a changeling boy, stolen from an Indian king, whom Oberon wants for one of his own attendants.

Oberon and Titania appear ("Ill met by moonlight, proud Titania!") and taunt each other with jealousies. Titania refuses to give the Indian boy up so when she leaves Oberon decides to play a trick on her. He calls on Puck to bring him a flower, love-in-idleness, the juice of which has a magic property. If it is dropped into a sleeper's eyes that person, on waking, will be besotted with the first living thing they see, whether human or animal. Puck sets off ("I'll put a girdle round about the earth in forty minutes.").

Demetrius comes past in search of Hermia and Lysander, followed by Helena; they cannot see the invisible Oberon. Helena declares her abject love for Demetrius but he spurns her. When they have gone Puck re-appears with the flower. Oberon, feeling sorry for Helena, tells Puck to put some of the juice in the eyes of Demetrius, who may be recognised by his Athenian clothes, so that he will fall in love with Helena. Meanwhile Oberon will use the juice on Titania, as planned ("I know a bank whereon the wild thyme blows,").

Scene 2

Titania's fairies dance and sing her a lullaby in another part of the woods ("You spotted snakes with double tongue....come not near our fairy queen"). As Titania dozes Oberon enters, squeezes some juice on her eyelids and vanishes. A weary Hermia and Lysander then come by, having lost their way. They decide to take a nap, lying apart as "becomes a

Act III, Scene 1

Bottom, investigating a noise, is given the head of an ass by Puck. Titania awakens and is instantly infatuated with him, through the magic of the love-in-idleness spell. She embraces him, observed by the invisible Oberon.

virtuous bachelor and a maid." Puck then appears, mistakes Lysander for Demetrius from his Athenian clothes and drops some juice in his eyes.

Demetrius comes along followed by the lovelorn Helena, now falling behind. As he runs on she discovers Lysander and awakens him. Under the magic spell Lysander immediately declares his love for her. Helena is affronted by this mockery and withdraws, pursued by the amorous Lysander. Hermia wakes up from a bad dream; finding no Lysander she goes off in search of him.

Act III

Scene 1

The tradesmen arrive in the glade where Titania is sleeping to rehearse their play. In discussion Bottom calls for a prologue that will reassure the ladies that the lion and the suicide of Pyramus are not real; also they will have to provide a wall and some moonlight. Puck turns up to enjoy the wrong words and missed cues of the clowning artisans. Bottom, playing Pyramus, withdraws to investigate a noise; when he re-appears Puck has given him the head of an ass, for a prank. When his friends flee in terror Bottom is taken aback but he affects indifference, singing a song to keep his spirits up.

Titania, awakened by the song, sees Bottom in his ass's head and is instantly infatuated, through the magic spell. She conducts him to her fairy bower and commands her elves, Pease-Blossom, Cobweb, Moth and Mustard-seed, to cosset him and attend his every wish.

Scene 2

Elsewhere in the woods Puck reports to Oberon that the Athenian has been given the love juice and that Titania is doting on a donkey-headed man. They watch as Demetrius, having found Hermia, renews his wooing. She, however, believing that he has abducted and killed Lysander, spurns him and leaves. Demetrius, heavy with sorrow, lies down to sleep.

Oberon realises that Puck has used the magic juice on the wrong man. He hastens to administer some of the juice to Demetrius and sends Puck to find Helena so that when Demetrius wakes up he will love her. Lysander arrives with Helena, before she is found by Puck. Still upset, she continues to reject Lysander who appears to be making fun of her. The enchanted Demetrius now awakens, sees Helena and declares his love for her fulsomely, telling Lysander to keep his Hermia. Helena is bitterly confused by the protestations of undying love from both men.

Hermia enters, pleased to have found Lysander, only to discover that both men are in love with Helena. She thinks that all three are making cruel sport with her whereas Helena is convinced that Hermia and the men are plotting against her. The two girls quarrel and insult each other. The men try to protect Helena from the smaller but fiercer

Hermia. This leads to an argument between them; they go off to have a duel, while Helena runs away from the aggressive Hermia.

Oberon, who has seen everything with the gleeful Puck, is annoyed. He tells Puck to go after the men, keep them apart and weary them till they fall asleep. Puck does his bidding, appearing to each man in the guise of the other and taunting them. He crushes a herbal antidote provided by Oberon into Lysander's eyes so that he will once again love Hermia.

Act IV

Scene 1

Still in the wood, all four lovers are asleep not far apart from each other. Titania approaches with Bottom who enjoys the ministrations of the elves; eventually he dozes off in Titania's arms. Oberon emerges from the background to inform Puck that Titania has relented and agreed to let him have the Indian boy. He therefore touches Titania's eyes with the antidote; she awakes to tell Oberon about a dream in which she was in love with an ass. He points to Bottom and she is horrified; together they watch Puck restore Bottom's head to normal.

Dawn breaks on May 1st. Hunting horns are heard and the Duke and his party come upon the lovers. Theseus and Egeus wake them. Lysander reveals his elopement plan to Theseus and asks his pardon. Egeus seeks vengeance but when Demetrius, still under the magic spell, declares his love for Helena Theseus perceives that all has fallen out well, although not as planned at first; he and Hippolyta invite everyone to the nuptial feast. Bottom is left to muse on the strange events of the past night ("The eye of man hath not heard, the ear of man hath not seen....what my dream was.").

Scene 2

Back in Quince's house the artisans, concerned over Bottom's disappearance, are delighted when he drops in and bids them gather at the palace to perform their play.

Act V

Scene 1

Theseus and Hippolyta with their courtiers assemble in a palace apartment; they are joined by the four lovers. Philostrate, Master of the Revels, offers various entertainments to the Duke, including the Battle of the Centaurs (to be sung by an Athenian eunuch), the Bacchanalian riot and the Three Muses mourning the death of Learning. Theseus opts for the romantic tragedy of Pyramus and Thisbe although Philostrate warns him that the acting is so bad as to be farcical. Despite Hippolyta's reservations Philostrate goes off to fetch the amateur actors.

Quince appears to give the prologue, in which he shows no understanding of speech rhythm ("All for your delight, We are not here."). He is joined by Pyramus, Thisbe, Wall, Moonshine and Lion in dumb show. He recounts the story to follow, in which the lovers whisper through a chink in a wall and arrange to meet at Ninus' tomb. He explains that Thisbe, arriving first, is scared away by a lion which leaves traces of blood on her fallen mantle. Pyramus, coming upon the mantle later, assumes that she has been eaten by the lion and kills himself. Thisbe, returning, finds his body and commits suicide in turn.

The stage is cleared and the audience is increasingly amused as Snout introduces himself as the Wall; Demetrius remarks that "It is the wittiest partition that ever I heard discourse,". Pyramus and Thisbe re-enter, thanking the Wall for making a chink for them, and arrange their rendezvous. The Wall then departs, to general hilarity.

Lion enters with Moonshine, who carries a lantern. The action proceeds, to audible comments by the audience, Pyramus stabbing himself with great passion on discovering the blood-stained mantle. Thisbe returns (by starlight, now) and does the same, Moonshine and Lion being left to bury the dead. The Duke hastily declines the offer of an epilogue and the company dance a Bergomask before going off to bed.

Scene 2

Oberon, Titania and their train appear with song and dance. When they depart Puck is left to excuse the play ("If we shadows have offended, Think but this and all is mended, That you have but slumber'd here While these visions did appear.")

Much Ado About Nothing

This work has no specific literary source but some of the incidents may be found in Ariosto's *Orlando Furioso*. The character of Dogberry may have been based on a real constable in Grendon, Buckinghamshire. The play was revived before King James I a few years before Shakespeare's death under the title *Benedick and Beatrice*.

Act I

Scene 1

In front of his house Leonato, the Governor of Messina [in Sicily], tells his daughter Hero and his niece Beatrice that Don Pedro, Prince of Arragon, is arriving that night fresh from a military victory. A messenger confirms that the prince was less than ten miles away when he left him. Beatrice asks if Signior Mountanto is with him; it transpires that she is referring to Benedick, a young lord of Padua. The messenger reports that he is returning a hero.

Don Pedro arrives with Don John, his bastard brother, Balthazar, his servant, Claudio, a young Florentine count and Benedick. Leonato introduces his daughter while Beatrice and Benedick exchange barbed witticisms. The party arrange to stay a month and go indoors, leaving Benedick with Claudio, who asks him for his opinion of Hero. Don Pedro rejoins them, to be told that Count Claudio is in love with Hero. He sends Benedick to assure Leonato that he will be there for supper; then he tells Claudio that he will woo Hero on his behalf and subsequently ask Leonato to accept him (Claudio) as a son-in-law.

Scene 2

Inside the house Leonato is informed by his brother Antonio that a servant has overheard Don Pedro telling Count Claudio of his (the prince's) love for Hero.

Scene 3

Don John reveals his gloom and discontent to one of his followers, Conrade, in another room. A friend, Borachio, comes in to report that he has overheard Don Pedro's plan to woo Hero on Claudio's behalf. As they go to supper Don John sees a chance to create mischief.

Act II

Scene 1

Leonato is chatting with Antonio, Hero, Beatrice and others in the hall. They are joined by Don Pedro, Claudio, Benedick, Balthazar, Don John and Borachio with Margaret and Ursula, two of Hero's waiting-gentlewomen; they are all masked. Don Pedro takes Hero aside while the others joke and gossip, Balthazar with Margaret, Antonio with Ursula and Benedick in flippant raillery with Beatrice, who affects not to know him and brands him 'the prince's jester'.

After they have danced Don John is left alone with Borachio and Claudio. Don John addresses the masked Claudio as Benedick and maliciously asks him to dissuade Don Pedro from pestering Hero. He and Borachio depart leaving Claudio to reflect on Don Pedro's duplicity. When Benedick returns to confirm that Don Pedro is pursuing Hero he replies bitterly, "I wish him joy of her" and leaves.

Don Pedro comes back and is told by Benedick of Claudio's resentment. In return he informs Benedick that Beatrice has been told that he (Benedick) has wronged her by "the gentleman that danced with her".

Benedick explains the situation and leaves as Claudio, Beatrice, Hero and Leonato return. Don Pedro warns Beatrice that she has lost Benedick's heart; he also tells Claudio that he has wooed Hero for him and obtained Leonato's consent to the wedding. Claudio is reluctant to wait a week for the ceremony; to divert him Don Pedro enlists his assistance in bringing Benedick and Beatrice together again. Leonato and Hero offer to help.

Scene 2

In another room Borachio proposes a cunning scheme to Don John. If Don John will tell Don Pedro and Claudio that Hero is really in love with him (Borachio) he will arrange for his sweetheart Margaret to be at Hero's window, dressed in her clothes; she will then converse with him while Don Pedro and Claudio look on, thus providing evidence of Hero's immodesty and disloyalty.

Scene 3

Out in the garden Benedick is determined not to become a lovesick fool like Claudio. He withdraws to an arbour but is spotted by Don Pedro when he comes along with Leonato and Claudio, followed by Balthazar and some musicians. Balthazar sings ("Sigh no more, ladies, sigh no more, Men were deceivers ever;") and departs with the musicians.

Don Pedro takes care to discuss Beatrice's great love for Benedick with the other two before strolling on. Benedick is at first surprised ("Sits the wind in that quarter?") and then convinced. He decides to ignore Beatrice's scornful jests ("Shall quips and sentences and these paper bullets of the brain awe a man from the career of his humour?")

Beatrice comes to call him to dinner (against her will, she says) but Benedick responds civilly to her tart remarks.

Act IV, Scene 1

Hero swoons in the arms of Beatrice at the wedding ceremony when Claudio accuses her of infidelity and immodesty. Friar Francis remonstrates and Leonato laments while Don Pedro, Don Juan and Benedick look on.

Act III

Scene 1

Still in the Governor's garden Hero sends Margaret to draw Beatrice into a bower. Beatrice enters the bower and overhears Hero and Ursula describing Benedick's great love for her, despite her disdain. As with the previous ruse Beatrice is convinced of Benedick's love and determines to requite it.

Scene 2

Inside the house Don Pedro tells Claudio, in the company of Benedick and Leonato, that he will stay for the wedding but must then go to Arragon. He and Claudio tease Benedick, saying that he must be in love since he is smartly dressed and perfumed. As Benedick and Leonato leave Don John comes to invite Don Pedro and Claudio to wait under Hero's window and observe her unfaithfulness on the night before her wedding.

Scene 3

Dogberry, a muddle-headed constable, is addressing Verges, a headborough [petty constable] and members of the watch [night patrol] in the street. George Seacoal, one of the watchmen, is handed the lantern to carry, because he can read and write. Dogberry tries to tells the watch how to deal with drunks and thieves but he confuses long words and his instructions are self-defeating.

Borachio comes along, telling Conrade that he has earned a thousand ducats from Don John for his success in getting Margaret to impersonate Hero at the window. Don Pedro was deceived, as was Claudio who swore that he would charge Hero with infidelity at the wedding ceremony. The watchmen, misunderstanding Borachio's words, arrest them both.

Scene 4

In Leonato's house Hero sends Ursula to fetch Beatrice while Margaret comments on Hero's costume. Beatrice comes in to assist the others in dressing Hero for the ceremony.

Scene 5

Dogberry introduces Verges to Leonato in another room as an honest witness ("Comparisons are odorous:"). Verges reports the arrest of Don John's followers; Leonato, called by a messenger to give his daughter away, delegates the examination of the two miscreants to Dogberry.

Act IV

Scene 1

Don Pedro, Don John, Leonato, Claudio, Benedick, Hero and Beatrice are assembled in a church with Friar Francis. When the friar asks if Hero or Claudio know of an impediment to their marriage Claudio taxes Hero with talking to a ruffian at her chamber-window.

Hero swoons as Don Pedro, Don John and Claudio leave and Leonato laments his daughter's infamy. The friar, however, is convinced of Hero's innocence. When she recovers he advises Leonato to conceal Hero and let it be known that she has dropped dead; then, he says, Claudio will be filled with remorse and will withdraw his allegations.

The friar takes Leonato and Hero away, leaving Benedick and Beatrice to declare their love for each other. Beatrice challenges Benedick to prove his love by avenging her wronged kinswoman, Hero. He is to kill Claudio, as she would do if she were a man. Benedick finally agrees.

Scene 2

In the presence of Verges, a sexton and members of the watch Dogberry begins his examination of Borachio and Conrade in the local prison, while Hugh Oatcake, a watchman, takes notes. Dogberry's comical hysteron proteron persists ("Masters, it is proved already that you are little better than false knaves, and it will go near to be thought so shortly.") Despite his complete misunderstanding of the evidence given by the watch the sexton orders the two offenders to be taken before the governor.

Act V

Scene 1

At his house Governor Leonato, giving out that Hero has died of grief, determines to challenge Count Claudio for slandering her. Antonio attempts to dissuade his brother but when Don Pedro and Claudio come along he sides with him in offering to duel with Claudio. He and Leonato leave as Benedick comes to challenge Claudio also. He is laughed off by Claudio and Don Pedro who insinuate that he is daring only because Beatrice has set him on. Benedick accuses them of causing the death of a sweet and innocent lady and mentions that Don John has fled from Messina.

As he leaves Dogberry arrives with Verges, Conrade, Borachio and the watch. Borachio informs the prince that the 'shallow fools' who arrested him have brought to light what his own wisdom could not uncover. He then tells the whole story of Don John's machinations, to Claudio's horror.

Leonato returns with Antonio and the sexton, who has already made his report. Claudio implores Leonato's forgiveness for his false accusation of Hero. As a penance Leonato commands him to marry a niece of his who is very like Hero; he is to meet her the next morning.

Scene 2

Benedick meets Margaret in Leonato's garden and asks her to call Beatrice to him. When Beatrice appears Benedick tells her that he has challenged Claudio. They resume their verbal jousting until Ursula arrives to tell them that Hero has been falsely accused and that Don John, the instigator, has fled.

Scene 3

Claudio mourns by the monument to Hero erected by Leonato in the church. He and Don Pedro depart to prepare for the second wedding.

Scene 4

Leonato, Antonio, Benedick, Beatrice, Margaret, Ursula, Friar Francis and Hero are assembled in Leonato's house. Leonato sends the ladies into another room and bids them don masks. He reminds Antonio that he is to give away his 'daughter' to Claudio. Benedick takes the opportunity to ask the friar to marry him to Beatrice.

Don Pedro arrives with Claudio and Antonio is sent to fetch his 'daughter'. He returns with the masked ladies and Claudio agrees to marry the daughter before she unmasks. He and the prince are amazed and overjoyed to discover that it is the living Hero.

Benedick asks Beatrice to unmask. Typically, they are too proud to commit themselves but Benedick tells Beatrice that her uncle together with the prince and Claudio have sworn that she loves him. Beatrice in turn says that Ursula and her cousin Margaret have sworn that he loves her. Benedick consents to take her 'for pity' and she yields 'to save his life'.

Before the friar takes the two couples off to the chapel a message is brought that Don John has been arrested and brought back to Messina. Everyone dances happily to the music of pipers.

Othello, the Moor of Venice

This play, a study of treachery and jealousy, is one of the major Shakespearean tragedies. It was written in about 1604. The action, which is set in Venice and a seaport in Cyprus, is drawn from the *Hecatommithi* of Giraldi Cinthio.

Act I

Scene 1

Late one evening in a Venetian street an ensign, Iago, is bitterly complaining to a gentleman called Roderigo. He says that his master Othello, a noble Moor who is a general in the Venetian forces, has made the inexperienced Michael Cassio of Florence his lieutenant instead of himself.

To get back at Othello he takes Roderigo along to the house of a senator, Brabantio; there they make a commotion outside, shouting, "Awake! what, ho!.... thieves! thieves!" When Brabantio comes to an upper window he recalls that he has refused to let Roderigo marry his daughter, Desdemona, and tells Roderigo not to bother him further.

Iago then informs him that Desdemona has eloped with "an old black ram", namely Othello. Brabantio, aghast, disappears indoors to check on Desdemona's whereabouts while Iago hastens to the commanding officers' residence to give false assurances to Othello of his sympathy and support.

Brabantio appears at street level with his servants. He has confirmed that Desdemona is missing and asks if she has indeed married Othello. Roderigo confirms it but says that the couple can be found.

Scene 2

In another street Iago warns Othello that Brabantio is on the way. Othello pays little heed, being confident that the Duke of Venice will not take action against a senior officer who has served him so well. Cassio and some companions come to tell Othello that the duke requires his immediate presence. Othello goes to leave word in his house; when he re-emerges Brabantio and Roderigo arrive with an armed party.

Both sides draw their swords as Senator Brabantio accuses Othello of enticing his daughter to his "sooty bosom" by witchcraft. He threatens to arrest Othello for sorcery but as the duke is waiting in council he agrees to lay his case before him.

Scene 3

The Duke of Venice is discussing the menacing movements of the Turkish fleet with senators in the council chamber. It is reported that over a hundred galleys have been joined by thirty more ships at Rhodes and are sailing towards Cyprus, which belongs to Venice.

Brabantio enters with Othello, Iago, Roderigo and others. The duke is about to send Othello to deal with the invasion when Brabantio accuses him of abducting Desdemona. Othello confesses their marriage ("I will a round unvarnish'd tale deliver"). He tells the council that Desdemona, beguiled by his tales of military prowess, fell in love with him and suggests that she be summoned to endorse his account.

Desdemona, fetched by Iago, shows respect for her father but her loving duty is to her new husband. Brabantio reluctantly accepts the situation. Desdemona asks to accompany Othello to Cyprus but he entrusts her to the care of Iago while he is travelling on active service.

After the council has left, Iago cunningly observes to a glum Roderigo that Desdemona will not long remain in love with Othello and suggests that she can be lured away with gifts of money and jewels. Privately Iago also plans to tell Othello that the Florentine courtier Cassio is after his wife.

Act II

Scene 1

Montano, Othello's predecessor as the governor of Cyprus, is talking to two gentlemen near the quayside of a Cypriot seaport. A third man arrives with the news that the Turkish fleet has been scattered by a gale. He is followed by Cassio who describes how he became separated from Othello in tempestuous seas. Another gentleman reports the arrival of Iago's ship; shortly afterwards Iago himself appears with his wife Emilia, Desdemona, Roderigo and attendants. Iago is pleased to note Cassio's airy kisses and flowery compliments to Desdemona, which suit his schemes well.

Finally Othello arrives with his attendants, to be greeted lovingly by Desdemona; they make their way to the castle leaving Iago alone with Roderigo. Iago assures him that Desdemona is now in love with Cassio, as he is with her. He urges Roderigo to pick a quarrel with Cassio; the Cypriots will then mutiny and Cassio will no longer be an impediment.

Scene 2

A herald proclaims that, the Turkish threat having been lifted, General Othello has ordered feasting and celebrations.

Scene 3

In the castle hall Othello tells Cassio to stand guard with Iago, before retiring with Desdemona. Iago invites Cassio to have a cup of wine; at first Cassio pleads a weak head but when he has fetched Montano and some gallants he consents, along with the others, to drink Othello's health repeatedly, to the sound of Iago's drinking songs. He then staggers drunkenly on watch; Iago sends Roderigo after him but Roderigo soon returns at Cassio's swordpoint. When Montano tries to intervene Cassio engages him in a sword fight.

Iago surreptitiously sends Roderigo to raise the alarm. Othello responds and is horrified to find that Cassio has injured the ex-governor of Cyprus. Iago, feigning reluctance, inculpates Cassio; Othello, believing his account, sadly dismisses Cassio from his service. He sees to Montano's wounds and when Desdemona appears escorts her back to bed.

Cassio, now sober, bewails the loss of his reputation; Iago slyly advises him to beg Desdemona to intercede for him with Othello. After Cassio has left, grateful for this counsel, the treacherous Iago muses on a plan to suggest to Othello that his wife is only pleading for Cassio because she lusts after him. When Roderigo returns Iago sends him to bed.

Act III

Scene 1

The following morning near the castle Cassio encounters some musicians with a clown. He gives the clown a gold piece and asks him to find out if Emilia has risen. Iago comes by and offers to send his wife out and keep Othello out of the way. Emilia appears and invites Cassio in so that he and Desdemona can confer in privacy.

Scene 2

Inside the castle Othello gives Iago some letters to go by ship to the Venetian senate; he then begins a tour of inspection with his men.

Scene 3

Close by the castle Desdemona promises to help Cassio, abetted by Emilia. They are seen from a distance by Othello and Iago. As Cassio scurries off he is half-recognised by Othello while the duplicitous Iago expresses doubts. However Desdemona innocently identifies Cassio and begs her husband to forgive him. Othello demurs but under pressure he consents to an approach by Cassio.

When Desdemona and Emilia have gone Iago refers to Cassio as an honest man but insidiously warns Othello to beware of jealousy and maintain his good name ("Who steals my purse steals trash....But he that filches from me my good name Robs me of that which not enriches him, And makes me poor indeed."). "Look to your wife; observe her well with Cassio;" he tells Othello, reminding him that she readily deceived her father in order to marry him. Left to himself, Othello is raised to a pitch of suspicion and jealousy.

Desdemona returns with Emilia to summon Othello to dinner. Distractedly, he pleads a headache; Desdemona tries to bandage his head with her strawberry-spotted handkerchief but, being too small, it falls to the ground as she helps Othello indoors. Emilia grabs the handkerchief, which Iago had already asked her to purloin. He now comes upon her and snatches the handkerchief from her, intending to leave it in Cassio's lodgings.

Othello returns, riven with suspicion; when he seeks proof of Desdemona's infidelity Iago tells him that he heard Cassio mumble in his sleep, "Sweet Desdemona, Let us be wary, let us hide our loves!". He says that he also saw Cassio wipe his beard with Desdemona's handkerchief. In a passion Othello orders Iago to kill Cassio within three days.

Scene 4

Elsewhere Desdemona requests the clown to find Cassio and call him to her. She is searching for the lost handkerchief when Othello appears. Pretending a cold, he asks for the handkerchief, which an Egyptian had given to his mother as a love charm; when Desdemona cannot produce it he sweeps off in a rage.

When Cassio arrives with Iago Desdemona tells him regretfully that her pleading has not gone well. Iago goes off, ostensibly to placate Othello, while Desdemona and Emilia wonder what to do next. As they move off Cassio's mistress, Bianca, comes along to complain that he has not visited her for a whole week. Cassio apologises; he hands her Desdemona's handkerchief, which he has found in his house, and asks her to sew him a copy of it. Bianca bridles, fearing that some other woman has given it to him, but she agrees to receive him soon.

Act IV

Scene 1

Iago again torments Othello with insinuations about Desdemona and Cassio until he falls into an epileptic fit. Cassio appears and offers aid but Iago asks him to step aside while Othello comes to himself. When Othello recovers Iago tells him that Cassio has been by and suggests that he eavesdrop on their conversation when he comes back. Othello withdraws as Cassio returns. Cassio laughs scornfully when Iago tells him that Bianca loves him and "gives it out that you shall marry her;". The watching Othello believes that they are discussing Desdemona.

In passing, Bianca throws Desdemona's handkerchief at Cassio, refusing to work on "some minx's token" and mentioning that he can drop in to supper or not, as he likes. Cassio, taken aback, hurries after her to mend matters.

Othello emerges, having seen the byplay with the handkerchief. By now his jealous fury encompasses Desdemona as well as Cassio. He tells Iago to procure some poison but Iago callously suggests that he strangle her on the marriage bed that she has contaminated.

Desdemona appears with her cousin Lodovico

Act V, Scene 2

Othello, riven with jealousy, enters his bedroom where Desdemona is lying asleep.
He is determined that she shall die but he cannot bring himself to shed her blood.

and attendants. Lodovico hands Othello a letter from the duke and senators of Venice, commanding him to return and appointing Cassio as governor in his place. It is the last straw. Othello cries out in anguish, strikes Desdemona and orders her out of his sight. Lodovico is amazed; when Othello has gone Iago hints to him that the Moor is mad.

Scene 2

Othello questions Emilia in a room in the castle. Emilia swears that she has seen no wrongdoing; she is sent to fetch Desdemona and leave her with him. Othello hurls accusations of infidelity at Desdemona who desperately maintains her bewildered innocence. When he leaves Emilia re-enters and attempts to console her. Emilia brings Iago in and Desdemona begs him on her knees to assure Othello that she is not the whore that he thinks.

As the women leave for supper Roderigo enters to remonstrate with Iago. His gifts of jewels, which were to have been passed to Desdemona by Iago, have had no effect and he now demands their return. To retrieve the situation Iago hastily informs him that Othello has been posted to Mauritania and will take Desdemona away with him unless Cassio, his replacement, can meet with an 'accident', requiring him to stay. Iago tells Roderigo to go to Bianca's house after midnight when he will help him kill Cassio.

Scene 3

In another room Othello sends Desdemona to bed before going for a stroll with Lodovico. Desdemona and Emilia lament together as Desdemona cries that she would not be unfaithful to her husband for all the world.

Act V

Scene 1

Out in the street Iago positions Roderigo behind a buttress with drawn rapier and retires. The outcome of the encounter doesn't matter to him; if Roderigo is killed he can keep the jewels previously entrusted to him while if Cassio dies he can gain the coveted position of lieutenant. When Cassio comes past Roderigo lunges at him but misses; Cassio strikes back, wounding Roderigo, and in the darkness Iago takes the opportunity to knife Cassio in the leg.

Othello, hearing the scuffle, thinks that Iago has killed Cassio as he had wished. He goes off to deal with Desdemona. Lodovico and Brabantio's brother Gratiano now hear the cries of the wounded men. As they hesitate Iago joins them and manages to stab Roderigo to death covertly. As Bianca arrives he goes to Cassio's assistance, bandaging him and calling for a chair to carry him away. Emilia also arrives and blames Bianca for the whole affair.

Scene 2

Othello enters his bedroom where a nightlight shows Desdemona lying asleep. He is determined that she shall die but he cannot bring himself to shed her blood ("Put out the light, and then put out the light".) Desdemona wakes as he kisses her and bids her offer up her last prayers. Othello is convinced, by the damning handkerchief, that she and Cassio have been lovers. Desdemona denies it and asks him to check with Cassio. When he replies that Cassio has been killed by Iago her entreaties become desperate but Othello loses control and smothers her with a pillow.

Hearing Emilia calling he unlocks the door and is shocked to learn from her that in fact Cassio has killed Roderigo in the street. With her dying breath Desdemona tells Emilia that no-one but she herself is responsible for her death. However Emilia turns on Othello who quickly confesses his guilt. She contemptuously informs him that "honest Iago" has basely deceived him.

Montano and Gratiano enter with Iago and others. In the ensuing conversation all is revealed. Emilia shrieks that Iago's lies have led to Desdemona's murder and tells Othello the truth about the handkerchief. Othello turns on Iago, who stabs Emilia in desperation and flees, pursued by Montano and Gratiano.

In deep remorse Othello takes up a favourite Spanish sword. When the others bring Iago back as a prisoner, with Cassio in a chair, Othello strikes at Iago, wounding him, but is restrained. Lodovico arrests Othello for murder, having found incriminating letters in Roderigo's pockets, and promises retribution for the "hellish villain" Iago.

In a final speech Othello beseeches them to speak of him as he was, as "one that lov'd not wisely but too well;". He stabs himself and falls beside the lifeless Desdemona with a dying kiss.

Pericles, Prince of Tyre

This work, a story of virtue rewarded, has acquired an unenviable reputation as the least well written play of the canon, to the extent that doubts have arisen as to whether Shakespeare was the sole author. The blank verse of the first two acts is certainly not of typical Shakespearean quality. The action is dispersed among a number of locations in the Middle East.

Act I

Prologue

Gower sets the scene in Antioch [then in Suria, now Antakya in Turkey], a city developed by the Seleucid king Antiochus the Great. The king has committed the crime of incest with the daughter of his deceased wife. He has decreed that anyone seeking her hand must answer a riddle or lose his life.

Scene 1

Pericles, a young prince of Tyre, has come to the palace of King Antiochus to attempt to win his daughter. When she enters he scans the riddle ("I sought a husband....He's father, son and husband mild, I mother, wife, and yet his child.") Antiochus, realising from his response that Pericles suspects that the answer lies in incest, gives him forty days to expound the answer. Pericles, left alone, appreciates that he is now in mortal danger however he answers and hurriedly departs.

Antiochus returns and commands Thaliard, a lord, to kill Pericles, giving him gold and some poison for the task. When he receives a message that Pericles has fled he sends Thaliard after him.

Scene 2

In his trepidation Pericles cannot relax in his palace at Tyre [southern Lebanon]. He sends some lords to check the shipping in port and relates what has happened in Antioch confidentially to his minister Helicanus, who shares his concern and advises him to absent himself for a time. Pericles decides to travel to Tarsus [where Anthony and Cleopatra first met] where he will await a letter from Helicanus.

Scene 3

Thaliard has arrived in Tyre and is waiting in an antechamber. He overhears Helicanus, Escanes and other lords discussing Pericles' flight. He greets them and is offered hospitality.

Scene 4

In his house in Tarsus [near Adana, in Turkey] the Governor, Cleon, is discussing the famine with his wife Dionyza. A lord enters to report that a fleet of ships under flags of truce is approaching. He is shortly followed by Pericles who offers Cleon grain in return for shelter in the harbour; the gift is gladly accepted.

Act II

Prologue

Gower introduces a mime featuring Cleon, Pericles and their train. A messenger brings a letter to Pericles who knights him and shows the letter to Cleon. Afterwards Gower explains that the letter was from Helicanus, warning Pericles of Thaliard's pursuit of him. Thereupon Pericles put to sea but was thrown ashore as sole survivor of a shipwreck.

Scene 1

On shore a bedraggled Pericles meets a master fisherman and two friends, Pilch and Patch-breech. The master wraps him in his gown and while the others go to pull up their fishing net he tells Pericles that he is in Pentapolis, the kingdom of Simonides in Greece. Pericles also learns that on the following day a tournament will be held to celebrate the birthday of Thaisa, daughter of King Simonides.

The fishermen return carrying a suit of armour that has been drawn up in their net. Pericles recognises it as his own, being a gift from his father. He begs it from the fishermen, promising to reward them in due course.

Scene 2

King Simonides emerges from his pavilion with Thaisa to greet his knights as they enter the lists. As each one passes by, his squire presents his shield to the princess. A Spartan knight is followed by a Macedonian prince, a knight from Antioch and three others, the last of whom is Pericles, in his rusty armour and offering only a withered branch.

Scene 3

Simonides is presiding over a banquet in the hall of state. Princess Thaisa presents a victory wreath to Pericles, the day's champion. She is much taken with him, especially when her father bids her drink a toast to him and enquire his name. Pericles presents himself as a gentleman of Tyre and joins in the feasting and dancing.

Scene 4

Back in Tyre Helicanus tells Escanes that the incestuous Antiochus and his daughter have been struck by lightning in their chariot and killed. Two or three lords come to tell Helicanus that if Prince Pericles is to be permanently absent they wish

Act III, Scene 1

Aboard a storm-tossed ship Queen Thaisa has apparently died in childbirth. Her attendant Lychorida brings the newborn infant to Pericles while, at the insistence of the crew, the queen's body is embalmed and consigned to the deep.

Helicanus to be their ruler in his place. Helicanus demurs and asks them to wait another year.

Scene 5

In the royal palace at Pentapolis Simonides, reading from a letter, tells the contending knights that Thaisa has vowed not to marry for another twelve months. On their departure he reveals that she has expressed her love for the 'stranger knight'. Simonides greets Pericles with praise for his musical ability and slyly suggests that he tutor Thaisa. Pericles refuses, suspecting a trap, but when Thaisa comes in their mutual love is discovered and a wedding is arranged.

Act III

Prologue

The audience learns from Gower that Pericles and Thaisa have married and that she is pregnant. Gower presents another mime in which a messenger gives a letter to Pericles, who shows it to Simonides. The lords kneel to Pericles as Thaisa enters with her attendant Lychorida. Simonides shows her the letter and she rejoices. She and Pericles take their leave of him and depart.

Gower explains that this letter, like the other, is from Helicanus, informing King Pericles that he can now return to Tyre in safety. Pericles and Thaisa embark on the journey but the ship again runs into a tempest.

Scene 1

Aboard the storm-tossed ship Queen Thaisa has apparently died in childbirth; Lychorida brings the newborn infant to Pericles who cries out in grief. Two sailors insist to Pericles that the queen's body must be thrown overboard, believing superstitiously that while it remains on board the storm will not abate. Pericles reluctantly allows the body to be embalmed with spices and placed in a caulked chest with a note of her identity. He alters course for Tarsus, thinking that the newborn baby will not survive the voyage to Tyre.

Scene 2

Cerimon is a skilful physician of Ephesus [a coastal city probably situated north of the Mandalya gulf in modern Turkey]. He calls his servant Philemon to provide food and warmth for some shipwrecked sailors in his house. Two gentlemen arrive seeking shelter; they are followed by two servants with a chest cast up on the shore. They open it and Cerimon, pronouncing that the body within (Thaisa) has been in a trance for five hours, revives her.

Scene 3

In the Governor's house in Tarsus Pericles is taking his leave of Cleon and Dionyza, leaving with them Lychorida and the baby, which he has named Marina since she was born at sea. He vows not to cut his hair until Marina grows up and is married.

Scene 4

Back in Ephesus Cerimon shows Thaisa, now recovered, some jewels and the note which was left in the chest. She decides to retire from the world and become a vestal (priestess) in the nearby temple of Diana.

Act IV

Prologue

Gower observes that Pericles has settled into his reign at Tyre and Thaisa remains at Ephesus. Meanwhile in Tarsus Marina has grown into a beautiful and accomplished girl, arousing the jealousy of Queen Dionyza, whose own daughter Philoten is being overshadowed. Upon Lychorida's death Dionyza orders a servant, Leonine, to kill Marina.

Scene 1

Marina, carrying a basket of flowers to strew on Lychorida's grave, interrupts the plotting of Dionyza and Leonine. Dionyza offers to be her nurse in place of Lychorida and sends her off for a stroll with Leonine. She tells him the story of her birth, as often related to her by Lychorida, but he bids her say her prayers before dying. As she struggles with him some pirates suddenly appear and carry her off. Leonine plans to report that she is dead, as instructed.

Scene 2

In a brothel in Mitylene a pimp sends his servant Boult to search in the market for more prostitutes, the madam having reported that the present three are not enough. Boult returns shortly with the pirates and Marina, whom the pimp buys for a thousand sequins [gold coins]. Boult and the madam discuss how to advertise Marina while she, in despair, wishes that Leonine had succeeded in killing her.

Scene 3

In Tarsus Dionyza has poisoned Leonine, the supposed murderer of Marina, while a shocked Cleon wonders what he will do when Pericles asks for the return of his daughter. Dionyza has erected a monument to Marina and is ready to brazen the affair out.

Scene 4

Gower appears to carry the story forward. He says that Pericles has left Escanes to rule Tyre and has come to Tarsus with Helicanus to find his daughter. In a mime, the long-haired Pericles and his entourage enter by one door and Cleon and Dionyza by another. Pericles, on being shown Marina's tomb by Cleon, dons sackcloth and departs in a paroxysm of grief. Gower reads out the fulsome epitaphs placed on the tomb by the duplicitous Dionyza.

Scene 5

Two men leave the brothel in Mitylene dumbfounded at having had divinity preached to them by Marina.

Scene 6

Inside the brothel the pimp and his two companions wonder how they can force Marina into prostitution. Lysimachus, the Governor of Mitylene, arrives looking for a whore with no disease. Boult produces Marina and the madam urges her to please Lysimachus. Alone with Marina he is overcome by her modesty and virtue; he gives her gold and leaves, saying that he will be in touch with her, to her benefit.

The madam returns with Boult, threatens Marina and leaves Boult to take her virginity. However Marina hands him the gold and reproaches him for abetting his master's vile trade. Boult relents and agrees to help her earn more gold by teaching singing, weaving, sewing and dancing.

Act V

Prologue

Gower relates how Marina has escaped from the brothel into an honest house and is captivating everyone with her music and embroidery. Meanwhile the mournful Pericles has arrived by ship and Lysimachus has gone to meet him.

Scene 1

Pericles is reclining on a couch in a pavilion on the deck of his his ship; a barge is lying alongside. A Tyrian sailor informs Helicanus that Governor Lysimachus is seeking to come aboard. Lysimachus and his suite appear and are ceremonially greeted. Helicanus takes him into the pavilion but warns him that Pericles will not speak for grief. A lord suggests that the beauteous Marina may be able to relieve his melancholy and is sent to fetch her.

He returns shortly with Marina and a young lady. Marina sings to Pericles and tells him that she has endured a grief as heavy as his. For the first time since leaving Tarsus she refers to her royal parentage. Pericles detects in her a likeness to his wife Thaisa

and enquires her history. He is stunned to learn that she is indeed his daughter Marina and calls upon Helicanus and Lysimachus to confirm the miracle of her restoration.

The entranced Pericles hears heavenly music and sees a vision of the goddess Diana who calls on him to come to her temple at Ephesus and offer up a sacrifice. Pericles is determined to obey but first he consents to the union of Lysimachus and Marina.

Scene 2

Gower describes the revelry in Mitylene at Marina's betrothal and the arrival of the royal party at Ephesus.

Scene 3

In the temple of Diana the high priestess Thaisa stands near the altar with Cerimon, who brought her back to life, and vestal virgins on either side. Pericles enters with Lysimachus, Helicanus, Marina and their suite. When he recounts the story of his wife and child Thaisa faints. Cerimon realises that Thaisa is his queen and pieces everything together. Thaisa recovers and shows Pericles a ring similar to one given to him by her father Simonides.

Pericles embraces Thaisa with joy and Marina kneels to her. Pericles introduces Helicanus and expresses his profound gratitude to Cerimon. He undertakes to shave and cut his hair for the first time in fourteen years, to grace the wedding of Lysimachus and Marina.

Epilogue

Gower informs the audience that the enraged citizens of Tarsus have burned Cleon and his wicked queen to death in their palace. He recalls how Antiochus and his daughter were struck down for their 'monstrous lust', how virtue has preserved Pericles, his wife and daughter from calamity and how Helicanus and Cerimon have been rewarded for their loyalty and charity.

Romeo and Juliet

The primary source of this archetypal love story is Arthur Brooke's narrative poem *Romeus and Juliet* published in 1562. Shakespeare may also have known an earlier work for the stage on the same subject. With the exception of one scene in Mantua the play is set in Verona [in the Italian see of Venetia] at about the time when Bartolomeo della Scala was ruler, i.e. 1301-04.

Prologue

Chorus proclaims that an ancient and bitter feud exists between the households of the Montagues and the Capulets. In the next two hours the tale of a pair of star-crossed lovers will be told, culminating in their deaths.

Act I

Scene 1

Two armed Capulet servants, Sampson and Gregory, encounter Abraham, a Montague servant, and Romeo's own servant Balthasar in a public place. They brawl until they are parted by Montague's nephew Benvolio; however Lady Capulet's nephew Tybalt prefers to fight. The four are joined by other supporters of both houses and a pitched mêlée ensues.

Capulet and Lady Capulet prepare to join in, followed by Montague and Lady Montague. Their quarrel is interrupted by the arrival of the ruler, Prince Escalus, who forbids more fighting on pain of death, having already had to deal with three similar incidents. He leaves, taking the Capulets with him.

Montague enquires of Benvolio how the trouble began while Lady Montague is thankful that Romeo was not involved. Benvolio reports that Romeo hid from him while walking before sunrise in a sycamore grove. Montague confirms that Romeo often grieves while out walking early, returning at first light to lock himself in his chamber; no-one knows why.

The Montagues retire as their son Romeo approaches. Romeo tells his cousin that he is in love with a beautiful girl who does not love him ("Love is a smoke rais'd with the fume of sighs;").

Scene 2

In another street Paris, a young nobleman related to the Prince, asks Capulet for Juliet's hand in marriage. Capulet considers her too young, being not quite fourteen, but he consents, subject to her agreement. He invites Paris to a feast that evening and hands a guest list to a servant so that he can convey invitations to others.

Unfortunately the servant is illiterate so when he comes across Romeo with Benvolio he asks him to read the names for him. As a Montague Romeo is not, of course, on the list but he learns from it that one of the guests is Capulet's niece Rosaline, his beloved. He arranges to gatecrash the feast with Benvolio in order to catch a glimpse of Rosaline.

Scene 3

In Capulet's house the Nurse calls his daughter Juliet to attend her mother, Lady Capulet, reminiscing about the day when she herself ceased wet-nursing her. Lady Capulet tells Juliet and the Nurse that Count Paris has proposed marriage and will be at the feast; she asks Juliet to take a look at him. A servant announces that all is ready for the festivity.

Scene 4

Outside in the street Romeo and Benvolio confer with Mercutio, a homosexual relation of Escalus, and various maskers and torch-bearers. Romeo regrets that he cannot dance; he is uneasy following a bad dream but dons a mask and takes a torch. Mercutio rallies him; he tells a poetic Warwickshire folk tale about Queen Mab, the fairies' midwife, and suggests that she caused Romeo's dream.

Scene 5

In the great hall the servants make ready for the ball and the musicians play. Capulet receives his guests and bids them dance, regretting that his own dancing days are over. Romeo, watching the couples, sees Juliet and is entranced. Tybalt recognises the masked Romeo and is prepared to throw him out but his uncle Capulet sternly restrains him. Tybalt goes off threatening to attack Romeo later.

Romeo goes up to Juliet, murmuring compliments, takes her hand and eventually steals a kiss. The Nurse brings a message to Juliet from her mother; Romeo is horrified to find that his new love is a Capulet. He departs with Benvolio while the others go on to the banquet leaving Juliet with her Nurse, from whom she learns in her turn that Romeo is one of the hated Montagues.

Prologue

Chorus comments on Romeo's new-found love and warns that he and Juliet will have to brave the enmity of their respective families in order to meet again.

Act II

Scene 1

Romeo, who has leapt over a wall to get into Capulet's orchard, hides from Benvolio and

Act II, Scene 2

Juliet is called in from the balcony by her Nurse but returns hurriedly to arrange a rendezvous concerning her wedding to Romeo. From the orchard he bids her a lingering farewell ("Parting is such sweet sorrow...")

Mercutio, who think that he has returned to find Rosaline. They leave him to his escapade.

Scene 2

Juliet appears at an upper window. ("But, soft, what light through yonder window breaks? It is the east, and Juliet is the sun!"). She sighs, "O Romeo, Romeo! Wherefore art thou Romeo?" and wishes that she or Romeo could renounce their surnames. ("What's in a name? That which we call a rose By any other name would smell as sweet:").

Romeo answers her from the bushes, saying that he will be happy to be a Montague no longer, for her sake. Juliet, recognising him by his voice, fears that he will be murdered by any of her family that come across him. Romeo scorns the danger and he and Juliet declare their passionate love for each other.

Juliet is called in by her Nurse but she returns to tell Romeo hurriedly that she will send someone to him at nine o'clock to find out the time and place of their wedding. She is again called in but returns once more for a lingering farewell ("Good-night, good-night! Parting is such sweet sorrow That I shall say good-night till it be morrow.")

Scene 3

At dawn in his cell a Franciscan, Friar Laurence, is preparing to gather medicinal herbs in a basket. When Romeo comes to see him he is surprised to learn that the object of Romeo's adoration is now Juliet and not Rosaline. Nevertheless he agrees to marry the young lovers, hoping that it will help to reconcile their families.

Scene 4

Meanwhile Benvolio and Mercutio are out looking for Romeo, knowing that Tybalt, an accomplished swordsman, has sent him a note challenging him to a duel. Romeo comes along in high spirits and jokes with them. They are joined by the Nurse with her servant Peter. She is introduced to Romeo and when Benvolio and Mercutio have left she tells him that she has been sent by Juliet. Romeo says that if Juliet will come to confession that afternoon Friar Laurence will marry them. He also tells the Nurse to wait behind the abbey wall; in less than one hour a man will come to her with a rope ladder.

Scene 5

Juliet is anxiously waiting in her garden for the return of her Nurse. When the Nurse arrives with Peter she chatters and prevaricates before telling Juliet about the wedding plans.

Scene 6

Back in the friar's cell Father Laurence warns Romeo against rushing into marriage. Nonetheless when Juliet arrives he takes them into the church for the ceremony.

Act III

Scene 1

Benvolio and Mercutio are walking with a page and some servants; they encounter Tybalt and his companions. They are joined by Romeo who is insulted by Tybalt and challenged to a duel. Romeo declines to fight, now that he is related to the Capulets by marriage. Mercutio, disdaining Romeo's apparent cowardice, draws his sword. Although Romeo and Benvolio try to intervene, Mercutio duels with Tybalt and is wounded. A surgeon is sent for and Mercutio is helped indoors by Benvolio ("I am hurt. A plague o' both your houses! I am sped.")

Romeo's shock turns to grief when Benvolio comes back to report that Mercutio is dead. Seeing Tybalt returning Romeo avenges his friend by attacking him. Tybalt falls dead and Romeo is spirited away by Benvolio.

Escalus, in the company of Montague, Capulet and others, comes upon Tybalt's body. While Lady Capulet laments the death of her nephew, Benvolio explains to the prince what occurred. Lady Capulet demands Romeo's execution but at Montague's pleading Escalus merely exiles him from Verona.

Scene 2

In the orchard Juliet longs for nightfall and Romeo's coming. Her Nurse rushes in with the rope ladder; she bears a confused tale of Tybalt's death and Romeo's banishment. Juliet weeps at the realisation that Romeo's visit will be a last farewell; she sends the Nurse to him with a ring.

Scene 3

Romeo, hiding in the friar's cell, is told by Father Laurence of his banishment. When the Nurse enters and tells Romeo of Juliet's sorrow he prepares to end his life. Friar Laurence tells him to go instead to comfort Juliet and then to depart for Mantua before the nightwatch comes on duty. He will then attempt to procure a pardon for him. The Nurse hands Romeo the ring and leaves.

Scene 4

Capulet, in the company of his wife, tells Paris that he can proceed to marry Juliet in three days' time. Her consent will no longer be a factor.

Scene 5

In another room in the house Romeo, having spent the night with Juliet, is preparing to leave ("I must be gone and live, or stay and die.") The Nurse enters to warn them that Juliet's mother is coming and with a final kiss Romeo climbs down the rope ladder.

Lady Capulet swears that she will have vengeance; she will get a friend in Mantua to poison Romeo for killing Tybalt. She goes on to tell Juliet that her father has arranged for her to marry Count Paris at St. Peter's Church. Juliet refuses and when

Capulet comes in with the Nurse she begs him on her knees to delay the wedding. He retorts that she is proud and ungrateful; she will marry Paris or be thrown out of his house.

Juliet appeals to her mother, who refuses to listen. When her parents have left she turns to her Nurse for advice but she coolly advises marrying Paris since Romeo cannot return to Verona except by stealth. Heartbroken, Juliet says that she will go to confess to Friar Laurence and seek absolution.

Act IV

Scene 1

Paris has come to Friar Laurence's cell to discuss the arranged wedding. When a tearful Juliet enters he reminds her of the arrangement and leaves her to confess to the Franciscan.

Finding that she is ready to commit suicide rather than marry Paris Father Laurence devises a plan. He tells her to go home and give her consent to the wedding; then, the following night when she is alone, she is to drink the potion which he gives her. It will make her appear lifeless and she will be carried on a bier to the Capulet vault. However forty-two hours later she will awake as from a pleasant sleep and he will have Romeo there to carry her off to Mantua.

Scene 2

In the hall of Capulet's house Juliet meekly asks her father's pardon for disobedience and undertakes to marry Paris. Capulet is so relieved that he brings the wedding forward by a day, to Juliet's alarm

Scene 3

The Nurse accompanies Juliet to her chamber in order to help with the wedding dress and other details but Juliet, saying she wishes to pray, dismisses her along with Lady Capulet. Juliet is beset by fears that the potion may be a poison or that she may awake before Romeo's arrival and be stifled in the tomb alongside Tybalt's decaying corpse. Eventually her love for Romeo gives her courage; she drinks the potion and falls across her bed.

Scene 4

Down in the hall Capulet and his wife supervise the preparations for the wedding banquet.

Scene 5

In the morning the Nurse enters Juliet's chamber to find her already dressed. On discovering that she is lifeless she screams for Lord and Lady Capulet. Their anguish greets Friar Laurence when he arrives with Paris to conduct Juliet to the church. The wedding procession becomes a cortège, with Peter arranging suitable dirges with the musicians.

Act V

Scene 1

In far-off Mantua Romeo has dreamed that Juliet has revived him from death with a kiss. Balthasar arrives from Verona. He brings no letters; instead he tells Romeo that Juliet lies dead in her burial chamber. Grief-stricken, Romeo purchases some poison from an apothecary for forty ducats and sends Balthasar to hire horses to ride to Verona.

Scene 2

Friar John joins Friar Laurence in his cell, back in Verona. He tells Friar Laurence that he and a brother monk have been quarantined after visiting people sick of the plague and that therefore he has been unable to deliver the letter to Romeo. Knowing that Juliet will recover in three hours Friar Laurence hurries to the vault, intending to keep her in his cell until Romeo gets back from Mantua.

Scene 3

Paris has come with his page to the Capulets' sepulchre in the churchyard to mourn for Juliet. He tells the page to extinguish his torch, loiter under some yew-trees and whistle if anyone approaches. While strewing flowers on Juliet's tomb he hears the page's signal and hides.

Romeo and Balthasar enter with another torch and a mattock. Romeo takes them and gives Balthasar a letter to be delivered to his father. He orders him on pain of death not to watch while he descends into the tomb to look upon Juliet's face and take a precious ring from her dead finger. Balthasar retires but when Romeo opens the tomb Paris emerges from the shadows and attempts to arrest him, suspecting that he is about to commit some felonious act. They fight, while the page runs to call the watch, and Paris is slain. Only then does Romeo discover who his adversary was.

He sorrowfully lays Paris in the tomb and after a passionate speech ("Eyes, look your last! Arms, take your last embrace!") he swallows the poison and falls dead.

At the other end of the churchyard Friar Laurence appears with a lantern, crowbar and spade. He bumps into Balthasar and, seeing a light in the Capulet vault, enquires who is there. Balthasar tells him that Romeo is inside but he will not accompany the friar to the tomb against Romeo's strict orders.

No sooner has Friar Laurence found the bodies of Romeo and Paris in the tomb than Juliet wakes from her coma. The friar, hearing the nightwatch approaching, quickly tells her of the fate of Romeo and Paris; he urges her to fly with him and take refuge in a nunnery. In a paroxysm of grief Juliet refuses to leave, waving him away. Seeing no poison left in Romeo's cup she kisses his lips, snatches his dagger and stabs herself. She falls across his body as the page leads members of the watch into the tomb.

The first watchman coming upon the bodies, one of which is still warm, sends some companions to search the churchyard and others to raise the alarm with the Capulets and Montagues. Some of the watch soon re-enter with Balthasar and the Friar, who is still carrying his spade.

Shortly afterwards Prince Escalus arrives with his attendants, followed by Capulet and Lady Capulet. They are all horrified by the scene and the unfortunate friar is suspected of murder. Montague appears with the news that Lady Montague has died of grief at Romeo's exile.

The prince demands an explanation for the slaughter. Friar Laurence tells them about the wedding of Romeo and Juliet, which could be confirmed by the Nurse, and their desperation over Tybalt's death and Romeo's banishment. He describes the plan involving the narcotic and the mischance that prevented his letter from reaching Romeo in Mantua. Remorsefully he offers his own life for the part he played in the tragedy.

Balthasar hands Romeo's letter to the prince while he and the page tell their stories. The letter confirms all that has been said. Escalus blames Capulet and Montague for the hatred that has led to the tragedy, noting that his own tolerance of the situation has meant the loss of two kinsmen. The two nobleman are reconciled and Montague offers to erect a statue of Juliet in pure gold. Thus the feud is ended.

The Taming of the Shrew

The story of the humbling of a termagant is a widespread folk tale, available to Shakespeare from Ariosto's *I Suppositi*, as translated in George Gascoigne's *The Supposes* (1566). The present version may also be an adaptation of a play entitled *The Taming of a Shrew* (sic) which had previously been performed by the theatrical company which Shakespeare joined. However it is also possible that the latter is a "bad" quarto of Shakespeare's play.

Introduction

Scene 1

Christopher Sly, a tinker, tells the hostess of an alehouse on a heath that he will not pay for some glasses he has broken, although she threatens to summon an under-constable. He reclines on the ground and goes to sleep.

To the sound of a horn a lord comes along with huntsmen and servants, ordering one of them to see to the hounds. Noticing Sly, the lord wonders what he would do if he were put to bed and, on waking, found a banquet served, music playing and minions to grant his every wish. He instructs the servants to carry Sly to his own bedchamber and practise the deception.

Some strolling players arrive whom the lord has seen before. He tells them that they are to perform before a 'lord' whose behaviour may seem strange to them. While they are preparing, the lord arranges for his page, Bartholomew, to go to Sly's chamber dressed as a woman and behave as if he were Sly's wife, welcoming his supposed recovery from a long illness with kisses and tears (with the aid of an onion). The lord goes into the tavern exulting in the elaborate practical joke.

Scene 2

In the bedroom Sly is dressed in a rich nightgown and surrounded by attendants (including the lord) carrying clothes, basins and other articles. Sly calls for ale, turning down the wine and fine clothes as unfitting for a simple pedlar turned tinker. The others, however, call him a lord and tell him he must have taken leave of his senses; they offer him music, pictures, horses to ride and first, a bowl to wash his hands.

Sly begins to believe in this fantasy and when his wife (the page) enters he bids 'her' undress and get into bed. 'She' has to tell him firmly that the physician has recommended abstinence. Another servant comes to tell Sly that a company of actors are ready to perform a comedy for him; he settles down to watch it.

Act I

Scene 1

Lucentio has come from Pisa to Padua with his servant Tranio to study philosophy. In a public place they see a rich gentleman, Baptista Minola, surrounded by his daughters Katharina and Bianca with Bianca's suitors Gremio and Hortensio. Baptista tells the young men that Bianca will not be allowed to become engaged before a husband has been found for her elder sister Katharina. They recoil from Katharina's rough demeanour.

Baptista sends Bianca indoors to her books and musical instruments, resolving to engage some tutors for both girls. He and Katharina follow. Gremio remarks glumly to Hortensio, "our cake's dough on both sides." They saunter off, agreeing that a husband must somehow be found for Katharina; after all, she does have a rich father.

Lucentio confesses to Tranio that he has fallen in love with Bianca at first sight; he decides to offer his services as her tutor. When Tranio points out that he will need a stand-in while thus occupied Lucentio changes clothes with him, planning to pass himself off as a Neapolitan or a Florentine.

When his other servant, Biondello, arrives Lucentio tells him that Tranio and he have had to swap clothes because he has killed a man in a quarrel and is seeking to escape undetected. He orders Biondello to play along and Tranio, as himself, to become another wooer for Bianca.

(Sly, who is nodding off, is nudged to attention by a servant and his 'wife').

Scene 2

Petruchio, a gentleman of Verona, has come to call on Hortensio at his house. He orders his servant, Grumio, to knock at the gate; when Grumio misunderstands he wrings his ears. Hortensio welcomes him and Petruchio explains that his father has died and he is looking for a rich wife, even if she is ill-favoured. It turns out that Baptista and Petruchio's fathers were acquainted. Hortensio quickly recommends a wealthy girl who is nevertheless perverse beyond measure. He plans to accompany Petruchio on his visit to Katharina, being anxious to gain access to Bianca as a teacher.

Gremio has met the disguised Lucentio and is taking him to Baptista's house to recommend him as a tutor for Bianca. Hortensio introduces Petruchio as someone who will woo the prickly Katharina and also present him to Bianca as a music teacher. Tranio comes along in fine clothes accompanied by Biondello. Gremio, learning that he is a third suitor for Bianca, warns him off but they all agree that Petruchio must first be supported in his wooing of Katharina.

Act II

Scene 1

In Baptista's house Katharina has bound Bianca's hands and is interrogating her spitefully as to which suitor she prefers. Baptista rescues Bianca and rebukes Katharina, who flounces out in a tantrum.

Gremio enters with Lucentio, who is simply dressed, Petruchio, Hortensio as a musician, Tranio and Biondello who is carrying Greek and Latin books and a lute. Petruchio introduces himself as a suitor for Katharina and presents Hortensio as Licio, a professor of music and mathematics from Mantua. Gremio presents Lucentio in turn as Cambio, a language student from Rheims. Tranio steps forward as Lucentio of Pisa and offers the lute and the books as gifts for Baptista's daughters. Baptista hands the lute to Licio and the books to Cambio before calling a servant to conduct the 'tutors' and Biondello to the girls.

Baptista suggests a stroll in the orchard and informs Petruchio that Katharina's dowry will comprise half of his lands and twenty thousand crowns. In return Petruchio is prepared to make her his sole legatee and proposes that a marriage covenant be drawn up.

Hortensio (Licio) re-enters, injured; he explains that when he told Katharina that she was fingering the wrong frets on the lute she broke the instrument over his head. Baptista takes him off to try his luck with Bianca, accompanied by Gremio and Tranio (Lucentio), while Petruchio plans his strategy for winning Katharina. When she comes in he plies her with droll flattery, insisting on calling her 'Kate' and telling her that he will marry her, as agreed with her father. She is contemptuous of him and slaps his face.

When Baptista returns with Gremio and Tranio Petruchio declares that since Kate and he are infatuated and will be married that Sunday he will be off to Venice to purchase the wedding garments ("We will have rings, and things, and fine array; And, kiss me, Kate...."). He goes out, Katharina pointedly leaving in the opposite direction.

Now that the way is clear, Baptista tells Tranio and Gremio that the one who can assure Bianca the greater dower shall have her hand. Gremio, the older man, offers his richly furnished house and a farm with a big herd of cattle. Tranio, as an only son, can offer three or four houses in Pisa and land yielding revenue of two thousand ducats a year. Gremio adds a merchant ship in Marseilles; Tranio retorts that his father has three such ships plus fifteen galleys, three of them large.

Baptista, impressed, tells Tranio that on the Sunday following Katharina's wedding he can marry Bianca if his father will sign over the property of which he has boasted. As he departs Tranio realises that as Lucentio he will have to produce somebody to be his father Vincentio.

Act III

Scene 1

Still in Baptista's house Bianca's suitors wrangle over which of them shall have the first hour with her, Hortensio (Licio) with a music lesson or Lucentio (Cambio) with a philosophy lecture. Bianca bids Hortensio tune his lute while Lucentio takes advantage of this to reveal his and Tranio's real identities, under cover of some fake Latin translation. She lightly rebuffs him using the same device.

The men continue to vie with each other as Hortensio manages to tune the lute and essays a lesson, to Bianca's dissatisfaction. Eventually a servant calls her away to help Katharina prepare reluctantly for her wedding on the morrow.

Scene 2

On the next day Baptista gathers with Gremio, Tranio, Lucentio, Katharina, Bianca and attendants outside the house. He asks Tranio (as Lucentio) why the bridegroom Petruchio has not returned for his wedding. Katharina, feeling scorned by her "frantic fool" of a wooer, sweeps off in tears, being consoled ineffectively by Bianca. Biondello rushes up to report that Petruchio is indeed on his way, dressed in ragged old clothes (but a new hat), carrying a rusty sword and mounted on a broken-down nag.

Petruchio duly arrives in tatters with Grumio and cheerfully asks for Kate. He turns down an offer of smarter clothes by the shocked Baptista and goes off with Grumio and Biondello to find Katharina, followed by Baptista, Gremio and the servants. Tranio tells Lucentio about the necessity of finding someone to be his father Vincentio while Lucentio contemplates absconding with Bianca.

Gremio returns to tell them of Petruchio's rowdy behaviour at the wedding, where he cuffed the priest, swore and afterwards threw dregs of wine at the sexton.

Petruchio himself arrives with his new wife Katharina in the company of Baptista, Bianca, Hortensio, Grumio and others. He announces that he must leave immediately with Katharina although the others entreat him to stay at least for the wedding feast. He carries off the protesting Katharina, accompanied by Grumio, while a forlorn Baptista invites the guests to the feast at which Bianca and Lucentio will stand in for the absent bride and groom.

Act IV

Scene 1

Grumio shivers in the hall of Petruchio's country house, having been sent on ahead to lay a fire. He calls another servant, Curtis, who truculently assures him that the house is swept, supper is ready and the

Act IV, Scene 1

*At dinner in his country house Petruchio pronounces the mutton
burnt and hurls it at the servants while his bride Katharina attempts
to mollify him. Grumio and Curtis go along with the charade.*

fire laid. Grumio relates how, when Katharina fell from horseback into the mud, Petruchio failed to help her, swore and pretended to blame him (Grumio) for the accident.

Some other servants Nathaniel, Joseph, Nicholas, Peter and Philip are paraded to receive Petruchio and the mutinous Katharina. Petruchio blames them for not helping him dismount, swears at Grumio and asks why Gregory, Gabriel, Adam and Ralph did not meet him in the park. He sings boisterously, calls for supper and boxes the ears of the servants when they remove his boots awkwardly and drop a basin of water.

At supper he pronounces the mutton burnt and hurls it at the servants while a dismayed Katharina attempts to mollify him. He and Curtis take her to the bridal chamber. Curtis returns to tell Grumio that Petruchio is still railing at the servants while sweet-talking Katharina. Petruchio re-enters, planning to keep Katharina not only hungry but sleepless by finding fault with the bed and scattering the bedclothes.

Scene 2

Back in Padua Tranio and Hortensio (Licio) loiter near Baptista's house while Bianca and Lucentio (Cambio) stroll up and down, conversing flirtatiously, to Tranio's feigned despair. Hortensio tells Tranio who he really is and Tranio as Lucentio agrees to forswear Bianca. Hortensio leaves, assuring 'Lucentio' in turn that he will give up Bianca and marry a wealthy widow within three days. Tranio conveys this development to Bianca and Lucentio as they depart.

Biondello comes running in to say that he has spotted a schoolmaster coming down the hill who can impersonate Vincentio. The man enters, informing Tranio that he is travelling from Mantua to Tripoli via Rome. Tranio says that Mantuans risk death when seen in Padua because of a quarrel between the dukes of the two cities [see *The Comedy of Errors*, Act I, Scene 1]. However he can pass himself off as Tranio's father Sir Vincentio of Pisa, whom he resembles, lodge with Tranio and assure his future father-in-law of the worth of the dower. The schoolmaster agrees to the plan.

Scene 3

When Katharina, in Petruchio's house, begs Grumio to let her have some food he taunts her with various dishes but refuses to serve them. Accompanied by Hortensio Petruchio brings in a dish of meat and sets it on the table. Katharina is made to thank him for the meal but Hortensio sits down with her and takes most of it.

A tailor enters with a haberdasher who produces a cap ordered by Petruchio. Katharina likes it "And gentlewomen wear such caps as these" but Petruchio dismisses it, telling her "When you are gentle, you shall have one too; and not till then."

The haberdasher withdraws while the tailor shows a gown which equally pleases Katharina.

However to her increasing fury Petruchio finds fault with it, bickering with the tailor over the details of the order, which was placed by Grumio. Petruchio waves it away while instructing Hortensio confidentially to see that the tailor is paid for it.

Finally he prepares to take Katharina to her father's house, intentionally mistaking the time and concluding "It shall be what o'clock I say it is."

Scene 4

In Padua Tranio (as Lucentio) brings the school-master, dressed as Vincentio, to Baptista's house. Biondello joins them, having told Baptista that Lucentio's father had come to Padua. Baptista and Lucentio (Cambio) arrive and the false Vincentio is introduced. Baptista is satisfied with the dowry arrangements but will not allow Tranio and Bianca to be betrothed in his house since "Pitchers have ears" and the elderly Gremio may interfere. They arrange to meet at Tranio's lodgings, together with Bianca and a scrivener.

Tranio, Baptista and 'Vincentio' leave Biondello with Lucentio, whom he advises to marry Bianca quickly at St. Luke's before she is wed to Tranio, in the guise of Lucentio.

Scene 5

On the way to Padua Petruchio continues to domineer waywardly, calling the sun the moon and correcting Katharina when she meekly agrees. On encountering the real Vincentio on the road Petruchio addresses him as a beauteous maiden. Katharina follows suit and is again crossed and apologetic when Petruchio points out that it is an old man. He informs Vincentio that his son is to be married to his wife's sister and they travel onward together.

Act V

Scene 1

Lucentio (Cambio) and Bianca scurry off to church with Biondello while Gremio waits for Cambio near Lucentio's house. Petruchio, Katharina, Vincentio and attendants arrive and knock at the door. The schoolmaster, as Vincentio, appears at the window; Petruchio asks him to advise Lucentio that his father has arrived from Pisa, only to be told that his father has come from Padua and is now at the window in front of him.

Petruchio and Katharina stand aside as Vincentio sees Biondello returning and appeals to him to identify the real Vincentio. When Biondello indicates the schoolmaster Vincentio beats him and drives him away. The schoolmaster descends and appears with Baptista, Tranio and their staff. Tranio demands to know why Vincentio is beating his servant. Vincentio unmasks Tranio (Lucentio), pointing out that his father is not himself but a sailmaker in Bergamo. Tranio brazenly calls an officer to arrest Vincentio but Gremio prevents his being taken to prison.

Biondello returns with Lucentio and Bianca, now married. They kneel to Vincentio while Biondello, Tranio and the schoolmaster make themselves scarce. Lucentio explains the whole situation to Baptista and asks pardon for Tranio, who has acted on his orders. They all go indoors leaving Petruchio to persuade the modest Katharina to kiss him in the street.

Scene 2

A banquet has been set out in Lucentio's house. Baptista, Vincentio, Gremio, the schoolmaster, Lucentio, Bianca, Petruchio, Katharina, Hortensio and his wealthy widow form a convivial group with Tranio, Biondello, Grumio and others. Petruchio remarks that Hortensio is afraid of his new wife, the widow, who retorts that "He that is giddy thinks the world turns round", provoking a riposte from Katharina.

When the ladies withdraw Tranio ventures the opinion that Katharina is holding her own with Petruchio. In refutation Petruchio proposes a wager of one hundred crowns, to be won by him whose wife comes obediently when he calls. Lucentio accepts and sends Biondello to 'bid' Bianca come; Biondello comes back with the message that she is busy and cannot do so. Hortensio then sends Biondello to 'entreat' the widow to come to him; Biondello returns to say that she bids Hortensio come to her instead.

Petruchio scoffs and tells Grumio to 'command' his wife to come to him. To the others' amazement Katharina immediately enters and is sent to fetch the other wives who were merely gossiping by the parlour fire. Baptista congratulates Petruchio and adds the dowry of twenty thousand crowns to the wager.

Katharina brings Bianca and the widow in. When Petruchio orders her to pull off her cap and throw it on the floor she does so. The other women are scandalised by this subservience, only to receive a lecture from Katharina on the virtues of wifely obedience as a complement to a husband's care and support. Hortensio acknowledges that Petruchio "hast tam'd a curst shrew."

The Tempest

Written in 1611, this is probably the last Shakespeare play of which he was the sole author (see *Henry VIII*). The plot seems to be loosely based on a pamphlet (1610) describing the shipwreck of Sir George Somers on Bermuda while on his way to colonise Virginia and may have drawn material from Montaigne's essay *Of Cannibals* (1603).

Act I

Scene 1

Alonso, King of Naples, is returning by sea from the wedding feast of his daughter Claribel to the King of Tunis. The ship has been caught up in a violent storm and the Master and Boatswain urge the mariners to greater efforts to avoid running aground.

Alonso comes on deck with his brother Sebastian, his son Ferdinand, a noble Neapolitan counsellor Gonzalo and Antonio, the self-proclaimed Duke of Milan. The Boatswain orders them back to their cabins; Alonso complies but the others return and get in the way of the sailors. Antonio and Sebastian curse the Boatswain but Gonzalo is more tolerant. As the ship appears to be running aground on an island the passengers leap overboard and swim for it.

Scene 2

On the island a young girl, Miranda, has seen the wreck and beseeches her father Prospero to abate the storm if he has used his magical powers to conjure it up. Telling her that nobody has been drowned and that all was done for her sake Prospero lays aside his magic gown, saying that the time has come for her to know her history.

Twelve years ago (when Miranda was not yet three years old) he was the proper Duke of Milan. He had immersed himself in the study of "the liberal arts", leaving the governing of Milan to his brother Antonio. In the course of time Antonio's greed for power led him to acknowledge the King of Naples and offer him annual tribute if the king would help to overthrow Prospero. King Alonso accordingly sent his forces to Milan, the gates being opened to them at midnight by Antonio.

Thus Antonio seized the dukedom but he and Alonso refrained from killing Prospero and his daughter, fearing the reaction of the Milanese citizens. Instead they ordered Gonzalo to cast the two adrift in an old, unseaworthy boat. He covertly put aboard a quantity of food, water, clothes and other requisites including especially a number of books from Prospero's library. Providence brought them to the island, where they have lived ever since.

Prospero resumes his gown, remarking that Fate has now brought his enemies to his shores. He sends Miranda to sleep by magic and summons Ariel, a spirit of the air who had called up the tempest for him. Ariel reports that he frightened the passengers into jumping overboard and they are now dispersed round the island. However he brought the ship safely into harbour, with the crew asleep below decks, while the remainder of the fleet has reassembled and is sailing on to Naples, thinking the king and his party lost.

When Ariel begs for his liberty as a reward for his honest labours Prospero accuses him of ingratitude. He reminds Ariel that when he and Miranda were cast away on the island they found a savage and deformed boy called Caliban, whose mother Sycorax was a witch who had earlier been banished from Algiers while pregnant. Ariel had been her servant at the time; because he would not obey her foul demands she had imprisoned him in a cleft pine tree. Later Sycorax died but Ariel had remained fast in the tree until Prospero arrived and freed him by his magic art.

Prospero then relents. If Ariel will transform himself into a nymph visible only to him he will free him in two days' time; otherwise he will be imprisoned again, in an oak tree. Ariel departs as Miranda awakes. She will not go with Prospero to visit his slave Caliban, whom she detests, so Prospero calls him to bring more firewood.

Caliban enters and accuses them of taking his island from him by magic arts and keeping him in a cave, after Prospero had initially educated him. Prospero points out that Caliban had repaid his kindness by attempting to rape Miranda, to which Caliban retorts that he regrets only that he was unsuccessful.

The invisible Ariel lures Prince Ferdinand to Prospero's cell with songs ("Come unto these yellow sands, And then take hands:" and "Full fathom five thy father lies;"). Miranda is enchanted by Ferdinand who seems godlike to her, being the first man she has seen apart from her father and Caliban. Ferdinand, in love at first sight and believing his father drowned, offers to marry her and make her Queen of Naples.

Prospero considers that Ferdinand may not value Miranda if he wins her too easily so he immures him as a spy. Miranda comforts Ferdinand, who feels that he can endure imprisonment as long as he can see Miranda every day.

Act II

Scene 1

Elsewhere on the island Gonzalo tries to console Alonso who believes that his son has been drowned, although according to Francisco, a nobleman, he was swimming strongly. Gonzalo expounds his theory of

Act I, Scene 2

Ariel, as a sea-nymph visible only to Prospero, lures Prince Ferdinand to Prospero's cell with songs. Miranda is enchanted by Ferinand, who is the first man she has seen apart from her father and his slave Caliban.

how the island could be run as a bucolic socialist community; he puzzles Adrian, another noble, wearies Alonso and is mocked by Antonio and Sebastian.

The unseen Ariel causes most of the castaways to drowse. Antonio tempts Sebastian to take the opportunity to kill Alonso and thus gain the throne of Naples (since Ferdinand is presumed drowned and the heiress Claribel is now Queen of Tunis), just as he himself usurped Prospero in Milan. They draw their swords; Sebastian recoils from fratricide but agrees to despatch Gonzalo if Antonio will kill Alonso.

Ariel hastily wakens Gonzalo by singing in his ear. Gonzalo rouses Alonso who enquires why the other two have their swords drawn. He accepts the explanation that they heard bulls or lions roaring and the party goes off to look for Ferdinand.

Scene 2

Thunder is heard as Caliban, carrying logs in another part of the island, sees someone approaching and hides under his gabardine cloak, fearing that it may be a tormenting spirit. In fact it is Trinculo, Alonso's court jester, who is seeking shelter from the rain. He spots the cloak and crawls under it also.

Stephano, Alonso's butler, reels in singing, having reached the island floating on a barrel of sack, some of which he is drinking. He is astonished to find a creature with four legs and two voices (the cloak) but when Trinculo answers him he shares the wine with the others. To Caliban, who has known no alcohol, it is a heavenly liquor and Stephano must be a god, or at least the man in the moon. He swears subservience to him instead of Prospero and the three stagger off so that Caliban can show them the treasures of the island.

Act III

Scene 1

Near Prospero's cell Ferdinand is piling logs. Miranda appears and offers to help, thinking that her father will be preoccupied with his books for three hours. In fact Prospero is listening in the background. Ferdinand assures Miranda that his task is lightened by the thought that his toil is for her. As the conversation develops they confess their deep love for each other, to Prospero's satisfaction.

Scene 2

In another part of the island Caliban tells Stephano and Trinculo that Prospero has taken his inheritance (the island) by cunning. The invisible Ariel arrives and, using Trinculo's voice, calls the other two liars. When, as a result, Trinculo is insulted by Caliban and struck by Stephano he attributes their behaviour to their tipsy state.

Caliban goes on to tell Stephano that as Prospero is powerless without his books Stephano should steal them and then murder Prospero while

he is taking his siesta. Stephano can then rule the island with the beautiful Miranda as his queen. Trinculo joins the conspiracy while Ariel flies off to warn Prospero.

Scene 3

Elsewhere the royal party searching for Ferdinand is weary. As they rest a hovering Prospero causes some weird dancing creatures to bring a table and spread a banquet in front of them, to the sound of strange music, and then disappear. However when they approach the food Ariel appears, dressed as a harpy, calling down perdition on them for their cruelty to Prospero and Miranda. In a crack of thunder he causes the banquet to vanish, after which the shapes dance in again and carry the table away. Alonso is filled with remorse but Antonio and Sebastian go off defiant, having plotted to kill him that evening. Gonzalo sends Adrian after them to try to prevent the crime.

Act IV

Scene 1

Prospero, feeling that Ferdinand has suffered enough, consents to his marriage to Miranda. He summons Ariel to organise a masque to celebrate the betrothal. The spirits appear, this time impersonating Greek goddesses. Iris, goddess of the rainbow and messenger of the gods, introduces Ceres, the goddess of fertility and of the harvest. Juno, the queen of the gods, confers with Ceres while Ferdinand delights in the entertainment. Iris, instructed by Juno and Ceres, calls up some naiads [water nymphs] and a group of reapers who dance together.

The masque ends suddenly when Prospero dismisses the spirits ("We are such stuff As dreams are made on,") recollecting that he must deal with Caliban and the other conspirators. Ariel reports that he led the three into a stagnant pool where they became stuck in the mud. Prospero tells Ariel to fetch some of his rich garments and hang them on a line as a decoy; he and Ariel then become invisible, in order to watch what happens.

The conspirators appear, all mud-spattered. The jester and the butler blame Caliban for losing their wine in the pool. They enter Prospero's cave quietly and discover the robes. Stephano and Trinculo quarrel over them while Caliban scolds them, telling them to concentrate on killing Prospero. The other two ignore him and prepare to steal the clothes but all three are driven away by spirits, now in the form of hounds, set on by Prospero and Ariel.

Act V

Scene 1

Prospero, invisible in his magic robes, orders Ariel to fetch the king's party. Ariel brings in Alonso, Gonzalo, Sebastian, Antonio, Adrian and Francisco; they enter Prospero's magic circle and stand in a trance while Prospero thanks Gonzalo for his kindness and rebukes the king, his brother and the usurping duke.

Nevertheless he forgives them and Ariel assists him to assume the clothes of the Duke of Milan, singing "Where the bee sucks, there suck I....Merrily, merrily shall I live now Under the blossom that hangs on the bough." Prospero then despatches Ariel to fetch the Master and Boatswain, still asleep in the ship.

When Prospero reveals himself King Alonso restores his dukedom and asks his pardon while mourning the loss of his own son. Prospero, remarking that he has similarly lost a daughter, reveals Ferdinand and Miranda playing chess in his cave. Alonso rejoices and Gonzalo adds his blessings on the couple. Ferdinand introduces a delighted Miranda ("O brave new world, That has such people in't!").

Ariel brings in the Master and Boatswain who report, in amazement, that their ship is fully rigged and seaworthy. Ariel is praised and then sent to fetch Stephano, Trinculo, and a penitent Caliban, who appear in their stolen clothes. After being reprimanded they are waved away by Prospero who invites the king and the others to spend a night in his cave while he tells them the tale of the last twelve years. He will then sail with them to attend the wedding of Ferdinand and Miranda in Naples before returning to Milan.

Epilogue

Prospero frees Ariel and tells the audience that he has regained his dukedom and divested himself of his magical powers. He asks to be released from his spell by their applause.

Timon of Athens

The sources for this work, which is the tale of a misanthrope, include Plutarch's *Life of Marcus Antonius*, Lucian's dialogue *Timon or Misanthropus* and Paynter's *Palace of Pleasure*. The textual anomalies have led some scholars to the supposition that it is an unfinished draft for an intended play.

Act I

Scene 1

At the house of Timon, an Athenian lord, some suitors meet in the hall. A merchant admires their gifts as a jeweller displays some jewellery, a painter his picture and a poet his book of verse. Seeing a group of visiting senators the poet predicts that they will cease to court Timon if his fortunes change.

To the sound of trumpets Timon enters accompanied by a messenger and followed by Lucilius and other servants. As he greets the suitors courteously the messenger tells him that a friend, Ventidius, is in the debtors' prison. He agrees to supply the five talents [about 30,000 drachmas] owed to Ventidius' creditors and the messenger leaves.

An old Athenian approaches Timon, asking him to forbid Lucilius to continue courting his daughter and saying that he will disinherit her if she marries him. Timon offers to provide the dowry of three talents so that the two can marry and a grateful Lucilius departs with the old man.

A philosopher, Apemantus, enters. He morosely turns down an invitation to dinner, calls the poet a liar and disparages the work of the painter and the worth of the jewellery. An Athenian captain, Alcibiades, turns up with twenty cavalry officers; Timon takes them and everybody else except Apemantus off to dinner.

Two lords arrive to attend the dinner, to Apemantus' scorn. Their comments confirm that the generous Timon is known always to reward donors with gifts many times more valuable than those he receives in return.

Scene 2

In a room of state Timon's steward, Flavius, serves a banquet, to the sound of oboes. Timon ushers in Alcibiades, Ventidius, senators, lords and attendants; a discontented Apemantus lurks behind. In the spirit of true friendship Timon politely declines when Ventidius offers to repay twice the sum that he provided. He notices Apemantus, who persists with his sour comments on the guests, and offers him a separate table.

Music plays as Cupid enters with a masque of ladies dressed as Amazons, playing lutes and dancing. The lords rise, bow to Timon and select ladies with whom to dance, while Apemantus reviles them as flatterers. After the masquers leave Flavius brings in a casket from which Timon dispenses jewels to the guests, to Flavius' disapproval.

Servants announce the arrival of more senators followed by Lucius, a noble who has brought a gift of four milk-white horses with silver trappings, and Lucullus, another noble who has brought two brace of greyhounds. Flavius goes out, muttering to himself that Timon's coffers are empty because of his profligacy. Timon continues to hand out gifts, to Apemantus' sullen despisal.

Act II

Scene 1

A senator scans some papers in his house. He finds that Timon owes nine thousand crowns to Varro and Isidore and considerably more to himself. He despatches a servant, Caphis, to Timon with some bonds for immediate repayment.

Scene 2

In Timon's hall Flavius shakes his head over many bills. Caphis arrives with servants of Varro and Isidore, followed by Timon, Alcibiades and lords. Caphis and the servants present requests for payment of debts outstanding for six weeks. Timon dismisses Alcibiades and the lords while he asks Flavius why these demands are being made; Flavius proposes that the business be settled after dinner.

After Timon goes out to continue conferring with Flavius Apemantus enters with a jester. Caphis and the others taunt them, together with a page who appears briefly; they retire as Timon and Flavius return.

Timon upbraids Flavius for allowing him to get into debt but Flavius reminds him that he has often ignored his advice and thrown out the accounts when they were brought to him. Timon suggests that all his land be sold but Flavius points out that some has already been forfeited and the remainder will scarcely cover his obligations. He reproaches Timon for his prodigality and offers to bring auditors in to verify his own honesty.

Timon calls in Flaminius, Servilius and other servants and sends them to borrow fifty talents from Lord Lucius, Lord Lucullus and Sempronius and a thousand talents from the senators. Flavius tells him that he has already tried that and been refused. Timon is reduced to sending to Ventidius for the five talents which he had paid on his behalf.

Act III

Scene 1

A servant receives Flaminius at Lucullus' house. Lucullus sees a box under Flaminius' cloak and, having dreamed of a silver basin and ewer, hopes that Flaminius has brought a further gift from Timon. However the box is empty and when Flaminius asks for fifty talents to put in it Lucullus deplores the fact that Timon has ignored his frequent advice to curb his spending. He gives the servant only three solidares [small coins] and suggests, with a wink, that Flaminius hasn't found him at home. Flaminius castigates Lucullus and throws the money away.

Scene 2

In a public place in Athens Hostilius and two other strangers tell Lucius about Timon's misfortunes and Lucullus' refusal to lend him money. Lucius avers that he would not have behaved so shamefully.

Servilius appears, to say that Timon has sent to Lucius; however what he has sent is not a gift but a request for a loan. Despite his previous remarks, Lucius regrets that a large purchase the previous day has left him unable to accommodate Timon and offers him only protestations of friendship. The three strangers philosophise on man's base ingratitude.

Scene 3

Another servant has come to Sempronius' house seeking a loan for Timon. Sempronius, learning that Timon has been turned down by Lucullus, Lucius and the wealthy Ventidius (now redeemed from prison), is annoyed that he is apparently regarded as a last resort. He tells the servant that he will be a laughing stock among his friends if he lends money when the others have declined. After he goes out the servant comments on man's villainy and Timon's fate.

Scene 4

Back at Timon's house in the morning Titus, Hortensius and other creditors' servants wait with servants of Varro and Lucius for Timon to emerge. Titus wryly observes to Philotus, another newly-arrived servant, that his master is dunning Timon while at the same time wearing jewels that Timon has given him.

Flaminius appears briefly, to tell them that Timon is not ready to see them. A muffled Flavius passes through, repulsing their advances, and Servilius comes to ask them to leave. Finally Timon comes out in a rage and scatters them. When they have gone Timon orders a disapproving Flavius to invite all the creditors to one more feast.

Scene 5

Captain Alcibiades appears before the senate sitting in the Senate House. He implores them to have mercy on a friend who has given valiant service to the Greeks but has been condemned to death for murder. However the senate is obdurate and insists on execution. When Alcibiades offers his own victories and reputation to save the man the senators banish him permanently from Athens.

Scene 6

The room of state in Timon's house is again set out for a banquet. Seeing the preparations the lords and senators are under the impression that Timon's recent poverty was a pretence, in order to test their friendship, and regret having refused his requests for loans. When he enters they fawn upon him and while the covers are brought in they discuss the banishment of Alcibiades.

Timon delivers an ironic speech culminating with "Uncover, dogs, and lap." The dishes are uncovered and found to contain nothing but lukewarm water and smoke. Timon bitterly flings the water in the guests' faces, curses them and throws the dishes at them as they scramble out, losing caps, gowns and jewels in the mêlée.

Act IV

Scene 1

Outside the walls of Athens Timon turns to look back at the city. He pronounces a comprehensive curse on all Athenians and resolves to live in the woods as a hermit among the kindly beasts.

Scene 2

Flavius shares out his little remaining money with the other servants in Timon's house. They all embrace each other and disperse while the downcast Flavius decides to follow Timon and still serve him as his steward.

Scene 3

Timon emerges from a cave near the seashore and digs for some roots. He discovers a hoard of gold and, hearing a drum and fife, takes a little of it and reburies the rest. Alcibiades marches in accompanied by his mistresses Phrynia and Timandra and followed by his loyal troops.

Timon proclaims himself a misanthrope. He disdains the two harlots and tells Alcibiades to keep his offer of money and be gone. When Alcibiades mentions his plan to sack Athens Timon urges him on and furnishes him with gold to pay his soldiers. The women ask him for more, are duly cursed and leave with Alcibiades.

Apemantus comes by as Timon resumes digging. He advises Timon not to be a curmudgeon like himself, to abandon the rigours of living rough and to become a courtier again. Timon retorts that unlike Apemantus he has reason to reject human society; he insults him and drives him away by throwing a stone at him.

Three thieves come along in the guise of needy soldiers. Timon sourly hands them some gold and tells them to go and steal in Athens. When they have left Flavius appears and grieves to see Timon's slave-like habit and careworn looks. At first Timon does not recognise him but when he realises that one

Act III, Scene 6

At his banquet Timon delivers an ironic speech to his fawning guests. He then curses them and flings the dishes of lukewarm water and smoke in their faces as they scramble out, losing their caps and gowns.

144

honest man still loves him and is ready to serve him he gives Flavius gold and bids him go and live happily but show no charity to anyone.

Act V

Scene 1

The poet and painter approach the cave, attracted by the stories of Timon's gifts of gold to Alcibiades, Phrynia, Timandra and the soldiers. Overheard by Timon the painter proposes to promise him "an excellent piece" while the poet is thinking of "a satire against the softness of prosperity."

Timon comes forward, hailing them as honest men but respectfully mentioning a small fault, namely that each trusts a cheating dissembler who deceives him. When they ask for names Timon refers each of them to the other and belabours them until they flee. He re-enters his cave.

Flavius now leads in two senators and calls Timon from the cave. The visitors bring Timon greetings from the Senate and an apologetic entreaty to return to Athens. He will be loved and rewarded, they say; further, he is to take charge of the garrison and repel Alcibiades' besieging force. Timon tells them that he cares nothing for them or the fate of Athens.

However he asks sardonically to be com-mended to his countrymen and suggests that if they wish to put an end to their afflictions they should hang themselves on a tree nearby. As he withdraws he sneers that his gravestone can be their oracle.

Scene 2

In front of the walls of Athens two senators and a messenger receive the senators who visited Timon and learn that no help will be forthcoming from him.

Scene 3

A soldier comes looking for Timon but finds only a tomb near his cave. Unable to read the epitaph he takes a wax impression of it.

Scene 4

Trumpets sound a parley as Alcibiades approaches the walls of Athens. The senators on the walls offer to allow him to enter the city if he will revenge himself only on those who have offended him. Alcibiades tosses them his glove as a symbol of agreement.

The gates are opened and the soldier who found Timon's tomb hands Alcibiades the impression of the epitaph. It reads, in part: "a plague consume you wicked caitiffs left! Here lie I, Timon; who, alive, all living men did hate:" Alcibiades calls for peace and reflects that "vast Neptune" will weep for ever on Timon's seashore grave.

Titus Andronicus

The first quarto edition was entitled *The Most Lamentable Romaine Tragedie of Titus Andronicus*. It is known that a production was staged on January 23rd, 1594, just before the closure of the theatres during the Plague. The blood-soaked play may have been a redraft of Henslowe's *Titus and Vespasian* which had appeared two years earlier. The source is obscure; set in the late fourth century A.D., it is the only one of the four Roman-period plays not based on North's *Plutarch*.

Act I

Scene 1

At the Andronicus tomb in Rome the tribunes and senators look down as Saturninus enters from one side and his brother Bassianus from the other with their respective followers. Saturninus calls on the patricians and plebeians to support his claim to the imperial diadem as the late emperor's first-born son. Bassianus asks for a straight election.

A tribune standing aloft, Marcus Andronicus, holds up the crown and declares that the people have already chosen his brother, Titus Andronicus surnamed Pius, a valiant general who has been summoned home by the senate after a ten-year struggle against the Goths [Dacians]. Saturninus and Bassianus withdraw their claims and everyone goes up to the senate-house.

A captain announces the arrival of a procession, to the sound of trumpets and drums. A coffin draped in black is borne in by two men; it is preceded by two of Titus' sons, Martius and Mutius, and followed by two others, Lucius and Quintus. Then comes Titus himself followed by Tamora, the captive queen of the Goths, with her sons Alarbus, Demetrius and Chiron. After them come Aaron, a Moor, and other Goth prisoners followed by soldiers and citizens. The coffin is set down.

Titus addresses the assembly and commits the coffin, containing one of his many sons, to the vault. Another son, Lucius, calls for the "proudest" Gothic prisoner to be immolated on a pyre to appease the gods. Titus nominates Tamora's eldest son, Alarbus, spurning the queen's desperate entreaties. The four sons take Alarbus out and return shortly with bloodstained swords to report that the sacrifice has been made.

Titus' daughter Lavinia enters and kneels to him. She is followed by Marcus, Saturninus, Bassianus and others. Marcus offers Titus a white candidate's robe but Titus declines the emperorship and asks the loyal tribunes to crown Saturninus. The grateful Saturninus announces that he will marry Lavinia in the Pantheon [Hadrian's rotunda] and make her his empress. Saturninus goes on to free the prisoners and assure the weeping Tamora that she will be treated as befits a queen.

However Bassianus suddenly seizes Lavinia, asserting that she is his. Before they can be stopped Marcus and Bassianus carry Lavinia off. They are aided by Lucius, Quintus and Martius while Mutius guards the door. Titus, barred by his youngest son, stabs him to death.

A horrified Lucius returns briefly and censures Titus. Saturninus tells Titus, to his distress, that he doesn't need Lavinia or any other member of his family. He turns to Tamora and offers to make her his bride and empress; Tamora gladly accepts and all leave except Titus.

Marcus re-enters with Titus' three remaining sons and adds his condemnation for the slaying of Mutius. Titus maintains that Mutius dishonoured his name and shall not be buried in the family sepulchre. The others plead with him until he relents.

Saturninus returns with his new wife Tamora accompanied by Demetrius (now her eldest son), Chiron and Aaron. He glowers at Bassianus who is returning with his new bride Lavinia and others. Bassianus and Tamora publicly entreat him to return Titus to favour while Tamora assures him privately that she will massacre the cruel Titus and his sons at some later time. She goes on to plead for Marcus also and Saturninus allows himself to be persuaded to forgive the Andronicus brothers and Lavinia.

Act II

Scene 1

In front of the palace Aaron muses on the opportunities opening up for him as a result of Tamora's elevation. Demetrius and Chiron swagger in, disputing their right to deflower Lavinia, and draw their rapiers. Aaron tells them not to be so foolish as to duel openly. He suggests that they waylay Lavinia jointly while the Roman ladies are watching the hunting in the forest.

Scene 2

At dawn in the moonlit forest Titus heads a band of huntsmen including Marcus, Lucius, Quintus and Martius, as hunting horns and the baying of hounds are heard. They are joined by Saturninus, Tamora, Bassianus, Lavinia, Demetrius, Chiron and a party of attendants. The emperor calls for horses and chariots to begin the hunt.

Scene 3

Elsewhere in the forest Aaron conceals a bag of gold under an elder tree overhanging a pit. Tamora comes along and invites him to dally in the shade like Aeneas and Dido in their cave. Aaron tells her that her sons are plotting to kill Bassianus and ravish

Act I, Scene 1

Bassianus and Marcus carry off Titus' daughter Lavinia, aided by Lucius, Quintus and Marcius.
Titus Andronicus, barred at the door by his youngest son Mutius, savagely stabs him to death.

Lavinia. Seeing the couple coming Aaron hands her a scroll for the emperor and goes to fetch her sons. Bassianus and Lavinia appear; they reprove Tamora for her involvement with Aaron and speak of informing her husband.

When Demetrius and Chiron arrive Tamora tells them that Bassianus and Lavinia have lured her to this spot and have threatened to bind her to a yew tree and abandon her to her fate as an adulteress. Demetrius immediately stabs Bassianus to death. Tamora is anxious to finish off Lavinia too but the two youths are intent on her violation. Tamora rejects her piteous pleas for mercy and looks on as Demetrius throws Bassianus' body into a pit and drags Lavinia away with his brother.

Aaron returns with Quintus and Martius; in the gloom Martius tumbles into the pit. Aaron goes to fetch the emperor, hoping that he will think that the two men were responsible for Bassianus' death. Martius tells Quintus about the corpse and beseeches him to help him out. Quintus is quaking with fear; when he weakly attempts to assist Martius he falls into the pit as well.

Saturninus is brought in by Aaron; he calls down and is told by Martius that his brother's body is in the pit. Tamora and her attendants appear with Titus and Lucius. She hands Saturninus the scroll which purports to be from the assassins and advises him to look among the nettles under the elder tree. Aaron produces the gold.

As planned, Saturninus is convinced that Quintus and Martius are his brother's murderers. He rejects Titus' plea for bail and orders that they be imprisoned until he has devised a suitable torture for them.

Scene 4

In another part of the forest Demetrius and Chiron leave the ravished Lavinia with her hands cut off and her tongue cut out. She is found by her uncle Marcus who is appalled at this butchery.

Act III

Scene 1

Senators, tribunes and judges are conducting Martius and Quintus, who are bound, along a Roman street to a place of execution. Titus pleads unavailingly for mercy for his sons. Lucius appears with drawn sword, having been banished for attempting to rescue his brothers. Titus' anguish is compounded when they are joined by Marcus and the mutilated Lavinia.

Aaron brings Titus a message from Saturninus that his sons can be ransomed if he or Marcus or Lucius will chop off a hand and send it to him. All three offer to sacrifice a hand. While Lucius and Marcus go to find an axe Aaron cuts Titus' left hand off, at his command. Lucius and Marcus return as Aaron goes to take the severed hand to the emperor. Titus and Lavinia kneel in sorrowful prayer.

A messenger brings Titus' hand back together with the heads of Martius and Quintus. In raging misery Titus swears a terrible revenge. He takes one severed head and Marcus the other, while Lavinia carries the hand in her teeth. Lucius is sent to raise an army with the Goths.

Scene 2

Titus is banqueting in his house with Lavinia, Marcus and young Lucius [his grandson]. Marcus swats a fly and Titus upbraids him, becoming slightly unhinged. When Marcus compares the black fly with the dark-skinned Aaron, Titus approves.

Act IV

Scene 1

Titus and Marcus have moved into the garden. Young Lucius runs in dropping some books, pursued by Lavinia making frantic signs. Lavinia finds Ovid's *Metamorphoses* among the books and manages to turn the pages to the story of Tereus and Philomela [in which rape and beheading feature]. Titus shows her how to manipulate a staff and with it she manages to write the names of Chiron and Demetrius in the sand together with the Latin word for 'rape'. The others renew their vows of revenge against the Goths.

Scene 2

Aaron, Demetrius and Chiron enter a room in the palace and see young Lucius and an attendant enter from the other side carrying weapons with verses wrapped round them. The boy tells them that their crime has been detected and that Titus has sent them some weapons. He leaves and they read a Latin quotation from Horace: "He who is whole and pure in life needs neither the Moor's javelin nor his bow." They scoff at the threat.

Trumpets sound and a nurse brings in a new-born dark-skinned baby. She tells Aaron that the shamed Tamora has sent his son to him to be killed. Aaron refuses and prevents Chiron and Demetrius from killing their new stepbrother. The three discuss what to do. Learning from the nurse that only she, the mother and Cornelia the midwife have seen the child Aaron stabs her. He tells the others that the wife of a fellow countryman of his, Muli, has recently given birth to a fair-skinned child. He proposes to substitute it for Tamora's. Demetrius and Chiron carry the nurse's body out and Aaron takes the baby to be brought up by the Goths.

Scene 3

Titus is now crazed with grief and hatred. He enters a public place with two of his relatives, Sempronius and Caius, young Lucius and Marcus with his son Publius. He gives them arrows with letters on them to shoot into the air and claims that they have hit various Zodiacal signs.

A carrier brings two pigeons in a basket. Titus gives him money and instructs him to take the pigeons to the emperor together with a supplication wrapped round a knife.

Scene 4

Near the palace the vexed Saturninus picks up some of the arrows, marked Apollo, Mars, Mercury etc. and shows them to Tamora, Demetrius, Chiron and other lords. Tamora tries to calm him as the carrier brings the pigeons and the document. Saturninus reads it and is infuriated; he orders the carrier to be taken away and hanged.

A nobleman, Aemilius, arrives to report that Lucius has raised an army of Goths to attack Rome. Saturninus fears that the people will turn to him.

Tamora sends Aemilius to Lucius with a request from the emperor for a parley at Andronicus' house; she proposes to coax Titus to win Lucius over.

Act V

Scene 1

Lucius and his men march over the plains near Rome. He has letters from Romans welcoming the Goths and expressing their loathing for the emperor. One of the Goths has come upon Aaron near a ruined monastery and brings him to Lucius with his dusky child in his arms. Lucius, recalling that Aaron amputated his father's hand, orders the two to be hanged from the nearest tree.

A ladder is brought as Aaron pleads for the baby's life. In return for Lucius' promise to spare it he flaunts his wickedness, informing the horrified Lucius that he is the father of Tamora's baby, that her sons mutilated his sister and murdered Bassianus and that he (Aaron) lured his brothers to the pit, hid the gold and wrote the incriminating letter.

Aemilius is brought in by another Goth. He delivers the message about the proposed parley and Lucius agrees.

Scene 2

Tamora, Demetrius and Chiron arrive in disguise at Titus' house. Titus appears at an upper window and recognises them. However she persuades him that she is Revenge and that her sons are Rapine and Murder. He comes down and welcomes them, telling them to go and slay their counterparts, the empress and her sons. Tamora assures him that if he will invite his son Lucius to a banquet she will produce not only the empress and her sons but the emperor and his other enemies, who will all kneel to him.

When Marcus arrives Titus sends him to Lucius

with the invitation, while Tamora leaves to report to Saturninus. Titus calls Publius, Caius and Valentine and orders them to seize Rapine and Murder and bind them.

Titus leaves and returns with a knife accompanied by Lavinia who carries a basin in her forearms. He tells Demetrius and Chiron that as they killed Lavinia's husband (for which her brothers were condemned to death) and ravished and mutilated Lavinia, he will serve their heads, cooked in their own blood, to their mother at the coming banquet. He cuts their throats while Lavinia holds the basin between her stumps, to collect the blood.

Scene 3

Lucius, Marcus and some Goths enter the court of Titus' house with Aaron as a prisoner. The Goths remove Aaron as trumpets sound the entry of Saturninus and Tamora with Aemilius, senators, tribunes and others. They take their seats as oboes play.

Titus enters dressed as a chef with young Lucius and Lavinia, veiled. He places some dishes on the table and welcomes the guests. Turning to Saturninus he asks him if Virginius [in a well-known tale] was right to slay his daughter to prevent her being ravished. Saturninus replies that he was. Titus then kills Lavinia, having "a thousand times more cause" than Virginius.

He fiendishly tells the shocked Saturninus that Tamora's sons were responsible for Lavinia's shame and torture and that Tamora is now eating a pie in which they are baked. He kills Tamora and is promptly slain by Saturninus. Lucius in turn kills the emperor.

In the ensuing tumult Marcus and Lucius go up to the balcony with their friends while the panic-stricken guests scramble out. Marcus calls on Lucius to explain the carnage and Lucius does so, calling attention to his own banishment. Marcus refers to Tamora's baby and recalls that Aaron is in the house.

Aemilius leads the Romans in hailing Lucius as the new emperor. Marcus orders attendants to fetch Aaron as he and Lucius descend from the balcony and bid young Lucius say farewell to his grandfather.

Aaron is brought in, still defiant, and is condemned to be buried breast-deep in the earth and left to starve to death. Lucius orders that the bodies of Saturninus, Titus and Lavinia be taken to their respective family tombs while Tamora's body be cast out to the beasts and birds of prey. He promises the people to govern Rome well and "wipe away her woe".

The Tragedy of King Richard II

This is the opening play of the eight which form Shakespeare's so-called 'history-cycle' and is based on Raphael Holinshed's *Chronicles*. It is written in verse throughout. The action revolves around Richard II of Bordeaux, the younger son of Edward the Black Prince and Joan the Fair Maid of Kent, and runs from the autumn of 1398 to his death in February, 1400.

Act I

Scene 1

At the royal palace in London John of Gaunt, the Duke of Lancaster, informs his nephew King Richard II that he has brought his son Henry Bolingbroke, Duke of Hereford, to court to resolve his dispute with Thomas Mowbray, the Duke of Norfolk. Attendants bring in Bolingbroke and Mowbray who greet the king.

Bolingbroke condemns Mowbray as a traitor and miscreant while he in turn brands Bolingbroke a slanderous coward and a villain. Bolingbroke throws down a challenge, disdaining to rely on the fact that he is the king's cousin. He asserts that Mowbray kept for his own use eight thousand nobles intended for the royal troops and also plotted the death of his father's youngest brother, Thomas of Woodstock, Duke of Gloucester [smothered in a Calais prison]. Mowbray denies that he slew Gloucester and retorts that three quarters of the money was properly disbursed and the rest set off against an outstanding debt owed him by the king.

Richard bids them desist; he will calm Mowbray if Gaunt will do the same with Bolingbroke. "Lions make leopards tame," he says, to which Mowbray responds, "Yea, but not change his spots," meaning that his name will still be dishonoured. Bolingbroke is equally defiant. Richard thereupon abandons his efforts and commands the two to settle the matter by a jousting duel at Coventry on St. Lambert's day.

Scene 2

Eleanor, the widowed Duchess of Gloucester, pleads with John of Gaunt in his palace to avenge her husband's murder but his allegiance to the king, as God's deputy, takes precedence. She bids him commend her to another brother-in-law Edmund of Langley, Duke of York, before she does away with herself.

Scene 3

Tournament lists and a throne have been set up in an open space near Coventry. The Lord Marshal checks with the Duke of Aumerle, son of the Duke of York, that Bolingbroke and Mowbray are fully accoutred. To a flourish of trumpets Richard takes his seat on the throne surrounded by Gaunt and the royal servants Bushy, Bagot and Green.

To the sound of more trumpets Mowbray enters in armour preceded by a herald. He formally states his name and his challenge. Bolingbroke makes a similar entry and affirmation. The king descends to embrace him and all resume their seats. The Lord Marshal equips the two with lances and the heralds proclaim the contest. However at the last moment, to avoid bloodshed, the king throws down his baton and decrees that the combatants be banished instead, Bolingbroke for ten years and Mowbray for life. He further orders the two neither to make contact in their banishment nor plot against him.

Mowbray laments that in banishment he must forego English, his native tongue, and leaves. Richard reduces Bolingbroke's sentence to six years while his father Gaunt fears that even in that period he himself will have died. The king departs with his retinue while Bolingbroke takes a dolorous farewell of his father and Aumerle.

Scene 4

Richard, with Bagot and Green in his London castle, receives Aumerle, who is offhand about Bolingbroke's departure. Noting glumly that Bolingbroke courted favour with the common people, Richard turns to the planning of his Irish campaign. Bushy enters to report that Gaunt is very ill at Ely House; Richard prepares to visit him, cynically hoping that he will arrive too late.

Act II

Scene 1

In Ely House Gaunt lies on a couch with his brother York and others standing nearby. While York decries Richard's susceptibility to flattery Gaunt hopes that he will come. He launches into a famous patriotic speech extolling the virtues of "This precious stone set in the silver sea....This blessed plot, this earth, this realm, this England."

Richard enters with his queen [Isabella, daughter of Charles VI of France], Aumerle, Bushy, Green, Bagot, Lord Ross and Lord Willoughby. Gaunt compares his own ailing condition with that of England under the king, whose poor reputation would have shamed his grandfather [Edward III]. He is carried out and Northumberland enters soon afterwards to report that he has died.

Richard at once seizes Gaunt's possessions to aid him with the expenses of the Irish expedition. Before York goes he protests, pointing out that Richard will be disinheriting Gaunt's son, the banished Bolingbroke, and warning him of dire consequences.

The king sends Bushy to fetch the Earl of Wiltshire, appoints York lord governor of England in his own absence in Ireland and leaves with his

Act II, Scene 1

In Ely House the dying John of Gaunt compares his illness with that of England under King Richard II, whose poor reputation would have shamed his grandfather, Edward III. Queen Isabella and Gaunt's brother, the duke of York, listen.

retinue. Northumberland is left to discuss with Ross and Willoughby the way in which Richard has alienated the aristocracy and commoners. He tells them that he has heard from Port le Blanc in Brittany that Bolingbroke and a group of nobles have been furnished with eight tall ships and three thousand men by the Duke of Britaine and will shortly be landing at Ravenspurgh [Ravenspur, a port south of Whitby, now washed away].

Scene 2

Queen Isabella confesses her sadness at Richard's departure to Bushy and Bagot in the palace. Green enters, hoping that the king has not set sail since Bolingbroke has now landed and been joined by Northumberland, Hotspur, Worcester, Ross, Beaumond and Willoughby. York comes and compounds the queen's despair. On ordering a servant to go to the Duchess of Gloucester to borrow a thousand pounds he learns that she has just died. He bids the others muster their men and meet him at Berkeley Castle.

When York has left with the queen Green and Bushy gloomily propose to take refuge in Bristol Castle with the Earl of Wiltshire but Bagot decides to join the king in Ireland.

Scene 3

Bolingbroke and Northumberland have reached Gloucestershire with their forces. Hotspur meets them and is introduced to Bolingbroke. He points out Berkeley Castle [near the Severn Estuary] where York awaits them with Lord Berkeley, Seymour and three hundred men. Ross and Willoughby arrive and are welcomed.

They are followed by Berkeley and then by York, with attendants. York brands Bolingbroke a traitor who has moreover been banished. Bolingbroke retorts that he is now the Duke of Lancaster just as Aumerle would be Duke of York if his father died. He has come to take back his inheritance, supported by Northumberland, Ross and Willoughby.

York acknowledges his rights but asserts that they do not excuse rebellion; however as his forces are weak he cannot oppose him. Bolingbroke accepts his offer to stay overnight in the castle and tries to persuade him to accompany the rebels to Bristol Castle later.

Scene 4

At a camp in Wales a captain tells the Earl of Salisbury that his men will wait no longer for Richard, who is thought to be dead. Salisbury cannot prevent their dispersal.

Act III

Scene 1

Bolingbroke has Bushy and Green prisoner in his camp near Bristol. In the presence of Northumberland, York, Hotspur, Ross, Willoughby and officers he condemns them to death, accusing them of not only causing a rift between the king and queen but procuring his own banishment and pillaging his estates. He sends his compliments to the queen and takes his supporters off to join Owen Glendower.

Scene 2

Richard has landed at Barkloughly Castle on the Welsh coast with the Bishop of Carlisle, Aumerle and soldiers. Salisbury arrives to tell him that 12,000 Welsh fighting men have defected to Bolingbroke. He is followed by Sir Stephen Scroop with the news that Bushy, Green and Wiltshire have been executed. Richard is despondent ("let us sit upon the ground And tell sad stories of the death of kings;"). Learning that York has also joined Bolingbroke he decides to retreat to Flint Castle [on the Dee estuary in North Wales].

Scene 3

Bolingbroke, York, Northumberland and their supporters arrive at Flint Castle with drum and colours. They are met by Hotspur who tells them that Richard is inside, with Aumerle, Salisbury, Scroop and the Bishop of Carlisle. Bolingbroke asks Northumberland to go and seek the repeal of his banishment from the king.

The trumpets sound a parley as Richard appears on the castle walls accompanied by the four nobles. Richard reminds Bolingbroke that he is king by divine right; Northumberland answers that Bolingbroke is asking only for his re-enfranchisement and will bend his knee to the king; Richard accedes to his demands. After further consultation Richard agrees to descend and Bolingbroke and the others genuflect. He and the king leave for London.

Scene 4

Queen Isabella and two ladies are idling in the Duke of York's garden at Langley. They withdraw as a gardener approaches and instructs one of his two under-gardeners to prune the apricot trees.

As the men gossip the queen learns of the deaths of the royal supporters and the seizure of Richard by Bolingbroke. She comes forward to reprove the gardener for talking of the king's deposition. Being assured that the story is true she makes ready to travel to London.

Act IV

Scene 1

In Westminster Hall the Lords spiritual face the Lords temporal with the Commons below. Bolingbroke enters with Aumerle, Northumberland, the Duke of Surrey, Hotspur, Lord Fitzwater, another lord, the Bishop of Carlisle, the Abbot of Westminster and officers with Bagot in the rear.

Bolingbroke calls Bagot forward and asks for the details of Gloucester's murder. Bagot accuses Aumerle of complicity and of opposing Bolingbroke's return to England. Fitzwater corroborates his account, saying that Mowbray had overheard Aumerle sending two men to Calais to assassinate Gloucester. He and Hotspur challenge Aumerle but Surrey comes to his support, calling Fitzwater a liar.

Bolingbroke defers Aumerle's trial until Mowbray returns to England but is informed by Carlisle that he has died in Venice. York enters with a message from Richard ceding the throne to Bolingbroke. Carlisle objects to a traitor's assumption of the crown in the absence of Richard; he is promptly arrested by Northumberland and placed in the Abbot's charge.

York is sent to fetch Richard, who enters with his officers and formally hands the crown and sceptre over to Bolingbroke. He refuses to read out a list of his 'crimes' produced by Northumberland and when a mirror is brought in he contemplates his reflection before dashing it to the ground. Richard asks leave to go and is escorted to the Tower.

Bolingbroke sets his coronation for the following Wednesday and departs, leaving the Abbot hatching a plot with Aumerle and Carlisle.

Act V

Scene 1

The queen and her ladies detain the king as he approaches the Tower under guard. Richard consoles her and advises her to cloister herself in a French religious house. He is overtaken by Northumberland who informs him that Bolingbroke has changed his mind; Richard is now to go to Pomfret [Pontefract, southeast of Leeds] and Isabella to France. The king and queen embrace each other before parting.

Scene 2

In his palace York describes to his wife Bolingbroke's arrival in London on the king's roan horse Barbary, to the cheers of the populace, followed by Richard, at whom they scowled and threw rubbish.

Aumerle, now to be known as Rutland, enters with a paper showing at his chest. York manages to snatch it and finds that a dozen men are conspiring to kill the king at Oxford. Despite the Duchess' pleas he orders his boots to be brought and his horse saddled, intending to impeach his son. After he goes out she urges Aumerle to take his horse, get to the king and ask his pardon before York arrives.

Scene 3

Bolingbroke, now King Henry IV, enters a room at Windsor Castle with Hotspur and other lords. He asks Hotspur for news of his son, the profligate Prince Hal who spends his time in London taverns. Aumerle enters and requests a private audience. He locks the door behind the others but York's voice is heard warning that he is a traitor.

Henry admits York and relocks the door. York shows him the paper that he took from Aumerle and the Duchess' voice is now heard outside the door. She is admitted by her son Aumerle and pleads for his life as all kneel to Henry. Eventually Henry pardons Aumerle and swears vengeance on the Abbot of Westminster and his colleagues.

Scene 4

In another room in the castle Sir Pierce of Exton [or Piers Exton], having heard Henry call for a friend to rid him "of this living fear", reveals to a servant that he is off to Pomfret to rid Henry of his foe Richard.

Scene 5

Richard muses on his fate in the dungeon of Pomfret Castle. A faithful groom who has obtained admittance cheers him. A keeper enters with a dish and dismisses the groom. When he refuses to taste the dish first, on Exton's orders, Richard strikes him. Exton rushes in with two armed servants; Richard grabs a sword and runs them through but Exton strikes him down.

Scene 6

Back in Windsor Castle Northumberland announces to Henry and York that he has despatched the heads of Salisbury, Spencer, Blunt and Kent to London. Fitzwater similarly reports that he has sent the heads of two plotters, Brocas and Sir Bennet Sely, from Oxford. Hotspur then arrives with the Bishop of Carlisle to state that the Abbot is dead. Finally Exton brings in a coffin with Richard's corpse but is sent into exile by Henry for the murderous deed.

The Tragedy of King Richard III

The action of this, the last play of the so-called history-cycle, runs from 1471 to the Battle of Bosworth in 1485 (the culmination of the Wars of the Roses). The main source, apart from Raphael Holinshed's *Chronicles*, was Edward Hall's *Union of the Two Noble and Illustrate Families of Lancaster and York* (1548). Both books drew on Sir Thomas More's *Historia Ricardi Tertii*. However Shakespeare compressed events, changed their order and invented new incidents to construct the play.

Act I

Scene 1

Richard Duke of Gloucester is musing in a London street. He notes that the people are enjoying peace under a Yorkist king ("Now is the winter of our discontent Made glorious summer by this sun of York;"). However being deformed and ugly he can take no pleasure in dalliance and will find satisfaction in villainy [as presaged in part 3 of *Henry VI*, Act III, Scene 2]. He plans to exploit the dissension that he has caused between two of his brothers, the King (Edward IV) and George Duke of Clarence.

Clarence is marched in, guarded by Sir Robert Brakenbury, Lieutenant of the Tower of London. He is to be imprisoned in the Tower because the king is heeding a prophecy that 'G' [signifying George] shall be the murderer of Edward's heirs. Richard falsely sympathises with Clarence, remarking that it is Queen Elizabeth (widow of Sir John Grey) and Earl Rivers (her brother Antony Woodville) that are responsible, having already persuaded the king to send the Lord Chamberlain (William Lord Hastings) to the Tower. He promises to do all in his power to have Clarence released.

When Clarence has gone the recently freed Hastings passes by, telling Richard that the king is extremely ill and that his physicians fear for his life. In a soliloquy Richard reveals his wicked plans to have Clarence killed before the King dies and to marry the Lady Anne Neville, despite the fact that he himself slew both her father, the Lancastrian king Henry VI in the Tower, and her husband, Edward Prince of Wales, at Tewkesbury [part 3 of *Henry VI*, Act V, Scene 5].

Scene 2

The funeral procession of King Henry VI is passing along another street, on its way from St. Paul's to Chertsey monastery. Lady Anne, as a mourner, laments the untimely deaths of her father-in-law and husband and vilifies their killer, Richard.

The man himself appears and halts the cortège funèbre. Despite Lady Anne's revulsion ("Avaunt! thou dreadful minister of hell,") he makes advances to her, even inviting her to plunge his own sword into his bared chest. Anne is sufficiently mollified to accept a ring from him and agrees to receive him later. When she has departed in procession with Tressel and Berkeley, her gentlemen-in-waiting, Richard exults in his oratorical skill ("Was ever woman in this humour won?") and reflects that he must be a more attractive man than he thought.

Scene 3

In the royal palace Queen Elizabeth voices her worries over the king's health to her brother, Lord Rivers, and Lord Grey, the son of her first marriage. They are joined by the Duke of Buckingham and Thomas Lord Stanley, later the Earl of Derby, who report that the king is more cheerful and is seeking to reconcile Richard and his royal relations.

Richard appears with Hastings and Elizabeth's other son, the Marquess of Dorset. He quarrels with Grey and the queen, accusing her of being responsible for the incarceration of both Hastings and Clarence. Queen Margaret of Anjou, widow of Henry VI, approaches and curses Richard for a murderous villain, as Anne had done. She extends her condemnation to all of them, especially Queen Elizabeth whose son, Edward of York, is now Prince of Wales instead of her son, Edward of Lancaster. She prophesies their downfall, with the exception of the innocent Buckingham, and departs.

Sir William Catesby summons the queen and courtiers to the king, leaving Richard to hand a warrant for Clarence's execution to two murderers.

Scene 4

Clarence, in the Tower, tells his gaoler Brakenbury about a nightmare of his in which he escaped and took ship to Burgundy, accompanied by his brother Richard. In tripping over a hatch Richard knocked him overboard; he drowned in agony and his soul was conducted to the underworld, where the spirits of his father-in-law and the Lancastrian Prince of Wales condemned him for perjury and murder. They called the Furies to torment him, whereupon he awoke.

As Clarence dozes off the two murderers enter; they deliver the warrant to Brakenbury who gives them the keys and leaves to report to the king. The murderers, somewhat conscience-stricken, debate whether to despatch Clarence as he sleeps. When he awakes and learns their intent he cannot believe that Richard is the instigator. He pleads for his life but one murderer stabs him and drags the body to be immersed in a butt of malmsey [a strong sweet wine, originally Greek], while the other repents, too late.

Act II

Scene 1

Back at the palace the ailing King Edward IV has apparently succeeded in reconciling the various factions. They embrace each other and swear fealty to the queen. Richard enters and joins in the professions of amity and good will. When the queen asks the king to extend his forgiveness to Clarence Richard pretends to be affronted since, he says, it is surely known that Clarence is already dead. The court is shocked by the news.

When Stanley enters to seek the king's pardon for one of his servants who has drunkenly killed a follower of the Duke of Norfolk, the king laments Clarence's death, reproaching all of them for failing to speak up for him and seek pardon, as they do for a mere servant. Hastings helps him away to his apartment while Richard slyly suggests to Buckingham that the queen's relatives procured Clarence's death.

Scene 2

Elsewhere in the palace Clarence's son and daughter question their grandmother, Cecily Neville the Duchess of York, about their father's death, believing Richard's story that the king was responsible. The queen enters, with Rivers and Dorset, to report that the king has died; the duchess laments the loss of two sons and all unite in mourning.

Richard comes in with Buckingham, Stanley, Hastings and Sir Richard Ratcliffe. Buckingham proposes that a small party be sent to Ludlow to fetch the young Yorkist Prince of Wales (later Edward V) to London to be crowned. Richard and Buckingham privately agree to go along, in order to keep the queen's relatives, the Woodvilles, away from the prince.

Scene 3

Three citizens meet in the street and discuss the prospects of being governed by a child who may be swayed by the queen's sons and brothers.

Scene 4

In the palace Thomas Rotherham, the Archbishop of York, looks forward to the arrival of Edward in the company of the ten-year-old Duke of York, Queen Elizabeth and the Duchess of York.

A messenger arrives with the news that the Woodvilles, Rivers and Grey, together with the chamberlain Sir Thomas Vaughan, have been arrested by Richard and Buckingham and imprisoned in Pontefract Castle, for no known reason. Queen Elizabeth, confronted by the ruin of her Lancastrian house, decides to seek sanctuary with the Duke of York and the elderly Duchess.

Act III

Scene 1

Prince Edward arrives in London with Richard, Buckingham, Catesby and Cardinal Bourchier, the Archbishop of Canterbury, to be met by the Lord Mayor of London and his train. Edward complains about the arrest of the Woodvilles and learns from Hastings that his mother and brother have taken sanctuary. Buckingham asks the Cardinal to get Queen Elizabeth to send the Duke of York to greet his brother; he persuades him that it would not be a breach of sanctuary to use force if necessary. The Cardinal goes on the errand, accompanied by Hastings. Meanwhile Richard advises the prince to reside in the Tower until his coronation.

Cardinal Bourchier and Hastings return with the Duke of York. The princes greet each other with small talk and go off to the Tower. Richard and Buckingham send Catesby to sound out Hastings. When he has gone Richard promises Buckingham the earldom of Hereford and assures him that if Hastings does not support them he will be executed.

Scene 2

At four o'clock in the morning a messenger from Stanley arrives at Hastings' house. Stanley's message is that Richard is holding two councils; he fears that at the first of them a plan will be hatched to arrest him and Hastings at the second council. He suggests that they ride away north together. Hastings, knowing that his friend Catesby will be at the council to warn him of any danger, confidently sends the messenger back to fetch Stanley to accompany him to the council, which is to be held in the Tower.

Catesby comes to tell Hastings that the queen's relatives will be put to death that day in Pontefract. When he welcomes the prospect of Richard's ascending the throne in due course Hastings flatly refuses to support him. Stanley arrives; he is still mistrustful but agrees to go with Catesby to the council. Hastings is summoned by a Pursuivant; after a word with a priest he leaves for the council with Buckingham.

Scene 3

Sir Richard Ratcliff conducts Rivers, Grey and Vaughan to their execution in Pontefract Castle. Rivers recalls that it was in this same castle that Richard II was murdered back in 1400, after his deposition by his cousin Henry IV [the act that precipitated the Wars of the Roses].

Scene 4

The council meets in the Tower of London to decide on the date of the coronation. Buckingham, Stanley, Hastings and Ratcliff are sitting with John Morton, the Bishop of Ely, and Lord Lovel. They are joined by Richard who asks the bishop to send for some strawberries from his garden in Holborn. He then withdraws with Buckingham to tell him about Hastings' opposition. The bishop returns and Hastings comments naively on Richard's good mood.

Richard re-enters with Buckingham and castigates the queen and Jane Shore, Hastings' mistress, for practising witchcraft against him, causing his arm to be withered. He accuses Hastings of traitorously protecting Mistress Shore and orders

Act III, Scene 5

Richard (not yet king) and Buckingham, in stained and rusty armour, pretend to quake with fear on the tower walls. Ratcliff, accompanied by Lovel, Catesby and the Lord Mayor, brings Hastings' severed head to Richard.

Lovel and Ratcliff to behead him immediately. Richard and Buckingham depart with other council members leaving Hastings to bewail his fate before he is led away to his execution.

Scene 5

Richard and Buckingham, in stained and rusty armour, pretend to quake with fear on the Tower walls. Catesby brings the Lord Mayor of London along, followed by Lovel and Ratcliff carrying Hastings' severed head. Buckingham convinces the Lord Mayor that Hastings had been plotting the murder of Richard and himself and regrets that he had to be executed without trial. The Lord Mayor agrees to go and explain matters to the citizens of London at the Guildhall. Richard sends Buckingham after him to denigrate Edward and convince the crowd of Richard's right to the crown.

Scene 6

In a soliloquy a scrivener reveals that Catesby sent him Hastings's indictment to be engrossed for proclamation some hours before Hastings was actually accused, thus affording evidence of double dealing.

Scene 7

Buckingham reports to Richard at Baynard's Castle that the people who listened to his Guildhall speech were unresponsive. However while Richard goes off, ostensibly to his devotions, the Lord Mayor arrives with aldermen and others. Catesby is sent more than once to fetch Richard from his prayers; eventually Richard appears in an upper gallery between two bishops.

On behalf of the deputation Buckingham calls upon him to become king, arguing that Prince Edward is debarred as illegitimate, being the son of Edward IV and Lady Elizabeth Lucy (before the king's marriage to Lady Grey). After twice refusing, Richard with feigned reluctance accepts the offer of the crown and is hailed as King Richard III.

Act IV

Scene 1

Queen Elizabeth, her son the Marquess of Dorset and her mother-in-law the Duchess of York meet Lady Anne, now Duchess of Gloucester, leading Lady Margaret Plantagenet, Clarence's young daughter. They seek to enter the Tower to visit the two young princes but are prevented by Brakenbury on the strict orders of the Lord Protector (Richard).

Stanley arrives to take Anne to Westminster to be crowned as Richard's queen. The women bemoan the news that Richard is on the throne. While Anne complies with the summons, Elizabeth bids Dorset to sail to Brittany and stay with Henry, Earl of Richmond, for his own safety.

Scene 2

Richard III ascends his throne with due ceremony. He reminds Buckingham that Edward still lives and tells him that he wishes the 'bastards' (princes) dead. Buckingham asks for time to consider, and withdraws. Richard suspects Buckingham's loyalty and sends a page to fetch Sir James Tyrrell, who can be bribed as an assassin.

Stanley enters with the news that Dorset has fled to be with Richmond in France. Richard orders Catesby to spread rumours that Queen Anne is ill and on the point of death, since he must be free to marry his niece Elizabeth, the sister of the young princes, to confirm his hold on the throne.

The page comes back with Tyrrell who is despatched to murder the princes in the Tower. Buckingham returns and claims the promised reward of the Earldom of Hereford. When he is contemptuously spurned he remembers what happened to Hastings and determines to depart at once for Brecknock [Brecon, in the Usk valley] before he loses his own head.

Scene 3

In a room of state Tyrrell reveals that the princes in the Tower have been murdered by two hirelings, Dighton and Forrest, and have been buried by the chaplain. Richard is satisfied with his report and continues with his schemes to confine Ned Plantagenet, Clarence's son, and marry off his daughter.

Catesby enters to tell him that the Bishop of Ely has fled to join the Earl of Richmond in Brittany and that Buckingham has raised an army of Welshmen and is in the field. Richard prepares for battle.

Scene 4

Near the palace Queen Elizabeth and the Duchess of York commiserate with each other while Queen Margaret comments grimly that it was one of their own family, Richard, who preyed on them; she prophesies his early doom and departs for France. When Richard comes past at the head of his army his mother the Duchess curses him comprehensively and leaves in her turn. Richard detains Queen Elizabeth and in a lengthy conversation seems to persuade her to allow him to woo her daughter Elizabeth.

Ratcliff, followed by Catesby, comes to report that a navy is off the west coast, probably under the command of Richmond. Richard sends Catesby to command the Duke of Norfolk to bring his forces to Salisbury. When Stanley arrives to confirm the news about Richmond Richard suspects that he is about to defect. Stanley protests his loyalty and is allowed to go to raise his own forces in the north; however Richard keeps his son George Stanley as a hostage.

Several messengers bring news of rebellions. Sir Edward Courtney and the Bishop of Exeter are in arms in Devon, the Guildfords have risen in Kent and Lovel and the Marquess of Dorset are under arms in Yorkshire. However Buckingham's army has been scattered by floods and the Breton fleet has been dispersed by a tempest. Catesby arrives to say that Buckingham has been captured but Henry, the Earl of Richmond, has landed at Milford Haven [south-west Wales]. Richard orders his men to march towards Salisbury to confront Richmond.

Scene 5

In his house Stanley instructs Christopher Urswick, a priest, to tell Richmond, who has reached Pembroke, that as his son is held hostage he cannot yet support him openly. However Queen Elizabeth has agreed that Richmond (not Richard) may marry her daughter Elizabeth.

Act V

Scene 1

It is All-Souls' day. The Sheriff of Wiltshire leads Buckingham through Salisbury to his execution under armed guard. Buckingham resigns himself to his fate.

Scene 2

Richmond marches over Tamworth plain with his supporters, the Earl of Oxford, Sir James Blunt, Sir Walter Herbert and their mercenaries. So far they have met no opposition and have received a letter of encouragement from Stanley. They are only a day's march from Richard's forces at Leicester.

Scene 3

Evening descends on Bosworth field [between Leicester and Birmingham]. To one side, soldiers erect Richard's tent while he stiffens the morale of the Duke of Norfolk and the Earl of Surrey. Richmond's tent is pitched on the other side while he confers with Oxford and Sir William Brandon.

Richmond sends Captain Blunt with a note to Stanley whose colours are half a mile to the south of Richard's forces. At the same time Richard tells Ratcliff to send a Pursuivant to Stanley with the message that he is to bring his regiment up by sunrise or his son will be killed.

Stanley stealthily visits Richmond in his tent and promises to aid him as much as he can, by delaying his own arrival on the field of battle. Richmond prays to God and composes himself to sleep.

Many ghosts arise between the two royal tents. Edward the Lancastrian Prince of Wales, his father King Henry VI, Clarence, Rivers, Grey, Vaughan, Hastings, the young princes, Lady Anne and Buckingham all encourage Richmond and utter dire threats to Richard, who lies awake in terror, tortured by guilty remorse. Ratcliff comes to tell him that it is time to don his armour.

At four o'clock Richmond is awakened by Oxford. He dresses and makes a speech to his soldiers. On the other side Ratcliff emboldens Richard who draws up his order of battle. He also makes a speech to his men, after which he learns that Stanley is not going to arrive. He calls for young George Stanley's head but there is no time to deal with this since Richmond's army is already emerging from the marshes.

Scene 4

Catesby tells Norfolk of the feats of Richard, whose horse has been slain. Richard comes by on foot, frantically seeking Richmond ("A horse! a horse! my kingdom for a horse!"). The two finally meet and go off, fighting. Richmond returns with Stanley to tell his men that Richard is dead; Stanley presents him with the crown which he has taken from Richard's head.

Stanley's son George is safe but many have been slain, including Norfolk, Walter Ferrers, Brakenbury and Brandon. Richmond proclaims a pardon for Richard's soldiers and confirms that he will marry Princess Elizabeth of York, thus uniting the Plantagenet houses of York and Lancaster and, as Henry VII, initiating the Tudor era.

Troilus and Cressida

This work is set in the earliest historical period of the canon, at the legendary siege of Troy by the Greeks (around 1200 BC). The play is based on Chaucer's *Troilus and Criseyde* with additional material from Caxton's translation *Recuyell of the Historyes of Troy* and Chapman's *Homer*. It was probably written in 1602.

Prologue

The audience is told that the haughty Achaean princes have sent sixty nine ships from Athens to Phrygia [modern north-west Turkey] to ransack the six-gated city of Troy [Ilium, near the Hellespont] where Menelaus' abducted queen Helen lies with 'wanton Paris'.

The Greeks have landed at Tenedos and pitched their pavilions on the Dardan plains [by the Dardanelles]. Prologue explains that the story begins not at the start of the ten-year siege but in its seventh year.

Act I

Scene 1

In front of the palace of King Priam in Troy the king's son Troilus tells Pandarus, brother of Calchas [a Trojan augur who has gone over to the Greeks], of his forlorn infatuation with Pandarus' niece, Calchas' daughter Cressida. He asks why he should fight the fierce Greeks outside Troy when he faces such "cruel battle" within the city. He deplores Pandarus' reluctance to continue to act as go-between; Pandarus counsels patience. After Pandarus departs Aeneas, a Trojan commander, comes to tell Prince Troilus that Paris has returned to the city, wounded by Menelaus of Sparta, the brother of the Greek commander Agamemnon.

Scene 2

In the street Cressida is told by her servant Alexander that Priam's wife, Queen Hecuba, and Helen have gone up the eastern tower to see the battle. He adds that Prince Hector that morning scolded his wife Andromache and his armourer, being angry at having the previous day been struck down by Ajax, a nephew of his fighting on the Greek side.

Cressida greets her uncle Pandarus, who notes that Troilus is adding his anger to his brother Hector's and remarks that whereas Hector is the better man Helen appears to favour Troilus, having joked with him and found a white hair on his chin. Cressida is non-committal.

They watch as the men return from the field. Aeneas leads, followed by his fellow commander Antenor and then Hector and his brothers Paris, Helenus, Deiphobus and Troilus. Pandarus comments on each, especially praising Troilus. As the troops pass by Cressida artfully suggests that one of the Greek commanders, Achilles, is a better man than

Troilus; Pandarus springs to his defence.

Troilus' boy comes to ask Pandarus to come to Troilus' house where he is removing his armour. After he goes Cressida soliloquises that she loves and admires Troilus more than Pandarus' high praise warrants but she resolves to appear cool in order to retain his interest.

Scene 3

The Grecian general Agamemnon attempts to rally his dispirited brother Menelaus and his commanders Ulysses and the elderly Nestor outside his tent. Nestor feels that the Greeks lack the challenge of combat after long inactivity. Ulysses blames the other commanders; he says that Achilles lolls on his bed laughing at Patroclus' parodies of Nestor and Agamemnon himself. Nestor adds that the brainless Ajax has become self-willed and incites Thersites, his deformed slave, to mock his colleagues with scurrilous comments.

To a trumpet flourish Aeneas appears looking for Agamemnon. Having identified him he issues a challenge from Hector to meet a man "who holds his honour higher than his ease" on the following day midway between the Greek tents and the walls of Troy. Agamemnon undertakes to find Hector an opponent and takes Menelaus and Aeneas off to a hospitable feast before Aeneas returns to Troy.

Ulysses remarks to Nestor that the challenge, although expressed in general terms, really relates to Achilles, the mightiest Greek warrior. But if Achilles were nominated and were to defeat Hector he would be insufferably proud whereas if he lost the Greeks would be humiliated. He suggests a lottery, rigged in order to ensure that Ajax fights Hector. Then if Ajax wins he can enjoy the acclaim while if he loses they can put up a better man for the next duel.

Act II

Scene 1

Elsewhere in the Grecian camp Ajax orders Thersites to find out what the recent proclamation is about; Thersites mocks and insults Ajax, who beats him. Achilles and Patroclus come up and are included in Thersites' ridicule. When Thersites has left Achilles tells Ajax that at five o'clock on the morrow Hector is to meet a Greek chosen by lottery.

Scene 2

Priam, in his palace, tells Hector, Troilus, Paris and Helenus that Nestor has again called for the return of Helen. Hector suggests that they let her go, as the burden of guarding her has become too great. Troilus and Helenus deplore the impugning of Trojan honour that would result. Troilus reminds Hector that he encouraged Paris to abduct Helen in the first place, to avenge an old woman whom the Greeks held captive.

Their deranged sister Cassandra passes through, raving that if Helen does not go Troy will burn and they will all weep. Paris deems it a disgrace to yield Helen up. Hector still feels that Helen should be returned to her husband but agrees to support his brothers and prepares for his challenge.

Scene 3

Thersites grumbles to himself near Achilles' tent, wishing that the positions could be reversed so that he could beat Ajax while Ajax railed at him. Patroclus and Achilles appear and, as before, suffer Thersites' contumely. Achilles and Thersites withdraw as Agamemnon arrives with Ulysses, Nestor, Ajax and Diomedes, another commander.

Agamemnon asks Patroclus to call Achilles from his tent, not believing that he is ill. Ajax takes Agamemnon aside as Patroclus re-emerges without Achilles. Agamemnon sternly orders Patroclus to fetch the over-proud Achilles and sends Ulysses into the tent after him. Ajax takes the opportunity to draw attention to his own lack of pride.

Ulysses comes out to report that Achilles will not go into the field the following day, loftily giving no reason. Agamemnon wants to send the eager Ajax into the tent next but Ulysses objects since that will merely "baste his arrogance". Agamemnon finally bids them leave Achilles and attend the council.

Act III

Scene 1

Pandarus accosts Paris' servant in the palace and receives some back-answers before Paris and Helen enter with their attendants. While Helen pesters him to sing to her Pandarus asks Paris to make excuses for Troilus if the king calls for him at supper. Paris consents, suspecting that Troilus wishes to be with Cressida, and Pandarus sings a love-song before leaving. As the lovers go to the hall Paris requests Helen to help Hector off with his armour.

Scene 2

Troilus' servant ushers him into Pandarus' orchard. As Pandarus goes to fetch a nervous and hesitant Cressida Troilus declaims his passionate love. When she appears he offers to perform great deeds for her, while Pandarus goes to procure a light. On his return Cressida confesses her love for Troilus, recoiling immediately from her own boldness. Pandarus brings their hands together and after they have sworn their fidelity he waves them away to a private room.

Scene 3

In the Grecian camp the priest Calchas addresses Agamemnon, Ulysses, Diomedes, Nestor, Ajax, and Menelaus. He reminds them that he has abandoned Troy, giving up everything, and now asks a favour in return. He wants them to return Antenor, who has been captured, in exchange for his own daughter Cressida, whom he misses; no obligation will then remain. Agamemnon assents; he sends Diomedes to Troy to effect the exchange and to tell Hector that his opponent will be Ajax.

Ulysses, noticing Achilles standing with Patroclus at the entrance to his tent, calls on the others to pass by without acknowledging him. Agamemnon, Nestor, Menelaus and Ajax either ignore Achilles or pointedly exchange a greeting with Patroclus on the way out.

Achilles is affronted; he accosts Ulysses who reads him a passage that a man should not boast even of what he has but must wait for his virtues to be reflected to him by others. He goes on to counsel forbearance in the face of inconstancy, for "One touch of nature makes the whole world kin" in praising novelty. He leaves, recalling that Achilles is in love with one of Priam's daughters and urging him not to let it be known that while Ajax bravely vanquished Hector, Achilles only won Hector's sister.

Patroclus calls Thersites who reports that Ajax is strutting about like a peacock. Achilles orders Thersites to go to Ajax and tell him to invite Hector to come unarmed to his (Achilles') tent, giving him safe conduct. Thersites fears that Hector will knock his brains out first.

Act IV

Scene 1

In the city Aeneas and a servant with a torch meet Paris with his brother Deiphobus, Antenor, Diomedes and others during a truce. Paris introduces Diomedes to his former opponent Aeneas and they exchange unsubmissive greetings. Paris informs Aeneas that he is taking Diomedes to Calchas' house to collect Cressida in exchange for Antenor and sends him ahead to warn Troilus. Diomedes tells Paris that he doesn't care whether he or Menelaus has Helen since she has been the cause of such losses to both sides. Paris thinks that he is dispraising what he desires to buy.

Scene 2

Troilus is taking leave of Cressida in a courtyard at Pandarus' house. Pandarus discovers the two and teases them. Hearing knocking at the outer door Cressida takes Troilus back to her room. Aeneas enters, seeking Troilus. Pandarus denies knowledge of him but Troilus re-enters and hears of the exchange agreement. He and Aeneas go to meet Paris' party while Pandarus curses Antenor as the cause of the trouble.

Cressida returns and wrings the story from Pandarus. She declares with high passion that she will not be parted from Troilus.

Scene 3

The party arrives and Troilus goes to fetch Cressida.

Scene 4

Inside the house Pandarus tries to assuage Cressida's grief. Troilus comes to confirm that she will have to leave him and Troy. Pandarus shares their woe and leaves. The lovers exchange tokens (his sleeve and her glove) as Troilus exhorts Cressida to remain true and not to succumb to Grecian wiles.

Aeneas enters with Paris, Antenor, Deiphobus and Diomedes. Troilus welcomes Diomedes and tells him that he will hand Cressida over at the city portal, after which he is to take good care of her. When Diomedes and the lovers have left Aeneas hears the trumpet that signals Hector's duel and remembers that he should have ridden before him to the field. He and the others scurry out.

Scene 5

In the Grecian camp Agamemnon commends Ajax in front of Achilles, Patroclus, Menelaus, Ulysses and Nestor as a trumpet sounds for the combat. The men see Cressida approaching with Diomedes and welcome her with kisses before Diomedes takes her to join Calchas.

Hector appears in armour in the lists with Aeneas, Troilus and their attendants. Aeneas hails the Greeks and identifies Achilles while Diomedes returns to stand by Ajax. Hector and Ajax take up their positions as Ulysses describes Troilus to Agamemnon as a man even greater than Hector.

Ajax and Hector fight until Diomedes and Aeneas call a halt. Hector is content, especially since Ajax is actually his cousin on his father's side. They embrace and Ajax invites Hector to Achilles' tent, as arranged. Hector is introduced to Agamemnon and all his commanders. Achilles and Hector confront one another and arrange to meet in combat the following day.

When the others have left Ulysses tells Troilus that Diomedes is being entertained by Calchas in his tent and is casting amorous looks at his daughter Cressida. Troilus asks him to indicate the tent to him after Agamemnon's dinner.

Act V

Scene 1

Near his tent Achilles reveals to Patroclus his plan to ply Hector with Greek wine that evening. The surly Thersites comes to hand Achilles a letter and quarrels with Patroclus while he reads it. The letter is from Queen Hecuba adjuring Achilles not to break an oath which he has sworn. Achilles and Patroclus depart for the banquet leaving Thersites muttering imprecations.

After dinner Agamemnon, Hector, Troilus, Ajax, Ulysses, Nestor, Menelaus and Diomedes, carrying lights, are met by Achilles. Agamemnon and Menelaus say goodnight and leave. Diomedes does

the same; Ulysses nudges Troilus to follow Diomedes' light with him; it will lead them to Calchas' tent. Hector, Ajax and Nestor join Achilles in his tent while Thersites vents his spleen on Diomedes.

Scene 2

Diomedes reaches Calchas' tent and calls Cressida out as Troilus, Ulysses and Thersites observe from a distance. Cressida appears to flirt with Diomedes while Ulysses attempts to draw an increasingly agitated Troilus away. Cressida refuses a request from Diomedes but promises to see him later. She fetches Troilus' sleeve token from the tent but then snatches it back and tells Diomedes to visit her no more. He demands to know whose token it is. Cressida will not reveal the name but eventually yields the sleeve to him. He departs, insisting on returning. Cressida laments her own weakness and retires.

Troilus is in despair. He rails at Cressida's falsity and swears to kill Diomedes when he is wearing the sleeve token in his helmet. Aeneas appears, to conduct Troilus to Ajax who is to accompany him home. Thersites exults in the situation.

Scene 3

In front of the palace in Troy Andromache pleads with her husband Hector not to fight that day. Cassandra comes up and also bids him disarm. When he refuses she goes to call her father. When Troilus appears Hector tells him not to don his armour as he will do all the fighting; Troilus insists, saying that Hector is too merciful, allowing his defeated adversaries to rise and live.

Cassandra returns with Priam who adds his entreaty not to fight. Hector maintains that he is honour bound to do so and dismisses Andromache. Cassandra prophesies Hector's death and leaves. [Her curse is that her predictions are all true but are never believed]. Hector and Priam also leave but Pandarus comes along in time to catch Troilus and hand him a letter from Cressida. Troilus tears it up and marches off.

Scene 4

Between Troy and the Grecian camp Thersites hurries to see the conflict. Troilus comes upon Diomedes wearing the sleeve and they move off, fighting. Hector challenges Thersites who hastily denies that he is a soldier.

Scene 5

Elsewhere Diomedes orders his servant to collect Troilus' horse and take it to Cressida with his compliments. Agamemnon appears, reviewing the Greek losses and calling on Diomedes to reinforce their men with him. He is followed by Nestor who orders him to convey Patroclus' body to Achilles and tell Ajax to arm quickly. Ulysses joins them and reports that Achilles and Ajax are preparing to repel the mighty Hector and Troilus. The two indeed appear and pursue their foes.

Act V, Scene 8

*Troilus' brother Hector, who has taken off his armour and dis-
carded his shield, is found by Achilles and speared to death by
the Myrmidons. Achilles trails the body round the walls of Troy.*

Scene 6

Ajax and Diomedes encounter Troilus and compete to fight with him. Achilles meets Hector but turns away from him. Troilus goes past, telling Hector that Ajax has driven Aeneas from the field. Hector chases another Greek warrior in resplendent armour.

Scene 7

Achilles gathers his Myrmidons and orders them to find Hector, surround him and kill him. Thersites is watching Menelaus and Paris in combat when he is challenged by Priam's bastard son, Margarelon; they go off, fighting.

Scene 8

In the dusk Hector takes off his armour and hangs up his shield. Achilles finds him and sets the Myrmidons on him. They spear him to death. Achilles ties Hector's body to his horse, to trail it over the field.

Scene 9

The news of Hector's death reaches Agamemnon, Ajax, Menelaus, Nestor and Diomedes who judge thereby that the Trojans have been defeated.

Scene 10

Aeneas orders his men to stand firm but Troilus comes to report that Hector has been slain. He shrinks from telling Priam and Hecuba but resolves to continue the war against the Greeks. Pandarus hails him but Troilus departs leaving Pandarus to lament the course of events.

Twelfth Night

or WHAT YOU WILL

The main source of the plot is *"The History of Apolonius and Silla"* from *Farewell to Military Profession* published in 1581 by Barnaby Rich. The action takes place in and around an unnamed city in Illyria, which is a part of the Balkan peninsula corresponding roughly with modern Dalmatia, Bosnia, Herzegovina and Montenegro. *Twelfth Night* was a working title unrelated to the story.

Act I

Scene 1

Orsino, the Duke of Illyria, is listening gloomily to music in his palace in company with Curio and other attendant gentlemen ("If music be the food of love, play on:"). He is in love with the rich Countess Olivia but Valentine, a courtier, comes to tell him that as she is in veiled mourning for her father and brother, both recently dead, she will not receive him.

Scene 2

On the nearby sea coast Viola, a young girl from Messaline, has survived a shipwreck together with the ship's captain and some of the crew. She is afraid that her twin brother, Sebastian, has been drowned but the captain assures her that he saw Sebastian clinging firmly to a mast in the sea. The captain, who was born in the region, goes on to tell her about Duke Orsino and his hopeless love for Olivia. Viola had hoped to be one of Olivia's ladies-in-waiting but now, being musical, she decides to disguise herself as a eunuch and serve the duke.

Scene 3

Olivia's uncle, Sir Toby Belch, lives in her house, drinking and roistering. Maria, Olivia's lady-in-waiting, reproves Sir Toby for his late hours and for inviting his simpleton friend Sir Andrew Aguecheek to drink with him, simply because wealthy Sir Andrew can speak several languages and play the viola da gamba.

When Sir Andrew enters, Sir Toby, for a prank, introduces Maria as a chambermaid by the name of Mary Accost. After some flirtatious talk Maria leaves and Sir Toby gets Sir Andrew to caper about, hinting that a talent for dancing will commend him to Olivia.

Scene 4

Three days later in the palace Valentine is talking to Viola, who is now dressed as a page called Cesario. Duke Orsino enters with Curio and other attendants. He takes Viola (Cesario) to one side and begs 'him' to do anything to gain audience with Olivia and convince her that he loves her. Viola is reluctant, having fallen for Orsino herself.

Scene 5

In Olivia's house Maria warns Feste, a clown, that he will be punished for being absent so often. She leaves as Olivia enters with Malvolio, the self-important steward of her household. Feste attempts to amuse Olivia, with little success. Maria comes in to say that a young man is with Sir Toby at the gate. Fearing that the visitor is Orsino's envoy Olivia sends Malvolio to turn him away.

Sir Toby lurches in to announce the young man and he and Maria are dismissed. Malvolio returns to say that the youth is 'well-favoured' and insists on speaking to Olivia. Donning a mourning veil Olivia consents to see him with Maria.

Viola, as Cesario, has prepared a speech and asks Olivia to unveil so that she can be sure that she is addressing the lady of the house; furthermore the speech is for Olivia's ears only. Maria and the attendants are sent away and Olivia unveils.

Viola praises her beauty and Olivia banteringly says that she will leave a copy of it when she dies. She rejects the protestations of Orsino's love delivered by Viola (Cesario), saying that she cannot love him. However she is much taken with young 'Cesario'; when he leaves she pretends that he has left a ring behind and sends Malvolio after him to return it and ask him to come back the next day.

Act II

Scene 1

Elsewhere on the coast Sebastian has been rescued from the shipwreck by a former sea venturer, Antonio. He thinks that his twin sister has been drowned and sets out for Orsino's court. Antonio follows him, despite having enemies at the court.

Scene 2

Malvolio delivers the ring to Viola in the street and departs. Viola, who had left no ring, realises that Olivia has fallen in love with 'him' as Cesario and despairs of untangling the situation.

Scene 3

Sir Toby Belch and Sir Andrew Aguecheek are drinking and talking in Olivia's house. Feste sings them a love song for sixpence ("What is love? 'tis not hereafter; Present mirth hath present laughter; What's to come is still unsure:"). As they are all singing a raucous catch Maria enters to beg them to keep quiet. She is followed by Malvolio who tells them that Olivia will have them thrown out if they do not stop their noise. Sir Toby laughs at him. ("Dost thou think, because thou art virtuous, there shall be no more cakes and ale?").

Act II, Scene 5

Malvolio finds a letter, apparently from Olivia, in her garden. Maria, who has dropped the forged letter, gleefully leaves Sir Toby Belch, Sir Andrew Aguecheek and a servant, Fabian, to observe Malvolio's reaction.

When Malvolio stalks off Maria concocts with the others a plan to make a fool of him. Being able to copy Olivia's handwriting she proposes to leave some 'obscure epistles of love' for him to find. He will then, in his conceit, think that Olivia is in love with him.

Scene 4

Back at the palace Orsino is still melancholy. While Curio goes to fetch Feste, Orsino talks to Viola (Cesario) about the suffering caused by love. She speaks of her own feelings and Orsino advises 'him' not to marry an older woman.

Feste arrives and sings to them. When he and the others leave Orsino gives Viola a jewel to take to Olivia. She warns him that Olivia is unlikely to respond to his advances since women are constant in love. She tells how her 'father's daughter' "sat like Patience on a monument, Smiling at grief." She is referring to herself but Orsino thinks she is speaking of her sister.

Scene 5

Maria joins Sir Toby Belch, Sir Andrew Aguecheek and a servant, Fabian, in Olivia's garden. Seeing Malvolio coming she drops a letter on the path and tells the others to hide in a box-tree to see what happens. Malvolio struts along, imagining himself as Count Malvolio with the power to make Toby curtsey to him. The watchers are consumed with mingled indignation and mirth.

Malvolio comes upon the letter, apparently from Olivia, and is transported since the phrase 'M, O, A, I, doth sway my life' seems to refer to him. Furthermore the writer goes on, "In my stars I am above thee; but be not afraid of greatness: some are born great, some achieve greatness, and some have greatness thrust upon them." He hurries off to comply with the instructions in the letter to don yellow stockings with cross garters.

A gleeful Maria returns to invite them to watch Malvolio's next meeting with Olivia who, as she knows, abhors yellow and detests cross garters.

Act III

Scene 1

Still in the garden Viola (Cesario), on her mission for Orsino, gives Feste sixpence to announce her arrival to Olivia; he departs on the errand. Sir Toby and Sir Andrew invite her into the house but Olivia and Maria come into the garden to meet her. Olivia orders the others to leave and shut the garden door behind them. Her blandishments cause confusion to Cesario, especially when she asks 'him' what 'he' thinks of her. Viola manages to escape, declaring (truthfully) that she will never love a woman.

Scene 2

Inside the house Sir Andrew Aguecheek, having witnessed Olivia's approaches to Cesario, considers that his cause is lost and prepares to depart. Fabian tells him that Olivia's behaviour was only designed to awake his jealousy. He and Sir Toby persuade Sir Andrew to write a note to Cesario challenging him to a duel and thus gain Olivia's favour. After he goes off to do so Maria calls the other two to take a peep at Malvolio, who is dressed in cross-gartered yellow stockings and is smiling fatuously.

Scene 3

Sebastian suggests to Antonio that they go sightseeing in the city but Antonio does not want to be seen and recognised by the police as an old enemy of the Duke. He hands over his purse and invites Sebastian to join him at an inn called *The Elephant* in the suburbs.

Scene 4

Olivia sends Maria to fetch Malvolio into the garden. He appears in his cross garters and affronts Olivia by smiling meaningly and addressing her as 'sweetheart'. A servant enters to tell Olivia that Cesario has come back again. As Malvolio seems to be suffering from midsummer madness she orders Maria and Sir Toby to look after him. They tease Malvolio and pursue him in order to lock him in a dark room.

Sir Andrew reads out his challenge to Cesario while Sir Toby, Fabian and Maria listen. Separately, Olivia requests Viola (Cesario) to wear a locket with her picture in it. On her departure Sir Toby and Fabian tell Viola that a duellist who is "quick, skilful and deadly" and has already slain three opponents is waiting at the end of the orchard. Viola is alarmed; Fabian guards her to prevent her running away.

Sir Toby now tells Sir Andrew in turn that his adversary is a fierce and accomplished fencer. Sir Andrew quakes with fear and wonders if he can buy Cesario off with the gift of his horse, Capilet [Capulet]. He and Cesario unwillingly draw their swords. Antonio comes to Cesario's defence, thinking him to be Viola's twin brother Sebastian, and he and Sir Toby draw.

However before any conflict can ensue two officers arrive to arrest Antonio for piracy. He asks Cesario, whom he believes to be Sebastian, for some of the money that he gave him in the city; he is taken aback when Viola (Cesario) denies having received it and offers him only a little of her own money. Antonio is dragged off, hurt by the apparent ingratitude of someone whom he saved from drowning. Since Antonio had addressed her as Sebastian Viola surmises that her twin brother must be alive after all.

Act IV

Scene 1

Feste, having been sent by Olivia to bring Cesario to her, meets Sebastian in the street and takes him for Cesario. Sebastian cannot understand Feste's entreaties. Sir Andrew Aguecheek and Sir Toby Belch come along with Fabian and, making the same mistake, start beating Sebastian. Feste scampers off to fetch Olivia. When she arrives she scolds Sir Toby and dismisses both of them. Sebastian is further confused when Olivia warmly invites him to her house (as Cesario).

Scene 2

At the house Maria is helping Feste to put on a gown and false beard in order to impersonate Sir Topas, the curate. She then fetches Sir Toby. Malvolio, imprisoned in his darkened chamber, calls to 'Sir Topas' to go to Olivia with a note and intercede for him. Feste tells Malvolio he is unhinged while Maria, enjoying the joke, points out that Feste had no need to disguise himself since Malvolio could not see him.

Scene 3

Sebastian is worried, having failed to find Antonio at *The Elephant*. However he is delighted when Olivia brings a priest to him in the garden and sweeps him off to the chantry to swear a formal betrothal.

Act V

Scene 1

In front of Olivia's house Feste and Fabian are joined by Orsino, Viola, Curio and their attendants. After some badinage Antonio appears in the grip of some officers of the law. Orsino recognises him as an old enemy but Viola pleads that Antonio saved her from a duel.

To Orsino's pleasure Olivia comes along with her attendants. However she informs him that she cannot marry him since she is formally engaged to Cesario. In a rage Orsino retorts that he will take his page Cesario away with him. Viola is happy to comply but the priest, fetched by a servant, confirms that Olivia and Cesario are indeed affianced. In disgust Orsino tells Viola to be gone with Olivia and never to come near him again.

Sir Andrew Aguecheek appears with a head injury. He says that he and Sir Toby Belch have been attacked by Cesario, although Cesario is there in front of him. A drunken Sir Toby arrives, leaning on Feste, to corroborate Sir Andrew's story and they stagger off to find a surgeon.

Sebastian now arrives to greet Olivia and Antonio with affection. Everyone can see that he and his twin are identical; moreover one of them is a girl! (Sebastian remarks to Olivia that she is "betroth'd both to a maid and man".) When an overjoyed Sebastian and Viola have compared notes Orsino is delighted to find that the page of whom he has grown so fond is not a boy; he realises why she could never love a woman and decides to marry her. She tells him that the ship's captain who saved her life has her woman's garments but that he has been detained by Malvolio.

At this moment Fabian comes back with Feste, who is carrying the letter from the 'madly-used' Malvolio given to him when he was Sir Topas. Fabian reads it out; in it Malvolio protests at being kept in darkness by Olivia's 'drunken cousin' when he did no more than comply with her own letter to him. Fabian goes off to fetch Malvolio, on Olivia's orders.

When Malvolio arrives with 'her' letter she recognises Maria's imitation of her handwriting and explains the trickery to him. In the same way Feste confesses that he was Sir Topas. Malvolio storms off, swearing revenge on the whole pack of them.

Thus it appears that Antonio is released, Sir Toby Belch has married Maria, Duke Orsino is to marry Viola and Countess Olivia will marry Viola's twin, Sebastian. As the play ends Feste sings, "When that I was and a little tiny boy, With hey, ho, the wind and the rain; A foolish thing was but a toy, For the rain it raineth every day."

The Two Gentlemen of Verona

The action of *The Two Gentlemen of Verona* takes place in Verona, Milan and the frontiers of Mantua in the Lombardy region of northern Italy. The plot may have been drawn from the story of the shepherdess Filismena in Jorge de Montemayor's *Diana*.

Act I

Scene 1

Valentine, a gentleman, is taking leave of his friend Proteus in Verona. He departs on a visit to Milan but cannot persuade the lovesick Proteus to accompany him. His servant, Speed, comes to report to Proteus that he has delivered Proteus' letter to his lady love, Julia, and thus missed his master's departure. Amid much joking about his sheepish behaviour Speed tells Proteus that Julia's attitude seems to be cold and uncaring.

Scene 2

In her garden Julia asks her maid, Lucetta, for an opinion of her suitors. Lucetta prefers Proteus to Sir Eglamour and the wealthy Mercutio. She hands Proteus' letter to Julia, apologising for accepting it on her behalf. Julia petulantly flings it at her and orders her to go and send it back but, repenting of her annoyance, recalls her on the pretext that it is dinnertime.

Lucetta retrieves the fallen letter, which Julia flightily suggests must be a love poem addressed to Lucetta. Getting nowhere with that suggestion, she snatches it and tears it up but when Lucetta has left she tries desperately to piece it together, kissing the fragments and tucking some of them in her bosom. Lucetta reappears to inform Julia that her father is waiting for her indoors.

Scene 3

Proteus' father Antonio, at home, learns from Panthino, his servant, that his brother is strongly advising him to send Proteus on his travels, preferably to Milan with Valentine where he can take part in tournaments, "hear sweet discourse" and so on. Antonio agrees to send him off at once with a party under Don Alphonso.

Proteus enters, sighing over Julia's loving reply to his letter. Seeing Antonio he pretends it is from Valentine and is told that he is to join him in Milan the very next day. Proteus has no wish to be parted from Julia but he is peremptorily ordered to comply with the arrangement.

Act II

Scene 1

Speed has caught up with his master Valentine in the palace of the Duke of Milan and is bold enough to tease him for falling instantly in love with Silvia, the Duke's daughter. When Silvia enters, Valentine tenders an amatory letter that he has written at her behest; she approves it, hands it back and leaves again, to Speed's amusement. He has to explain to his master that Silvia is coyly declaring her love for him by means of this device.

Scene 2

Back in Verona Proteus bids farewell to Julia at her home. They exchange rings with vows of constancy before Panthino calls Proteus to depart.

Scene 3

Proteus' servant Launce is exercising his dog, Crab, in the street. He makes a pantomime of his parting from his family, using his two shoes and the hard-hearted Crab. He too is called away by Panthino.

Scene 4

In the Duke's palace in Milan Valentine, Silvia and Speed are talking with Thurio, a young courtier, who is irritated by Valentine's nimbler wit. The Duke looks in, telling Valentine that his old friend Proteus has arrived and requesting Silvia to welcome him. Silvia greets Proteus when he appears and is then summoned to her father by a servant; she goes off with Thurio and Speed.

Left with Proteus, Valentine goes into raptures over Silvia and asks him to help the two of them to elope, which requires Valentine to climb a rope ladder to her window. Proteus says he must unpack first, having suddenly realised that he is blinded by love for Silvia himself, to the effacement of Julia.

Scene 5

Speed meets Launce in the street and welcomes him to Milan. Launce tells him of the looming rift between Proteus and Julia as they saunter off to the alehouse.

Scene 6

In a soliloquy Proteus manages to justify to himself his abandonment of Julia and his betrayal of Valentine. He decides to let the Duke know of the planned elopement, to baulk Valentine, and subsequently to outwit the simple Thurio, who is preferred by the Duke as a son-in-law.

Scene 7

Meanwhile in Verona Julia insists on journeying to Milan to be with Proteus, over Lucetta's objections. She plans to dress as a page and tie her hair up rather than cut it; however she balks at wearing a cod-piece.

Act III, Scene 1

*The Duke of Milan, on a pretext, plucks open Valentine's cloak,
revealing a coiled rope ladder and a conspiratorial letter to the
duke's daughter, Silvia. Thus the planned elopement is thwarted.*

Act III

Scene 1

The Duke dismisses Thurio from an anteroom in order to listen to Proteus' report of his daughter's intended elopement. After Proteus has left he detains Valentine who is on his way to despatch some letters. The Duke pretends that he is tired of trying to persuade Silvia to accept Thurio and has decided to take a lady of Verona for his own wife. He asks Valentine for advice, since this fictional lady is guarded by day and locked in an upper room at night.

Valentine naturally recommends the use of a rope ladder with grappling hooks, which can be concealed easily beneath a cloak. The Duke plucks open Valentine's cloak, ostensibly to verify the feasibility of the idea, and discovers not only a coiled rope ladder but a conspiratorial letter to Silvia. He wrathfully banishes Valentine and strides off, leaving Valentine to lament his predicament.

Shortly afterwards Proteus enters with Launce; he tells Valentine complacently that the Duke has imprisoned Silvia, who is in floods of tears. Valentine goes off with him to quit the palace, Launce being left to send Speed after him to the North gate of the city. When Speed comes in Launce passes on the message but not until he has forced Speed to go through a description of a milkmaid sweetheart of his, item by item.

Scene 2

In another room the Duke assures a despondent Thurio that Silvia will come to favour him in due course. Proteus enters and allows himself to be persuaded to go to Silvia, vilify Valentine and flatter Thurio. He also suggests that Thurio sing an elegy or two at her window.

Act IV

Scene 1

Valentine and Speed are held up by a band of outlaws in the forest [near Brescia] between Milan and Verona. Learning that Valentine is a poor but educated man suffering banishment, like many of them, the outlaws make him their captain, honourably agreeing not to prey on women or poor travellers while under his command.

Scene 2

Proteus, in the role of tutor, conducts Thurio and some musicians to Silvia's window. Behind them, unseen, an innkeeper has brought a doleful page (Julia) to be cheered by the music. However Julia is heartbroken when she hears Proteus singing a serenade ("Who is Silvia? what is she....") After Thurio and the musicians leave Julia overhears Silvia rebuking Proteus for wronging both her Valentine and his Julia, although she agrees to let him have a picture from her room.

Scene 3

Eglamour, an elderly man, now arrives under Silvia's window. She begs him to escort her on the road to Mantua so that she can escape from Thurio and overtake Valentine. He agrees to meet her at Friar Patrick's cell.

Scene 4

Launce appears with his dog which he has been ordered to present to Silvia as a gift. Proteus brings in the page (Julia) who is in his employment under the name of Sebastian. Launce tells him that Silvia has rejected Crab and is sent to find Proteus' own dog. To Julia's chagrin Proteus then sends her, as 'Sebastian', to deliver a letter to Silvia with the very ring that Julia had given him in Verona.

When he has gone she encounters Silvia who gets an attendant, Ursula, to give Julia (Sebastian) the picture which she had promised Proteus. Julia offers her the letter and the ring; she is pleased when Silvia tears up the letter and refuses the ring. She confides that she knows Julia, who is the same size and colouring as herself (Sebastian) and is rewarded with a purse.

Act V

Scene 1

Eglamour meets Silvia in the abbey, as arranged, and takes her out by the postern gate to the nearby forest.

Scene 2

In the palace a spineless Thurio asks Proteus what Silvia thinks of him while 'Sebastian' adds sotto voce comments. The Duke enters and calls on them to join him in his pursuit of Silvia and Eglamour, who have been seen in the forest by Friar Laurence.

Scene 3

Silvia has fallen into the hands of the outlaws (despite their vow) but Eglamour has dashed off through the forest.

Scene 4

Elsewhere in the forest Valentine laments his banishment from Silvia. He withdraws as Proteus and Sebastian come along with Silvia, whom they have recaptured from the outlaws. He watches as Silvia continues to fend off Proteus' advances and then confronts Proteus as a faithless ruffian. Proteus confesses his guilt with shame; Valentine, deeply touched, forgives him and selflessly yields Silvia to him, at which Sebastian swoons.

Recovering, Julia (Sebastian) shows Proteus the ring that she had 'forgotten' to deliver to Silvia; Proteus recognises it as the one he had given to Julia. She excuses her 'mistake' and produces the second ring, which he had had from her. Proteus now realises that Sebastian is Julia and the two pairs of lovers are reconciled.

The Duke and Thurio arrive with the outlaws, still pursuing Silvia. Thurio sees and claims her but when he is rebuffed by Valentine he cravenly cowers. The Duke, in disgust, spurns him and bestows Silvia on the worthy Valentine, who takes the opportunity to ask for a pardon for all the outlaws. The Duke assents and they all depart for some festivities as Valentine begins to tell him the whole story.

The Winter's Tale

This is among the last group of plays to be written by Shakespeare, in or about the period 1609-1611. The plot is taken from Robert Greene's *Pandosto, the Triumph of Time*, or *Dorastus and Fawnia* (1588). The action is set in the island of Sicily and in Bohemia [part of the modern Czech Republic]. Shakespeare interchanged the two countries, which is why Act III, Scene 3 is set on the shore of Bohemia, a country that has no coastline.

Act I

Scene 1

In an antechamber of the royal palace Camillo, a Sicilian lord, is chatting to Archidamus, a nobleman who is visiting Sicily with the Bohemian king Polixenes. He recalls the close friendship, from infancy, between Polixenes and the Sicilian king Leontes which has been maintained over the years by exchanges of letters and gifts. He hints that in the summer Leontes may pay a return visit to Bohemia.

Scene 2

Queen Hermione, Camillo and young Prince Mamillius listen as Polixenes tells Leontes that after a stay of nine months he must finally leave the next day to return home to Bohemia to see his son. Leontes presses him to remain and the queen persuades him to stay another week. Leontes wryly observes that only once before had his wife Hermione spoken to such good purpose — when she agreed to marry him. Hermione begins to arouse his jealousy by treating Polixenes with affection while Leontes talks to his young son Mamillius.

Polixenes and Hermione go for a stroll in the garden and Mamillius is sent away to play. Camillo unwittingly fans Leontes' jealousy by noting that Polixenes prolonged his stay only at Hermione's request. To Camillo's distress Leontes suddenly accuses his wife of adultery with his old friend and commands Camillo to poison Polixenes.

Leontes leaves, pointedly shying away from the returning Polixenes. Under close questioning Camillo admits to Polixenes that he has been ordered to murder him. Polixenes agrees to his suggestion that they and the Bohemian attendants slip away that night unobtrusively in twos and threes. Camillo has the keys to the posterns and can aid their escape.

Act II

Scene 1

Elsewhere in the palace Queen Hermione's attendant ladies gossip with Mamillius about her coming confinement. He settles down to tell them a 'winter's tale' [i.e. an old wives' tale] of sprites and goblins. Antigonus and other lords enter with Leontes, whose suspicions have been confirmed by the flight of Polixenes and Camillo. He dismisses Mamillius and accuses Hermione of being pregnant by Polixenes. Despite her protestations of innocence he sends her off to prison under guard with her attendants.

Antigonus and the others plead Hermione's cause, to little avail; Leontes is convinced of her infidelity. However he has sent two noblemen, Cleomenes and Dion, to the Delphic oracle at the temple of Apollo to endorse his suspicions.

Scene 2

Paulina, Antigonus' wife, summons the gaoler in an outer room of the prison. He refuses to allow her to see Hermione but permits her to speak to Emilia, one of her ladies, in his presence. Emilia tells her that Hermione has given birth to a baby daughter. Paulina proposes that if Hermione will trust her with the child she will show it to the king, hoping thus to soften him and heed her eloquence on Hermione's behalf. Emilia knows that she will agree, since Hermione had hit on the same idea herself but found no-one to carry it out.

Scene 3

In the palace Leontes is informed by an attendant that Mamillius is pining away, sleepless, in grief at his mother's dishonour. On Leontes' orders Antigonus attempts to prevent Paulina from bringing Hermione's baby in but she over-rides him. She lays the child of the 'good queen' before the king and draws his attention to its likeness to himself.

Leontes, enraged, orders Antigonus to take his wife and the baby away; Paulina implores his mercy and departs, leaving the baby at his feet. In a fury Leontes turns on Antigonus, accusing him of complicity and ordering him to take the 'female bastard' to some remote and desert place outside his dominion and leave it to its fate. As Antigonus carries the baby out news is brought of the return of Cleomenes and Dion from Delphos; Leontes convenes a trial at which the oracle's answer may be heard.

Act III

Scene 1

Cleomenes and Dion, down at the seaport, compare notes on the impressive temple of Apollo and the awesome voice of the oracle.

Scene 2

Leontes opens Hermione's trial in the court of justice. An officer reads out an indictment charging Hermione with high treason (by adultery) and plotting the king's death with Camillo. Hermione, as a proud and honourable daughter of the Emperor of Russia [an anachronism], delivers a passionate speech protesting against being deprived of her newborn baby and also being branded an adulteress.

Cleomenes and Dion are summoned to bring in the oracle's pronouncement; they swear that the seals on it are unbroken. An official unseals the document and reads it out: 'Hermione is chaste; Polixenes is blameless; Camillo a true subject; Leontes a jealous tyrant; his innocent baby truly begotten; and the king shall live without an heir if that which is lost [i.e. the baby] be not found!'

At first Leontes dismisses the oracle's words as false. However before the trial can proceed a servant comes to report that Mamillius has died. Hermione faints at the news and is carried out. Leontes fears that Apollo's wrath has been aroused by his arrogant refusal to believe the oracle and repents of his suspicions of Polixenes and his treatment of Camillo. Paulina enters, reports that Hermione is dead and rails bitterly at Leontes. In despair Leontes belatedly acknowledges his wrongdoing and asks to be taken to the bodies of his queen and son to do penance.

Scene 3

Antigonus, having landed with the newborn child in Bohemia, sends an accompanying sailor back to the ship as a storm brews. He muses on a dream that he had in his cabin, in which a weeping Hermione appeared in pure white robes telling him to name the child Perdita [i.e. the Lost One] and prophesying that he would not see his wife again. As the rain begins to fall he lays the baby down together with a bundle with a note attached to it and leaves, followed by a bear.

A shepherd appears, looking for two lost sheep, and finds the baby. He is joined by his son Clown who relates how he has seen Antigonus slain by the bear and the ship wrecked in the storm. Noting the babe's rich clothing and the gold jewellery in the bundle the shepherd decides to keep it secretly while Clown goes off to bury what is left of Antigonus.

Act IV

Prologue

Time tells the audience that over the next sixteen years Leontes has abandoned himself to sorrow and Perdita has been raised as the shepherd's daughter. He adds that the name of Polixenes' son is Florizel.

Scene 1

In the Bohemian royal palace King Polixenes begs the homesick Camillo not to return to Sicily. He diverts him by referring to a certain shepherd who has somehow become very wealthy; Prince Florizel, who has frequently been absent from court, has been seen at the cottage of this shepherd, who is rumoured to have a most beautiful daughter. Polixenes asks Camillo to pay a visit to the shepherd with him, in disguise.

Scene 2

Autolycus, a light-fingered rogue, is walking along a road near the shepherd's cottage, singing. He confesses that he is, like his father, "a snapper-up of unconsidered trifles" and is pleased to come across Clown, a potential victim. He falls to the ground and wails that he has been robbed and beaten; when Clown comes to his aid he picks his pocket.

Scene 3

A sheep-shearing festival is taking place on a lawn in front of the shepherd's cottage. Florizel pays Perdita compliments while the shepherd welcomes Polixenes and Camillo, both in disguise. They are presented with flowers by Mopsa and Dorcas, two shepherdesses, and are enchanted by Perdita's gentility and grace.

Clown bids the musicians strike up and the rustics dance. Polixenes asks the shepherd for the name of the swain dancing with Perdita and is told that it is Doricles.

A servant enters to announce a linen pedlar at the door. It is Autolycus, singing the praises of his "Lawn as white as driven snow;". Mopsa asks Clown for the lace and gloves he promised her but he has no money after Autolycus' theft. He is offered a ballad by Autolycus who sings it with Dorcas and Mopsa; they all go off together. A dozen country folk dressed as satyrs then present a dance.

Polixenes asks Doricles (his son, Florizel) why he has let the pedlar go without buying a gift for Perdita. Florizel asks the others to witness that he is offering her instead his hand in marriage, to the approbation of the shepherd.

Polixenes, taken aback, urges him to consult his father first. When Florizel refuses he throws off his disguise in anger, forbids the lovers to see each other again, on pain of disinheriting Florizel, and abruptly departs.

Perdita is affronted and is prepared to return tearfully to her ewes. However Florizel is willing to give up Bohemia for Perdita and proposes to elope with her on a vessel that he has riding at anchor. Camillo, who has also put off his disguise, suggests that the couple sail with him for Sicily where he is confident that Leontes will welcome them.

When Autolycus returns Camillo gets him to exchange clothes with Florizel; he then leaves with the lovers. Clown, re-entering, advises the shepherd to tell the king about the foundling Perdita and her jewels. They are joined by Autolycus who manages to persuade them to let him approach the king on their behalf, in return for payment in gold.

Act V

Scene 1

Leontes is still grieving in his Sicilian palace. Cleomenes, Dion and Paulina recall the oracle's prediction that King Leontes should not have an heir until his lost child be found. Leontes promises not to remarry without Paulina's consent. A courtier announces the arrival of Florizel and Perdita; Cleomenes is sent to fetch them.

Act V, Scene 3

Perdita kneels in wonder to kiss the hand of the 'statue' of her mother Hermione. Although Hermione looks a little older King Leontes is astonished at the lifelike form and imagines that the 'statue' is breathing.

When they enter Florizel brings Leontes greetings from Polixenes and explains that he met Perdita in Libya. Leontes welcomes them but a lord enters to tell Leontes that he has just seen Polixenes and Camillo in the city. Polixenes has caught up with Clown and the shepherd and threatened them with death. He wishes Leontes to arrest Florizel for fleeing with the shepherd's daughter.

Scene 2

Near the palace, however, Autolycus is told by Paulina's steward and two other gentlemen how the two kings and Camillo have now in amazement confirmed Perdita's identity, from one of Hermione's jewels round her neck and also from the note left with the baby by Antigonus; his identity in turn was confirmed by Clown who produced rings and a handkerchief belonging to him.

They describe how Leontes embraced everyone with delight while Paulina was torn between distress at the manner of her husband's death and joy at finding Perdita. One of the gentlemen mentions that Perdita has gone to a chapel in Paulina's house to see a statue of her mother Hermione, recently finished by the Italian sculptor Julio Romano [who, in reality, died in 1546!].

As the men depart to see the statue of Hermione Autolycus is joined by Clown and the shepherd. They are pleased by their newfound status of gentlemen and take him off to look at the stone figure.

Scene 3

Leontes, Polixenes, Florizel, Perdita, Camillo and Paulina have gathered in her chapel with their lords and attendants. Paulina opens a curtain, revealing the statue of Hermione. Perdita looks at the figure of her mother in wonder and kneels to kiss its hand. Leontes is astonished at the lifelike form although he notes that it is older than Hermione as he remembers her sixteen years ago.

Paulina goes to draw the curtain again but is prevented by Leontes who imagines that the statue is breathing and moving its eyes — so much so that he wishes to kiss it. At this, Paulina tells everyone to prepare for a further marvel; she calls for music and commands the statue to descend from its plinth.

Queen Hermione comes alive, blesses Perdita and embraces Leontes. She tells him that Paulina, taking hope from the oracle's words, originally reported her death but has been sheltering her ever since.

King Leontes is filled with happiness; he now has a wife, a daughter and a son-in-law and is reconciled with his old friend Polixenes. Overcome with gratitude to Paulina he suggests that she take Camillo for an honourable husband.

Historical Chronology

A speculative list of the plays by historical period is as follows

	BC
Troilus & Cressida	1197?
The Winter's Tale	700?
A Midsummer-Night's Dream	580?
Coriolanus	493
Timon of Athens	408
Twelfth Night	350?
The Comedy of Errors	230?
Pericles	190?
Julius Caesar	44
Antony & Cleopatra	40 - 30

	A.D.
Cymbeline	4?
Titus Andronicus	380?
King Lear	600?
Hamlet	960?
Macbeth	1040 - 1058
King John	1202 - 1216
Romeo & Juliet	1303?
All's Well That Ends Well	1345?
As You Like It	1350?
The Two Gentlemen of Verona	1350?
Richard II	1398 - 1400
Henry IV, Part 1	1403
Henry IV, Part 2	1403 - 1413
Henry V	1413 - 1419
Henry VI, Part 1	1422 - 1445
Henry VI, Part 2	1445 - 1455
Henry VI, Part 3	1455 - 1471
Richard III	1471 - 1485
Othello	1499?
Much Ado About Nothing	1500?
Henry VIII	1520 - 1523
Love's Labour's Lost	1530?
Measure for Measure	1560?
The Merchant of Venice	1570?
The Merry Wives of Windsor	1580?
The Taming of the Shrew	-
The Tempest	-